Historic
Canada

LANCASTER

Historic Canada

LANCASTER

Harold E. Wright

ARCADIA PUBLISHING

ISBN 978-0-7385-7285-7

Published by Arcadia Publishing
Charleston, South Carolina

Printed in the United States of America

Library of Congress control number: 2009939568

For all general information contact Arcadia Publishing at:
Telephone 843-853-2070
Fax 843-853-0044
E-mail sales@arcadiapublishing.com
For customer service and orders:
Toll-Free 1-888-313-2665

Visit us on the Internet at www.arcadiapublishing.com

Dedicated to Bert Huestis

"Bert Huestis' passing this past week removes from our midst a fine man and a good citizen". Thus ended an editorial in the *Evening Times Globe* four days after Bert's death. The editorial said he was a "big man with a hearty laugh and an engaging personality". Bert was Mr. Lancaster.

Bert served his community beginning with a seat on the Lancaster Parish Council in 1951. He led the polls in the new City of Lancaster's first election in 1952, serving as deputy mayor until being elected mayor in 1958. In 1967 Bert led Lancaster into amalgamation with Saint John, serving as deputy mayor on that first consolidated council.

His public service did not end there. He was chairman of the old General Hospital Board of Trustees, a Past Worshipful Master of the Masons, vice president of the Canadian Home & School Association, a governor of Acadia University, and a most active member of his church, Lancaster Baptist.

Bert's resume could go on for pages, but it is not necessary for those who knew him. His legacy to them is "his association with [the] people" of Lancaster. For those who did not know him, his public legacy is evident in the public documents of Lancaster and Saint John. The story illustrated between these covers is largely of his doing or influence.

Bert's love of photography began in 1938 with his first job with the *Saint John Citizen*. His picture appeared in my first book, *Saint John*, with Charles Lynch and Hoot Gibson. His camera kept clicking until the day he died—capturing the spirit and vitality of his community. I took Bert to Partridge Island a few times and on several occasions we talked about our common love—the heritage of Saint John today. Bert may be in a better place now, but I bet his camera is still clicking. Thanks Bert.

I also wish to recognize two other individuals who gave me information for this book but passed away this year: former Lancaster city solicitor Lyman Purnell, and Ida Harris, both of whom you will see later in this book.

Harold E. Wright
November 1998

Contents

Acknowledgements

I wish to thank the following individuals who provided photographs and information for this book. Your love of Lancaster was evident through your support. If I have inadvertently omitted a name, please accept my humble apologies.

Penny Hovey
Norm Garey
Willard Moore
Fred Hazel
Ken Steen
Frank and Lena Perry
Carol and the late Ida Harris
Kay Ryan
Rose Poirier
Louis Poirier
Heather and Keith Dow
Val Dexter
Mitchell Franklin
Pat Franklin
Rick Smith
Mr. and Mrs. Byard Herrington
Eileen Boyd
Lodge family
Marjory Bernard
Margaret Kingston
Bill Butler
Gerry Butler
Margaret Logue
Vince Richards
Moosehead Breweries Ltd.
Ken Olsen
Bob Campbell
Pat Valardo
Evelyn Small
Arlene Donovan
Abbie Colwell
Barry Ogden
Jean Neal
Doris Taylor
Laurette Gogan
the late Lyman Purnell
Mary Munford
Bernard McHarg
Janet Reed
Grace Huestis
Marlene Ross
Elaine Reid
the late Ken Kierstead
Dave Goss
Doris Webb
Don Coholan
Rose Riley
Annette McManus
Melodie Melanson
the late Hartley Green family—Judy and Carol
the late Buzz Devenne family
Jerry Arseneau
Harold Mayes
Linda Rolston
Saint John Jewish Historical Museum
Carol Craig

INTRODUCTION

Lancaster—A Community of Communities!

For many, the city of Lancaster lasted less than one generation. Incorporated as Canada's newest city on January 1, 1953, Lancaster was swallowed up in an amalgamation with Canada's oldest incorporated city, Saint John, on January 1, 1967, Canada's centennial year. For more than 30 years the name Lancaster has conjured up images of that part of Saint John now known as the west side, or Saint John West, two appellations which also mean different things for other older residents of the city. Today the name lives on at the Lancaster Mall and the Lancaster Centennial Arena, or with some of the local sports teams. For thousands of others, the name Lancaster evokes images of the former communities of Fairville, Beaconsfield, Randolph and Milford, and South Bay. These communities incorporated to form Lancaster in 1953.

Few in Saint John are as ferocious at remembering their heritage as west siders. Even today, some kindergarten children identify as living in Fairville, a handover from their grandparents' days! While these children may use the name, only their parents and grandparents will remember the familiar area politicians like Tommy Horsler, Bill Golding, Arthur Carton, Bert Huestis, and Hartley Green. Memories of Lancaster include businessmen such as George Chittick, Les Spragg, Willard Moore, Louise Poirier, Parker D. Mitchell, C.R. Nelson, and Russell Webb; or residents like Tom Butler, Louis Murphy, Albert Perry, Lyman Purnell, or Paul Phillips, and countless others. Gone are the Fairville Fountain, the Fairville Department Store, Willard Moore's grocery, Buzz Devenne's Champlain Street grocery, Purdy's Sales & Service, and Boyle's Hardware—the list could go on and on.

On January 1, 1953, the city of Lancaster became the newest and youngest of Canada's cities. With a population of more than 10,000 it was New Brunswick's fifth city. "CANADA'S NEWEST CITY IS BORN"! was the banner of the first newspaper of the new city, *The Lancaster Advertiser*. With 15 pages of articles, it stands today as an important historical document of Lancaster and Saint John. Costing only 10¢, it introduced the new mayor, Thomas Horsler, and his council, the community's educational facilities, and opportunities for this new city. As observed by A.R. Jones: "Lancaster citizens are determined to move forward, and to make this community a model of progressive and efficient government". Mayor Horsler said "Let us hope and pray that there is much good in store for our new City, and the road over which we must make our way will lead us to build a progressive and prosperous City".

Lancaster was home to the Provincial Hospital, a landmark since 1848, the DVA Hospital for Veterans, the Ridgewood Health and Occupational Centre, and the New Brunswick Protestant Orphans' Home. The DVA hospital is gone, as is the Protestant Orphanage. The Provincial Hospital (later Centracare) was a fixture on Lancaster Heights from 1848 until its relocation in 1998. The building is scheduled to be demolished in 1999. Stalwarts of the local economy, T.S. Simms and Moosehead Breweries, remain true to their location.

T.S. Simms & Co. Limited is one of the largest brush manufacturing companies in the world. The Simms plant is a huge concrete building, 4 stories high, 52 feet wide, and 400 feet long. To guard against fires, the Fairville plant had its own fire protection system that included hoses, hydrants, a 1,000-gallon water pump, water sprinklers, and a large water storage tank on the roof that proudly carried the name Simms.

Moosehead Breweries spans over a century—back to 1867 with Susannah Oland brewing beer in Turtle Grove, Nova Scotia. After her death in 1886, the Oland family brewing legacy was kept alive by her sons. "The same Oland Family is at the helm of Moosehead Breweries Limited, Canada's oldest independent brewery, the third largest in the country and the only brewery to be locally owned and operated in the Maritimes". The Saint John brewery uses the latest technology in brewing and bottling: "The brew house is among the most modern in North America with its fermentation and storage systems". Today the products of Lancaster's Moosehead Breweries are known for "The taste of a distinctive beer, tinged with history, touched by tradition and mellowed with the unique spirit of the Maritimes".

Other Lancaster businesses are also etched into the minds of those from this part of Saint John. There was George Chittick's, Val Dexter's, and Harry Tippett and Murray Long's construction companies. Prominent Fairville resident Fred Hazel wrote that there was "the Palm Restaurant, run by the McManus brothers, John Hooley's poolroom, Joe Boyle's hardware, Chittick's shoe repair, Koven's clothing store, Reid's diner, Olsen's Fairville Fountain . . . [and] Eddie Snodgrass's ice cream parlour". He notes that "Billy Reid had a second-hand store", mentions the "bowling alley run by John Kern and Clarence Cogswell", and writes of the grocery stores run by the "Barker Brothers and Johnny and Joe Seargeant, Johnny Collin's butcher shop, Sam McCormack's general store, John Allison's, Nellie McKinnon's, Hobart's and McColgan's groceries, and Tommy Horsler's drugstore".

Names such as Prospect Point, Kingsville, Randolph, Milford, Goose Alley, Raynes Beach, and Fox's Alley are also no longer part of the main stream vocabulary of Lancaster. While gone, the people, businesses, places, and events of Lancaster are not forgotten. A browse through these pages will rekindle the sights, sounds, and emotions of this "Proud Community of Communities"!

The name Lancaster relates to both the city of Lancaster from 1953 until 1967 and to the Parish of Lancaster, which basically covers the area from South Bay to Musquash. Instead of continually switching back and forth in the photograph captions between Fairville, Beaconsfield, Milford, and the other community names, I have tried to be consistent and use the name Lancaster regardless of the time period depicted in the photograph.

One

CELEBRATIONS

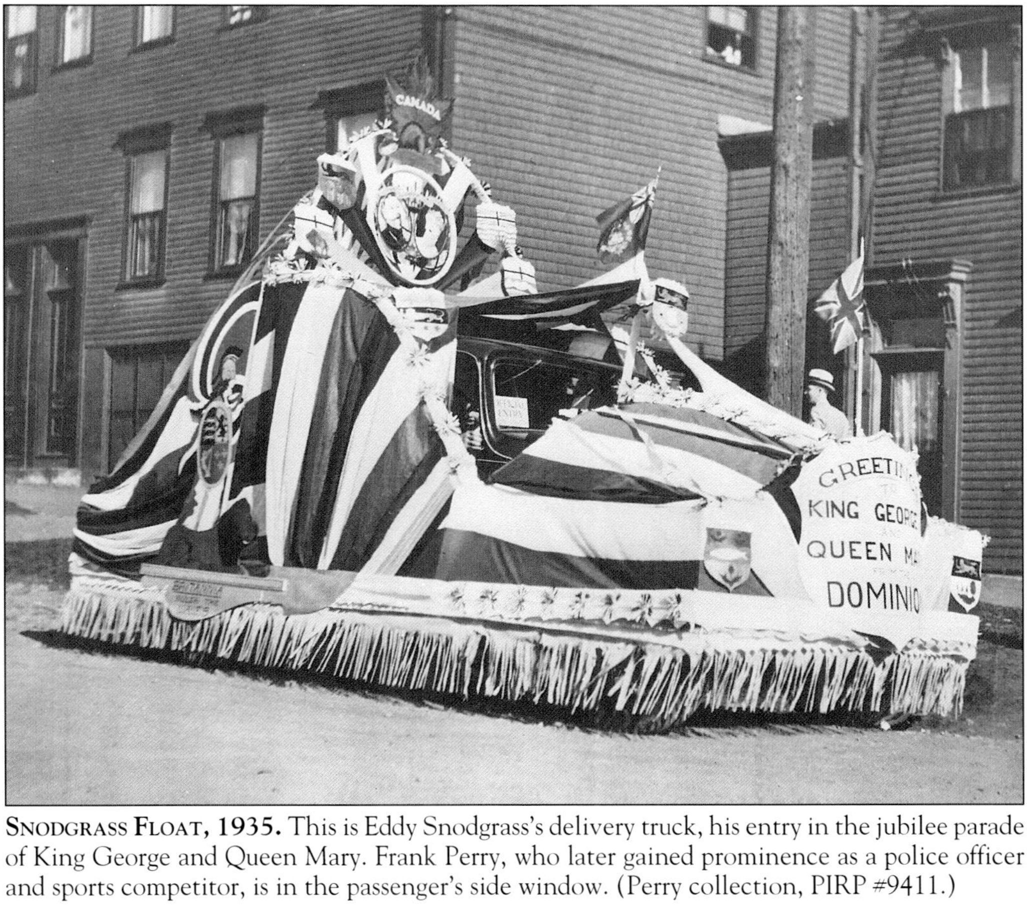

SNODGRASS FLOAT, 1935. This is Eddy Snodgrass's delivery truck, his entry in the jubilee parade of King George and Queen Mary. Frank Perry, who later gained prominence as a police officer and sports competitor, is in the passenger's side window. (Perry collection, PIRP #9411.)

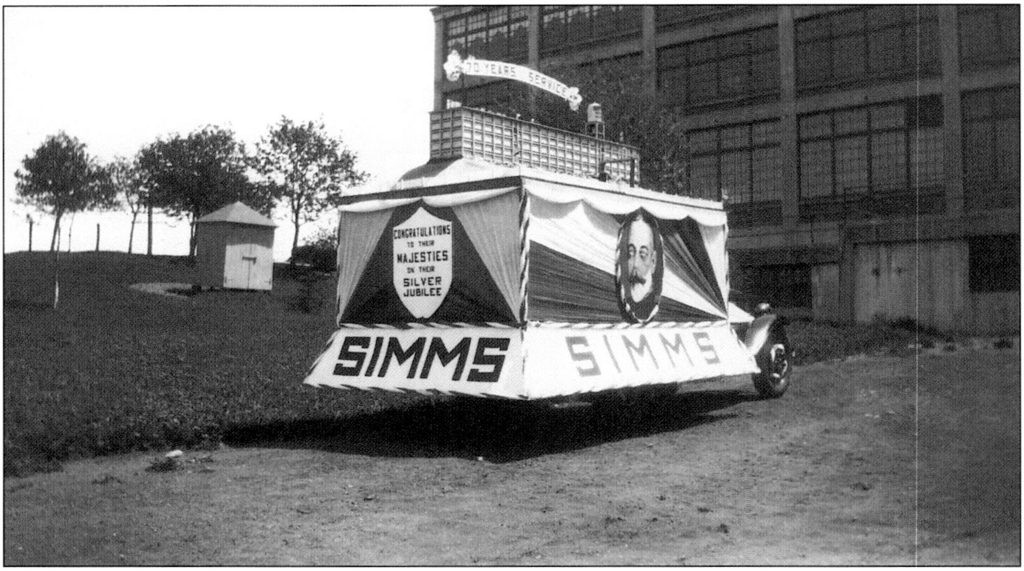

Simms Float, 1935. To mark the jubilee of King George and Queen Mary, Simms put this truck, with a model of their plant on the roof, in the citywide parade. It is believed that Tom McHugh, who worked in the graphics department, did the decorations. (Canavan collection, PIRP #7910.)

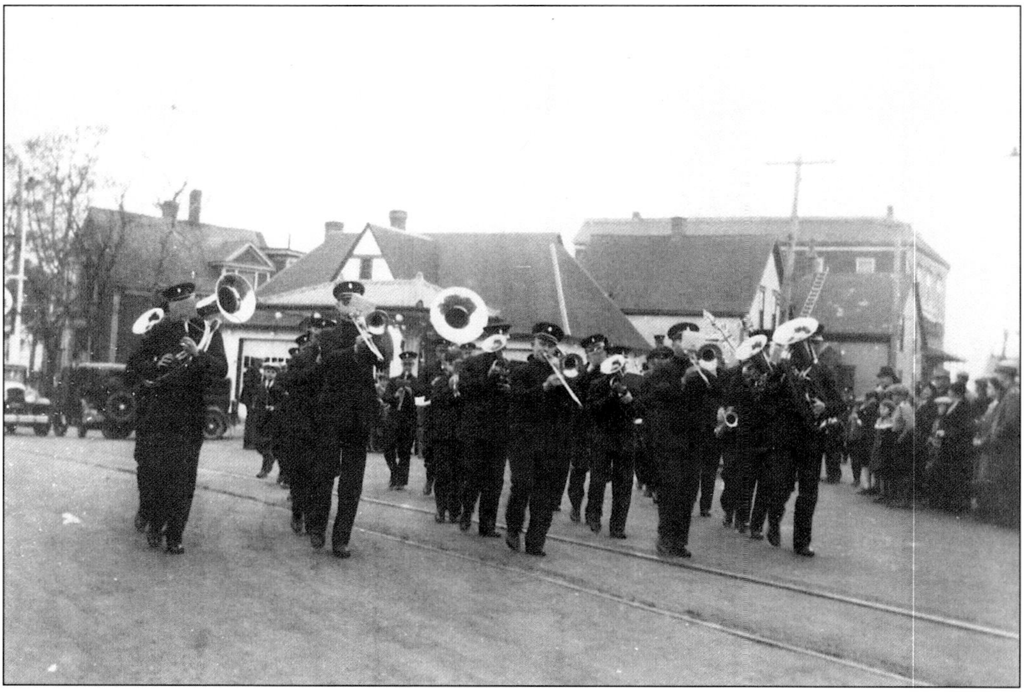

Fairville Band, c. 1935. The Fairville Citizen's Band is on Church Avenue, in front of Webb's service station. This may also have been the jubilee Transportation Day parade. The photograph was taken by Bert Huestis. (B. Herrington collection, PIRP #9106.)

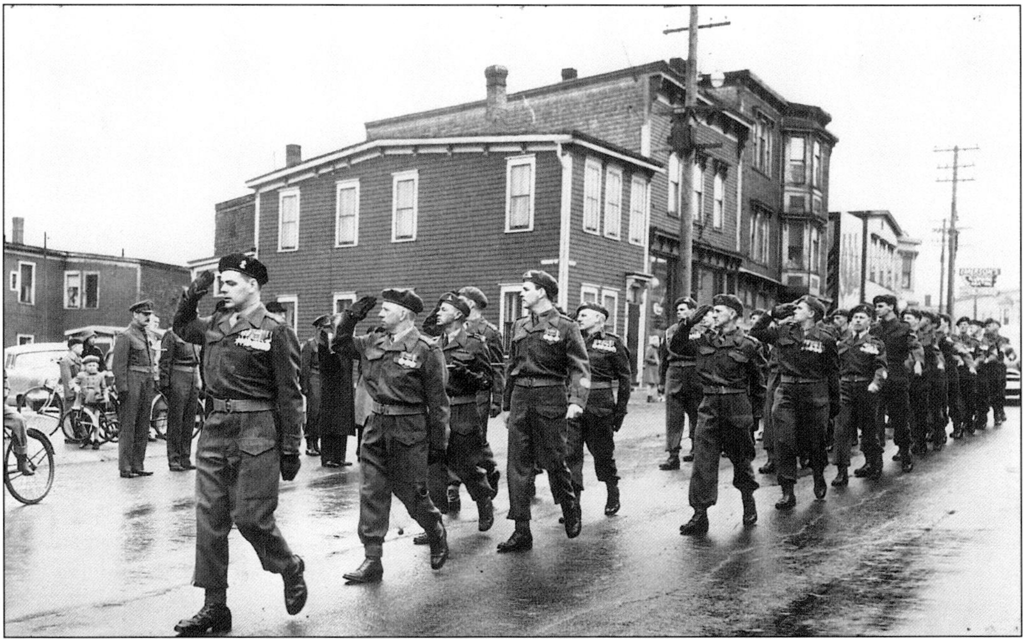

Artillery Parade, 1957. Major James H. Turnbull, Battery Commander of the 104th Battery, 3rd NB Medium Anti-Aircraft Regiment, is returning his battery from service at the Church of the Good Shephard on Manawagonish Road. Also in attendance was His Honour Lt. Gov. D. Laurence MacLaren, a former gunner on Partridge Island during World War I. In the background is Parker's grocery store and Billy Reid's second-hand shop. (McGoldrick collection, PIRP #5129.)

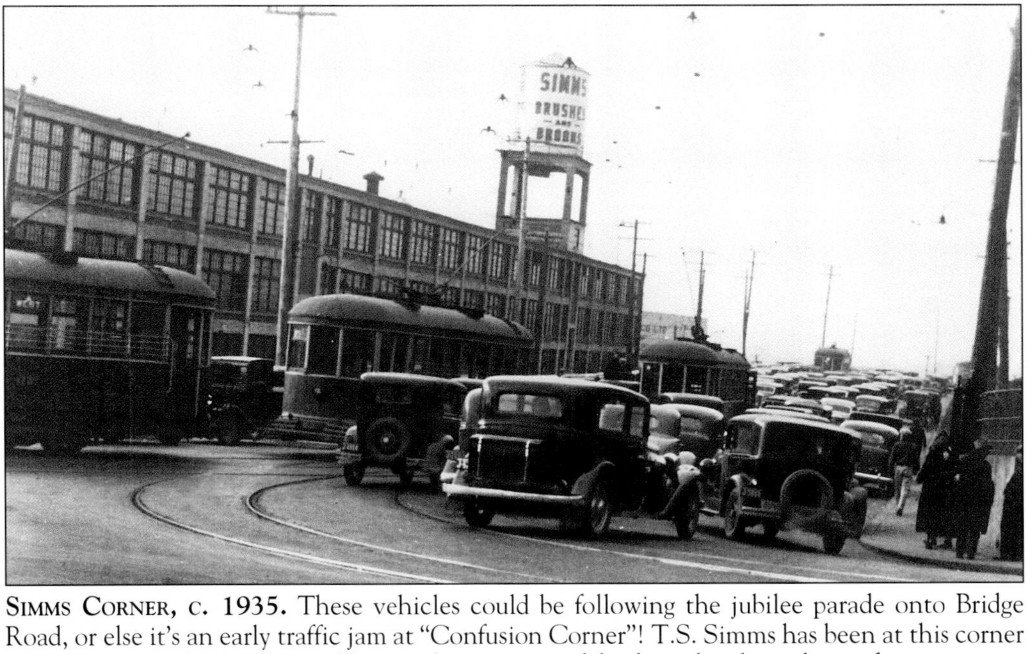

Simms Corner, c. 1935. These vehicles could be following the jubilee parade onto Bridge Road, or else it's an early traffic jam at "Confusion Corner"! T.S. Simms has been at this corner since 1912. The firm prides itself on producing some of the finest brush products of any company in the world, a boast that they have earned with over a century of business. This photograph was taken by Bert Huestis. (B. Herrington collection, PIRP #9110.)

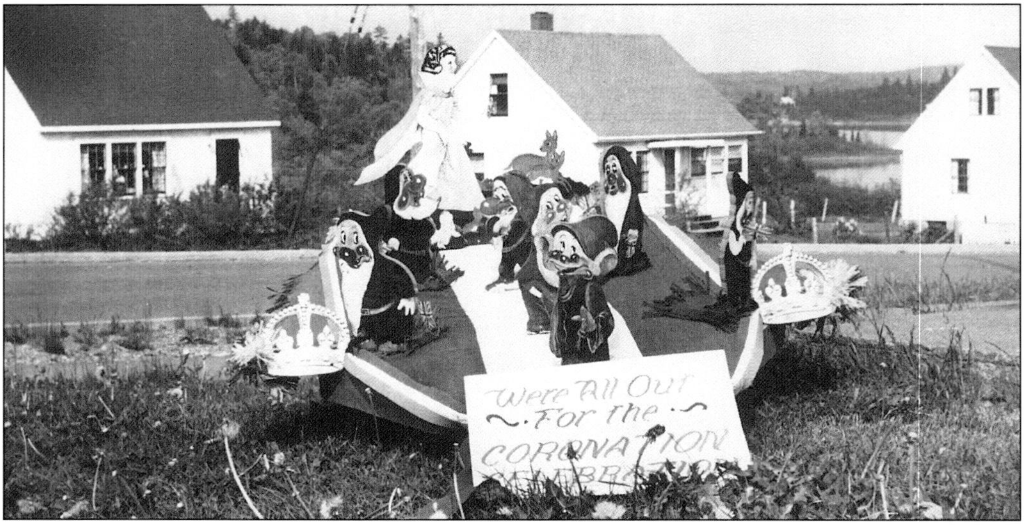

Snow White and Friends, 1953. While policeman Albert Perry was popularly known for his sports abilities, it was he who decorated the Dennis Morris Memorial School for its official opening. For the coronation celebration of Queen Elizabeth in June 1953, Albert decorated many of the businesses on Main Street, most of which are shown in this book. He also made Snow White and the Seven Dwarfs, shown here on his front lawn on Greenhead Road. (Perry collection, PIRP #9465.)

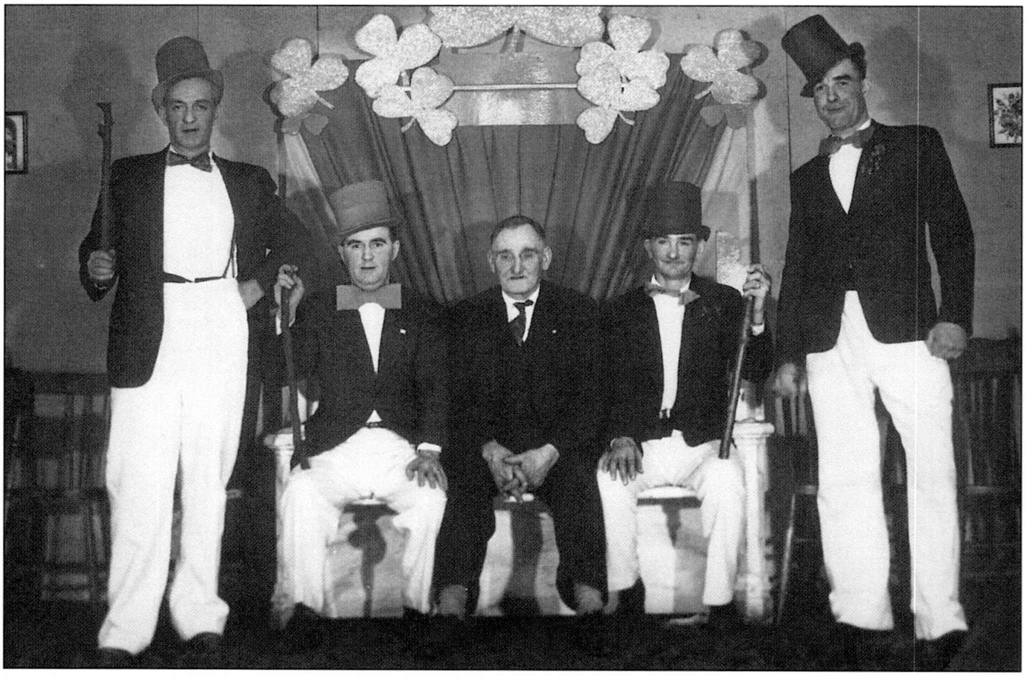

St. Patrick's Show, c. 1940. For years, an annual minstrel show was held at St. Patrick's Hall. In 1933 the St. Rose's Women's Society presented "A Plain Old Irishman", directed by J.J. O'Toole. The business manager for this performance was Charles Melanson, and scenic effects were done by A.J. Quigg. This photo is not of this play, but the performers shown here, from left to right, are unidentified, John Garey, Joe O'Toole, Albert Perry, and ? McEwain. (Perry collection, PIRP #9412.)

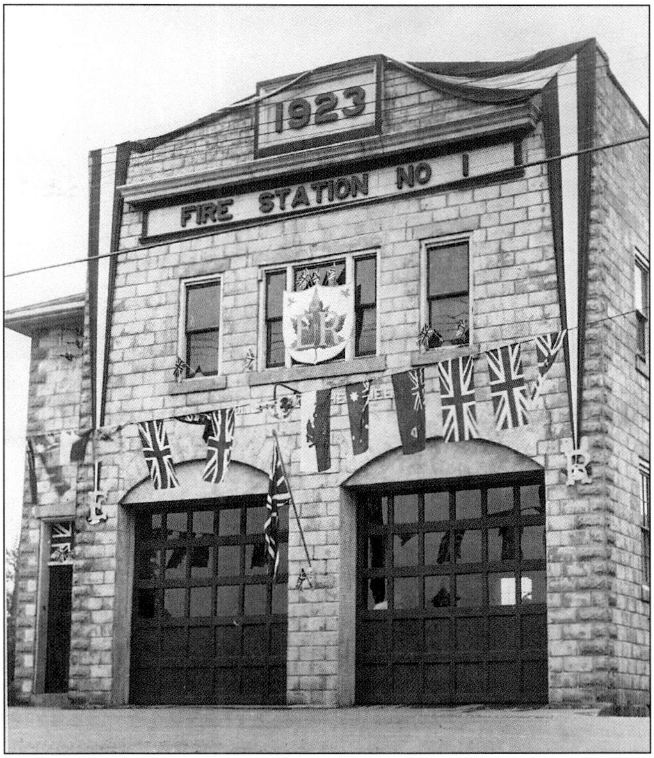

Coronation, 1953. In June, Saint John and Lancaster hosted a series of week-long events to mark the coronation of Queen Elizabeth II. Fire Station No.1 was also decorated by Albert Perry. One wonders . . . what ever happened to the large shield at the second-floor window. Does it still exist? Handsomely decorated for the occasion, the Gaiety was also home to the law office of the late Lyman Purnell, Richard & B.A. Ryan, contractors, the House of Jewelry, and Peggy's beauty shop. (Perry collection, PIRP #9499, #9463.)

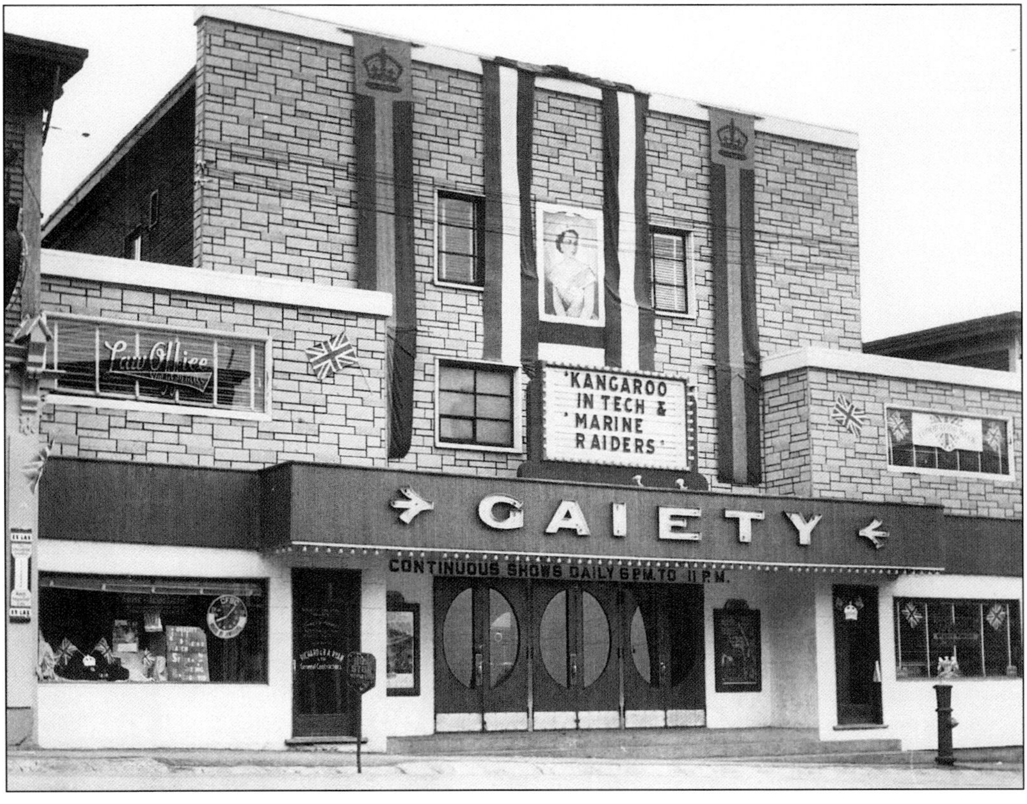

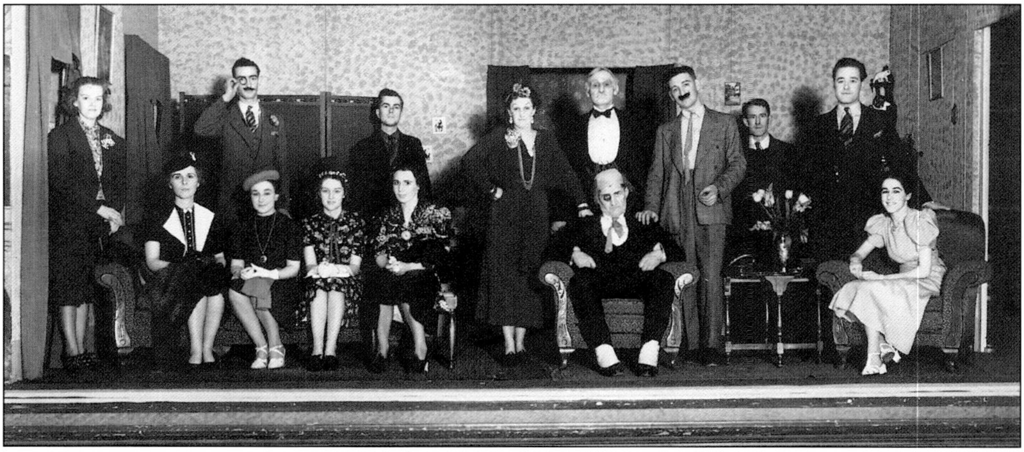

"BRINGING UP FATHER", C. 1948. These performers, from left to right, are Verna Keena, Kay Leger, Jim Palmer, Mary Hickey, Dot Logue, Charlie LeBlanc, Dorothy Butler, Helen O'Toole as "Maggie", John J. O'Toole, Elmer McGiviney as "Jiggs", Ed Maloney, Jim Fox, Charlie Melanson, and Margie Babineau. (R. Riley.)

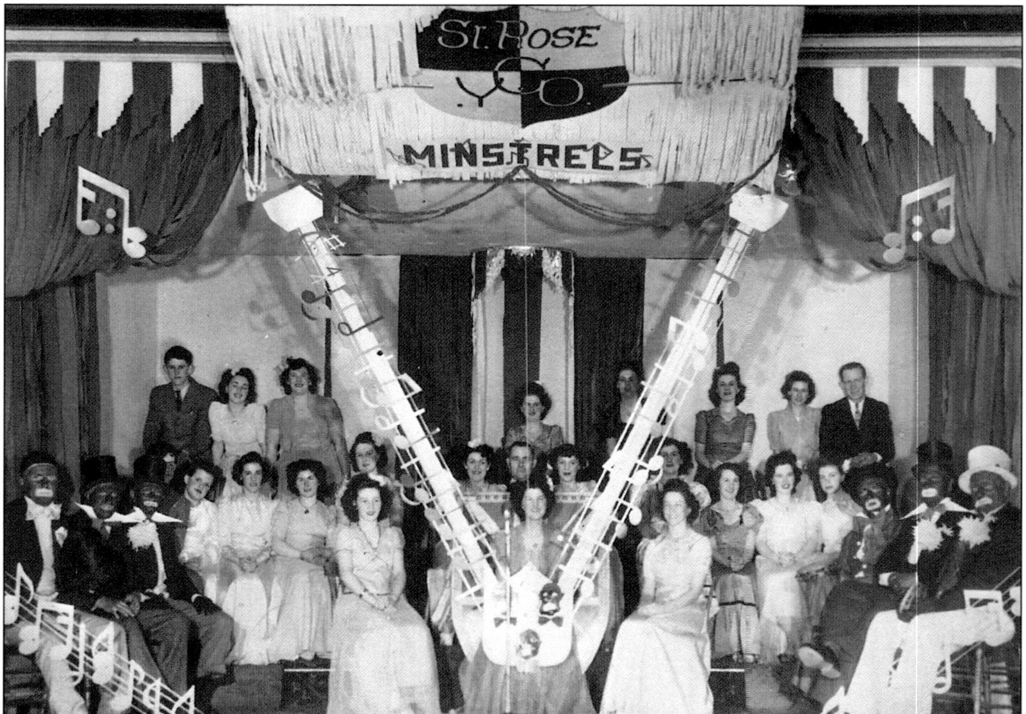

ST. ROSE'S MINSTRELS, 1945. St. Rose's CYO Minstrels held annual shows to raise money to aid orphans in the diocese. The minstrels are pictured here, from left to right: (front row) Walter Garey, Willie Ouellette, Albert Perry, Lena Joyce, Dot Melanson, Pauline Babineau, Joe Murphy (the singing mailman), Charlie Melanson, and J.J. O'Toole; (middle row) Francis Doyle, Treva Barry, Josephine Babineau, Dorothy Carton, Dorothy Logue, Regina Robichaud, John Garey, interlocutor, Mary Reid, Bernadine Burns, Mary McGovern, Dean Riley, and Mary McCann; (back row) George Jenkins, Helen Ferguson, Theresa Massaro, Lorraine Jenkins, Lil Garey, Edna Garey, Rita Babineau, and Tom Butler. (Garey collection, PIRP #9425.)

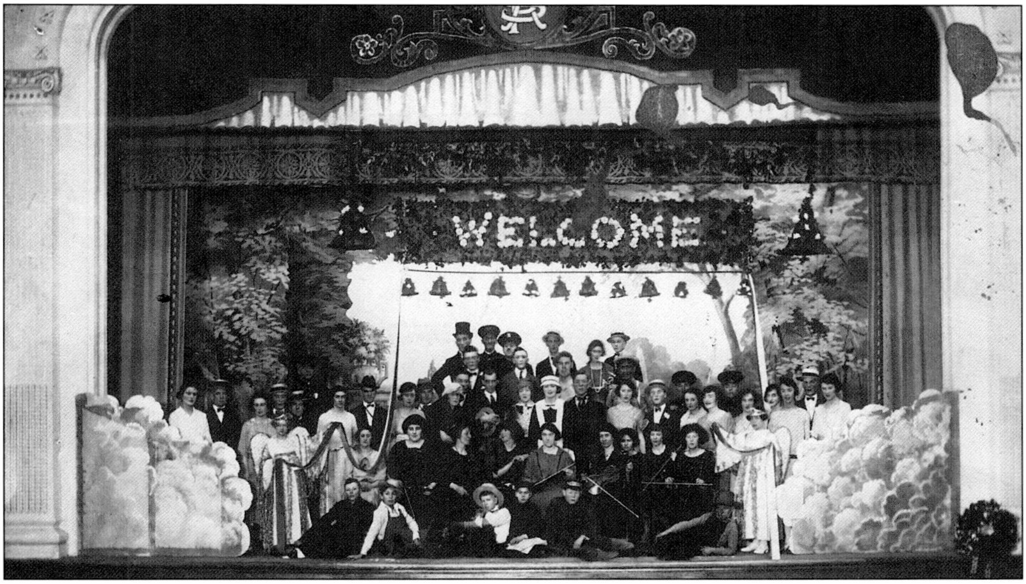

St. Patrick's Day, c. 1920. St. Patrick's Hall was a magnificent site for these community-based performances. On March 17 and 18, 1920, the St. Rose Dramatic Club presented Rose O' My Heart, with J.J. O'Toole in the lead role. (Perry collection, PIRP #9413.)

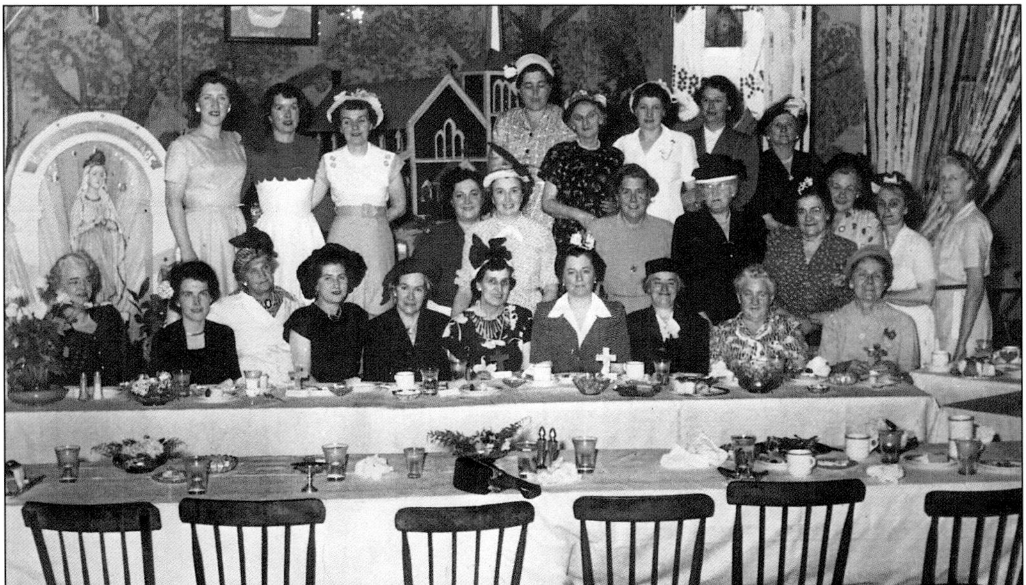

Anniversary Dinner, June 1950. On the 25th anniversary of Monsignor William J. Osborne's ordination, the ladies of St. Rose's CWL held a dinner in the old St. Rose Hall on Church Avenue. The ladies, shown here from left to right, are as follows: (front row) Vera Keenan, Irene Brennan, Elizabeth Massaro, Helen Cormier, Irene Malloy, Tina Duffy, Geraldine O'Brien, Blanche O'Keefe, Lena Ferguson, and Alice Crowley; (middle row) Helen Logue, Loretta Lahey, Agnes Barry, Margaret Maloney, Elizabeth Clark, Alice Coholan, Beatrice Joyce, and May Tibbett; (back row) Rita Logue, Hortense Garey, Mary Haslam, Jenny Hayes, Margaret Barry, Lena Perry, Edna Sprague, and Gertrude Crilley. (Garey collection, PIRP #9424.)

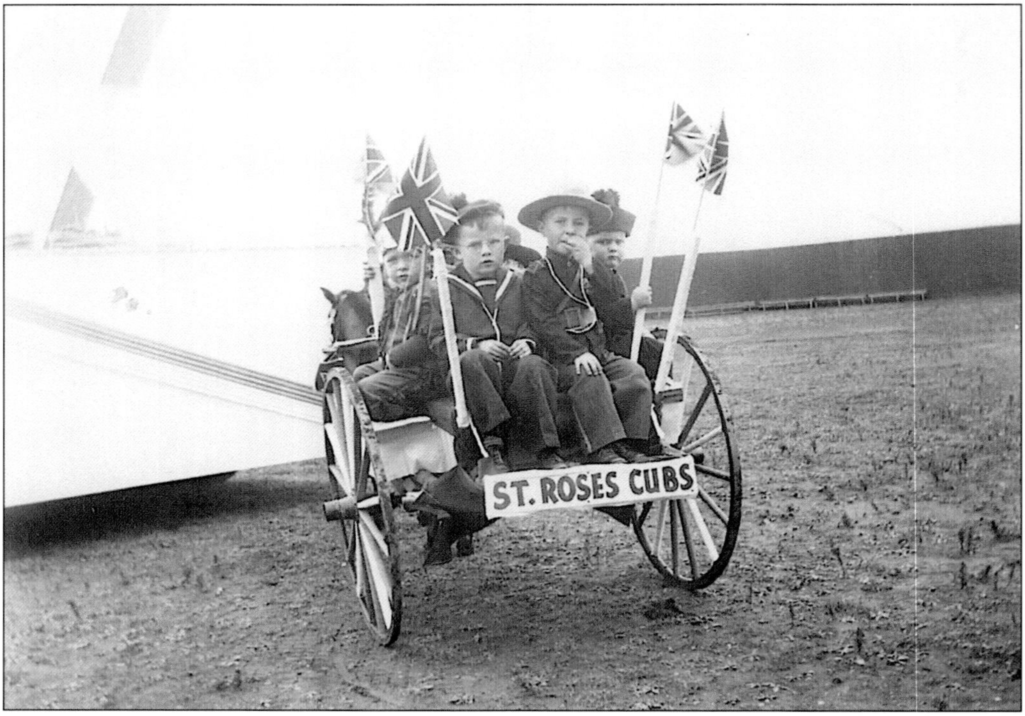

St. Rose's Wolf Cub Pack. The 1950s and 1960s were great times to be a Cub in Lancaster. Every church had a large successful wolf pack. In the top photo Terry Garey (with hand on mouth) and his pals ride this pony-hauled wagon, while below we find Paul Bordage, Rudy Poirier, Ron McCann, Philip Wright, and Gerry Butler. (Top photograph courtesy of N. Garey; bottom photograph courtesy of Poirier family.)

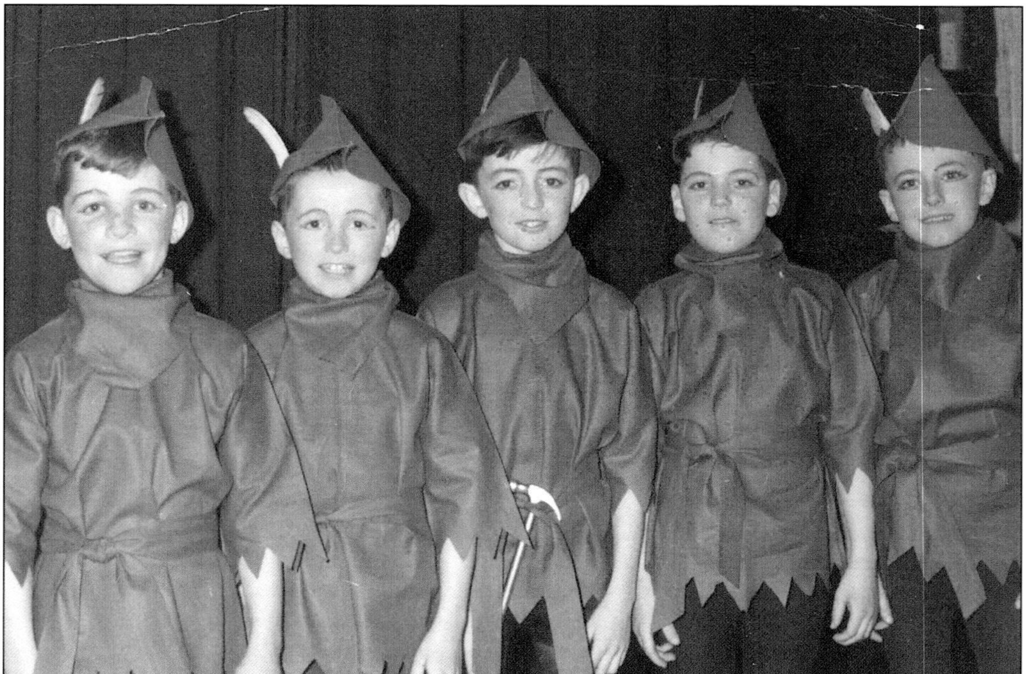

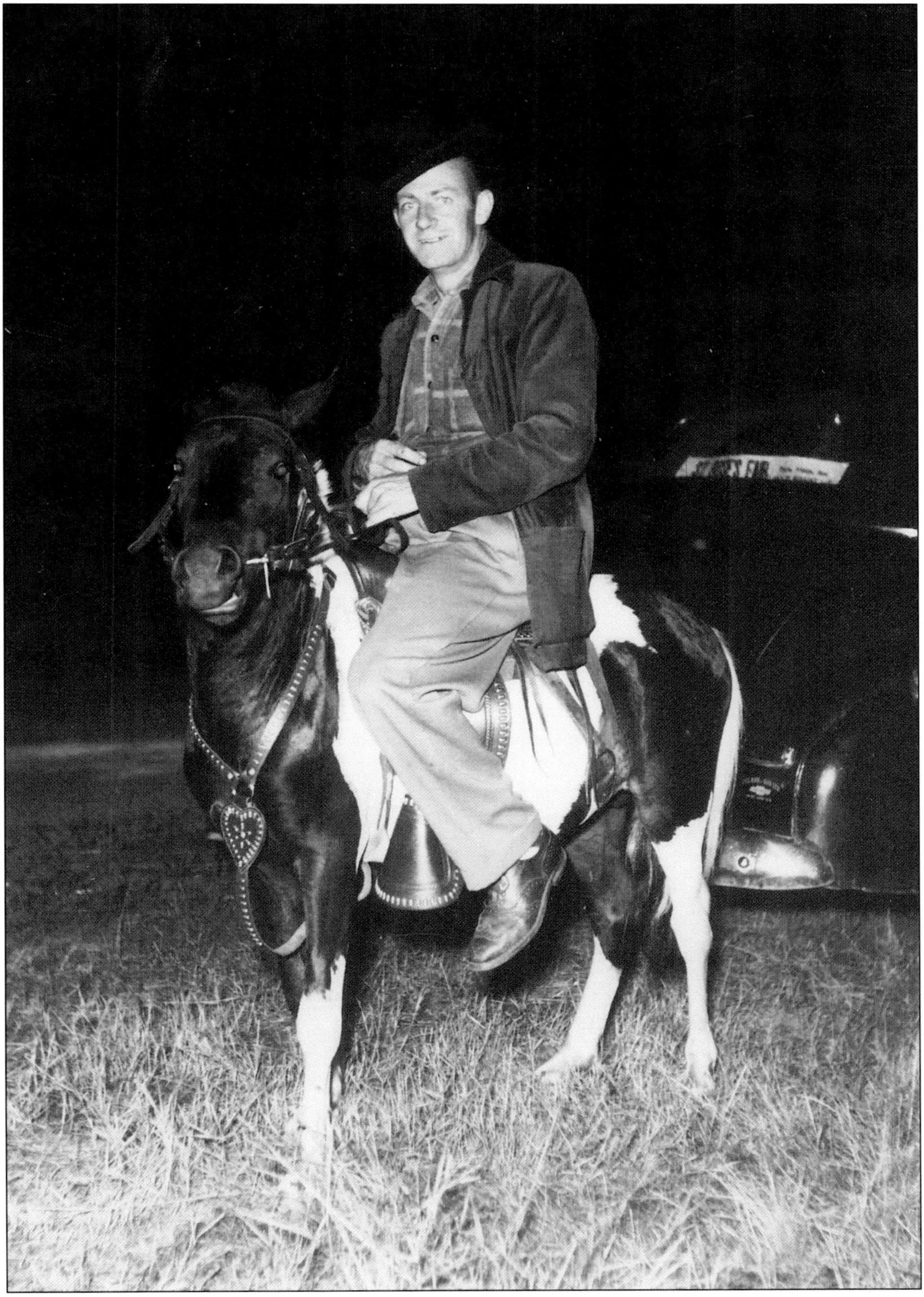

WHO'S TOO OLD TO BE A KID? Tommy Butler is proof positive that at St. Rose's fair, everybody could be a kid if they so chose. He does look a bit too big for the pony though! Tom was a member of the Boy Scout Group Committee and the parish council. He died on August 17, 1963. (G. Butler.)

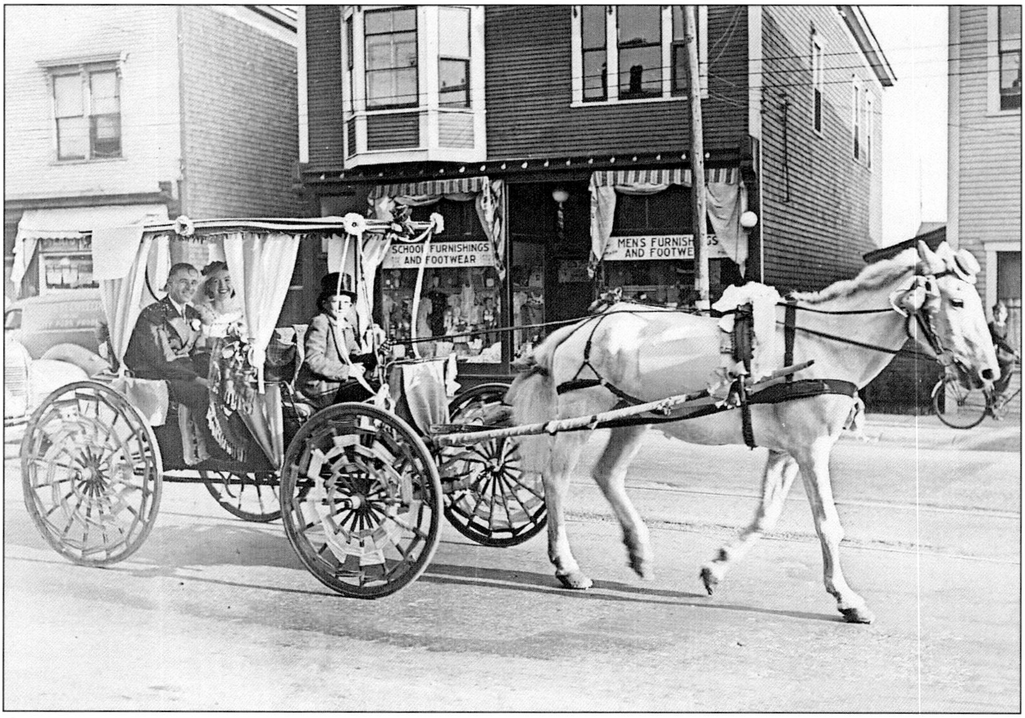

Garey Wedding Bells. It seems the horse and carriage was a wedding tradition for the Garey family. John and Hortence (O'Connor) Garey, married on August 21, 1939, are just passing the Fairville Department Store. In the bottom photo are Vince Richards and his bride, Edna Garey, sister of John. They were married on August 11, 1947. The children are Mary O'Herne, Vince's niece, and Kenny Garey, Edna's nephew. Note the sign on the Richards wagon "Sentenced For Life". Both couples were married at St. Rose Church in Milford. (Top photograph courtesy of M. Bernard; bottom photograph courtesy of Vince Richards.)

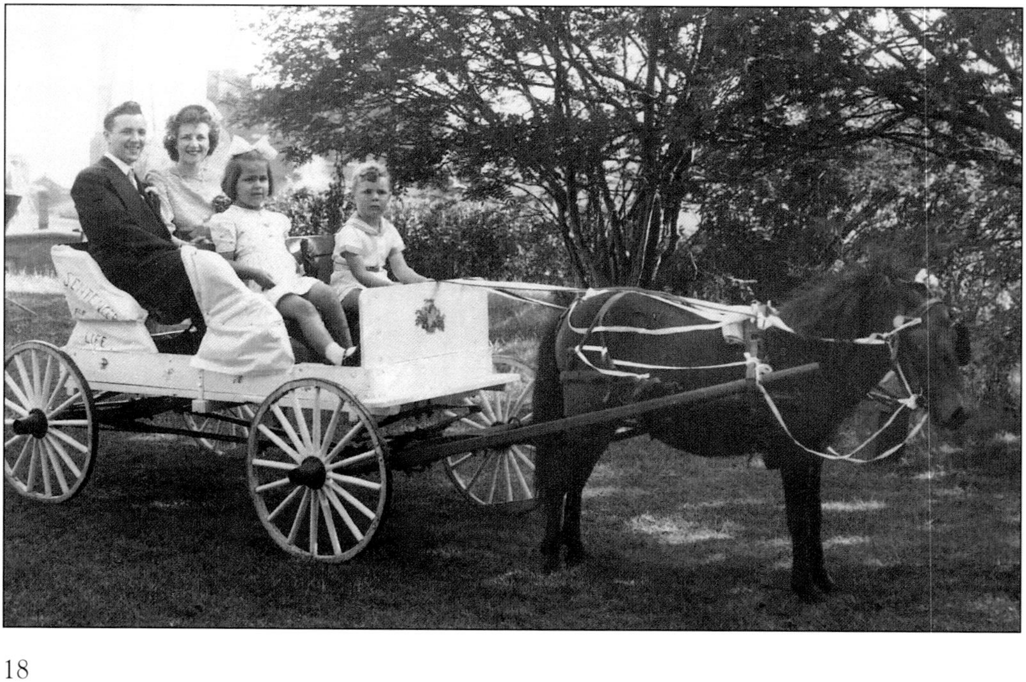

Two

PUBLIC BUILDINGS

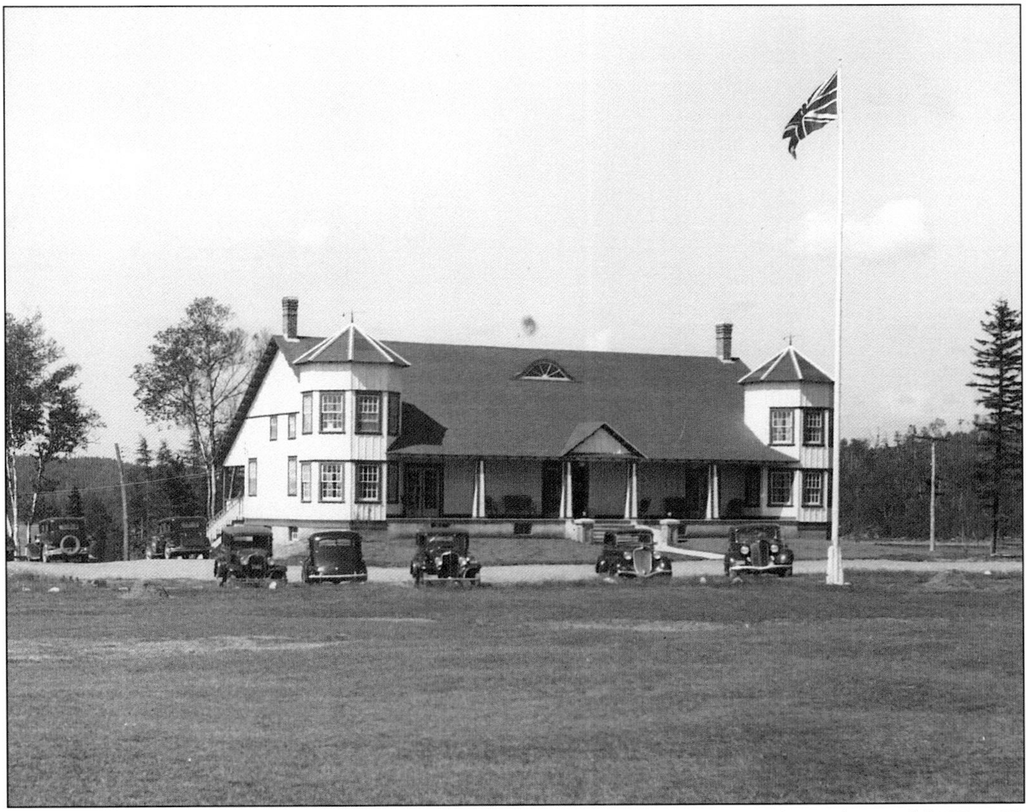

GOLF, C. 1930. The Ridgewood Golf Course at South Bay operated until World War II. The property was then used as the Health and Occupational Centre (for veterans from the Lancaster Military Hospital), the Workers Compensation Board, and now, it serves veterans again as a wing of the Regional Hospital. It is also the site of the new Centracare. (Steen collection, PIRP #7843.)

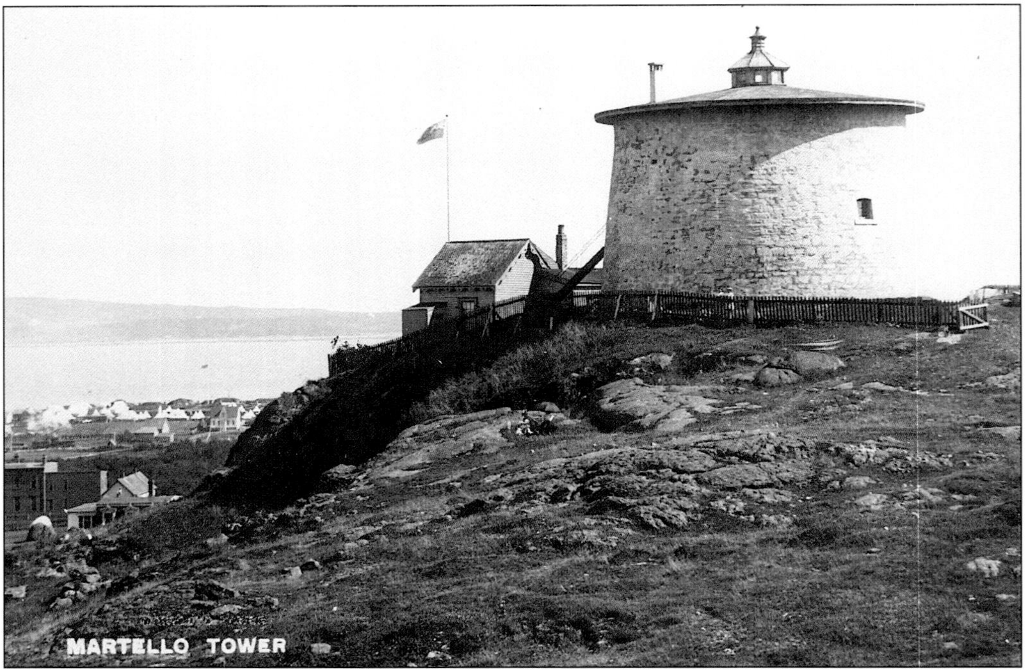

MARTELLO TOWER, C. 1910. The Carleton Martello Tower was built in 1815 just after the end of the War of 1812. The tower's first call-to-arms was in 1866 when a local battery of the NB Regiment of Artillery manned it against a feared Fenian attack. During World War II the same artillery regiment manned the Fire Command Post established there. Today it is operated by Parks Canada. (NB Museum.)

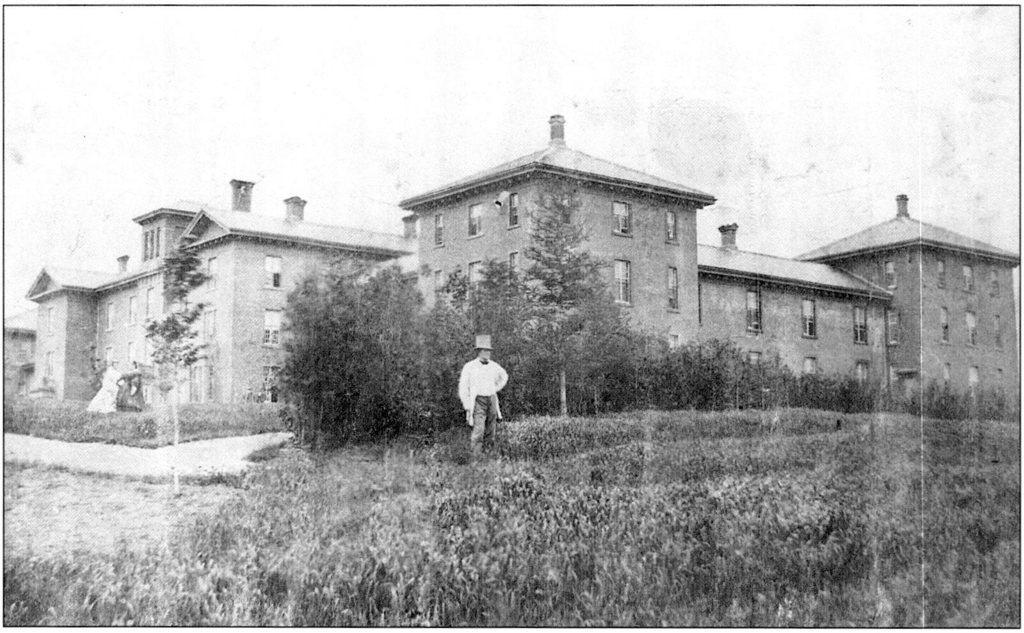

LUNATIC ASYLUM, C. 1860. Opened in 1848 to house the mentally ill, this oldest asylum in Canada was closed in 1998, its 150th anniversary. The buildings will be demolished. (HSJ collection, PIRP #6044.)

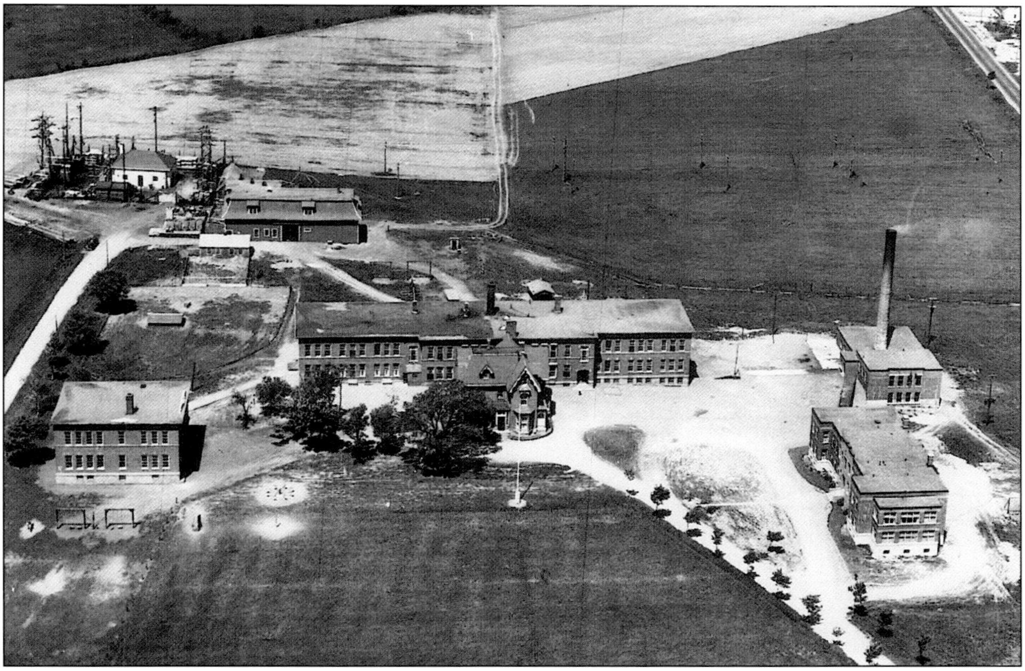

ORPHANAGE, C. 1955. The NB Protestant Orphans Home on the old Manchester Farm operated from the 1920s until 1979. The house of James Manchester, one of the founders of MRAs, is seen at the centre. Some of the buildings were incorporated into the current seniors residential complex. (HSJ collection, PIRP #9285.)

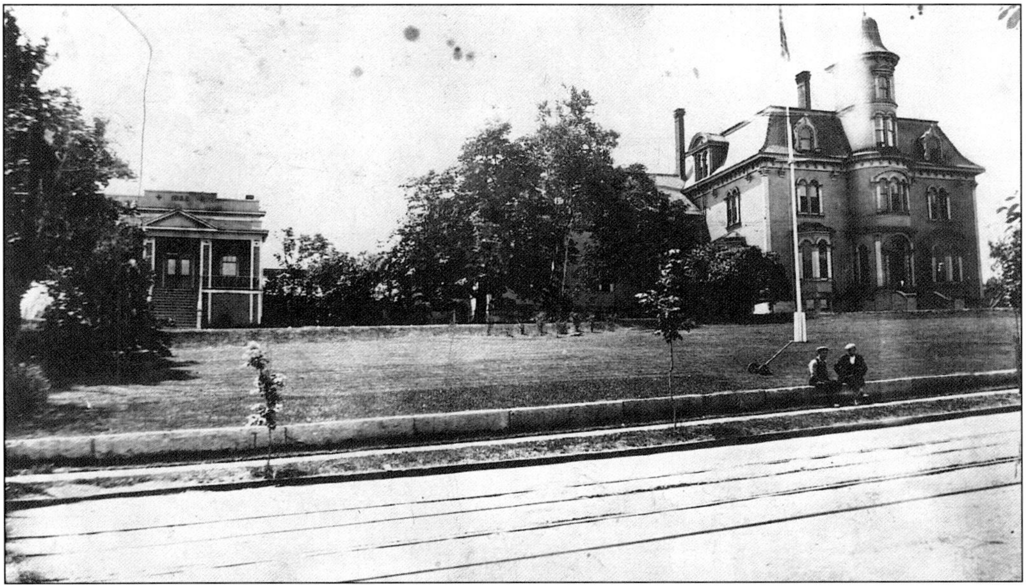

JEWETT'S CASTLE, C. 1925. E.D. Jewett's home served as the Union Baptist seminary and the Deaf & Dumb Institution before becoming a military hospital in 1919. Shortly thereafter it became a veterans hospital. In 1951 the original Jewett home was demolished for a new hospital entrance. After serving as the western division of the Regional Hospital, a dormitory for the 1985 Canada Summer Games, and government offices, the old DVA was demolished in the 1990s. (Bury collection, PIRP #5785.)

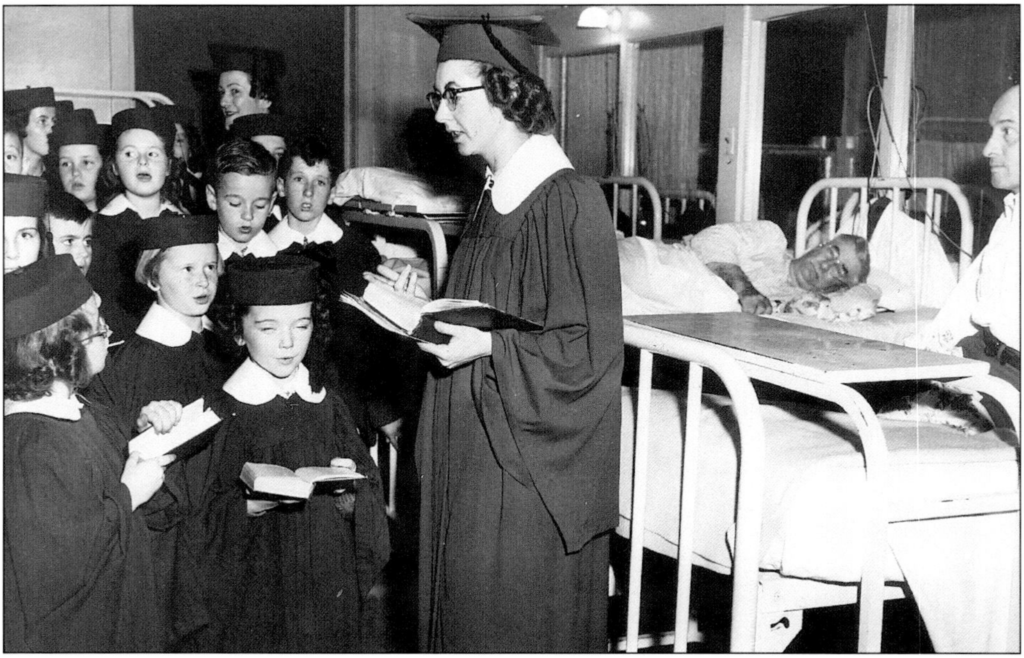

VETERANS ENTERTAINMENT, C. 1960. Under the guidance of Carol Harris, choir pianist of the Lancaster Baptist Church, the church choir visited the veterans in the DVA hospital on Christmas Eve. The veterans at the right are H. O'Connor and J.F. ?. (Harris family.)

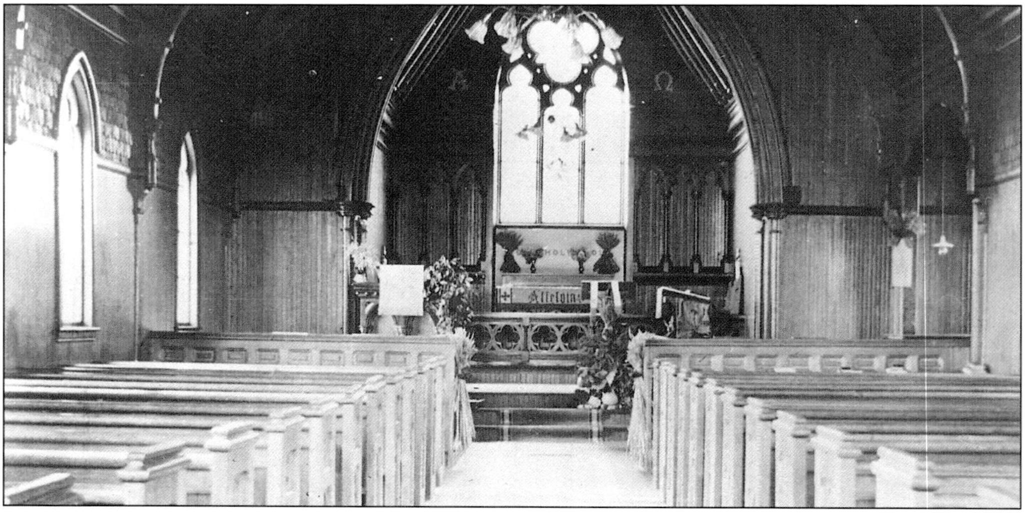

ST. JUDE'S CHURCH, C. 1906. St. Jude's, off Queen Square, Carleton, is one of the oldest Anglican churches in the west side. Although changes to the interior have been made, the ambiance of St. Jude's is still there today. Lancaster had its fair share of significant churches. The Church of the Good Shepherd was built on its present site in 1956, but the cornerstone was laid in 1877. Between 1831 and 1877, an Anglican church was located on or near the present Church of the Good Shepherd cemetery on Manawagonish Road. Lancaster United Baptist Church was built in 1881 and Rev. J.F. Bartlett was the first minister. After its construction, Baptists of the Carleton Free Christian Baptist Church living in Randolph and Fairville transferred their membership to the newly organized First United Baptist Church of Fairville. (Boyd collection, PIRP #7929.)

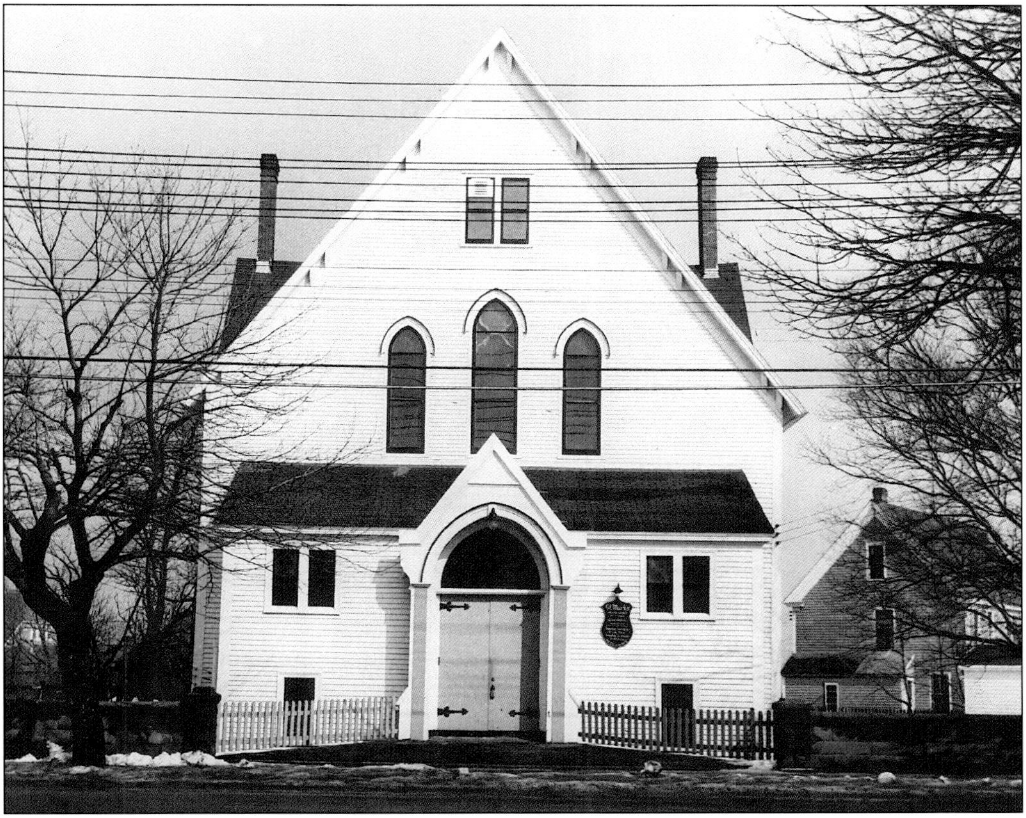

St. Mark's, c. 1950. The first Protestant church in Fairville was in the block between Church Avenue and Walnut Street. It was destroyed by fire in 1892 and replaced by St. Mark's. By the mid-1950s, St. Mark's had outgrown this building so a magnificent new church and centre was built in Greendale in 1960. (McPherson collection, PIRP #9492.)

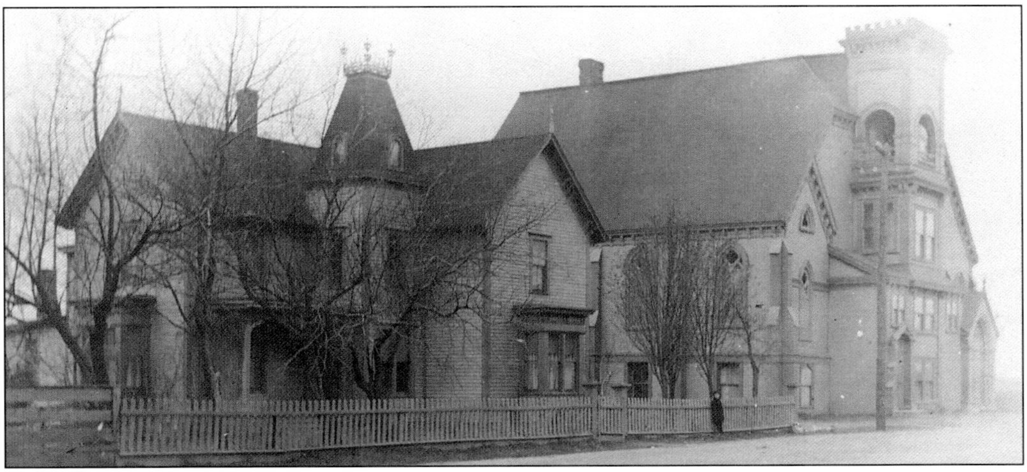

Fairville Baptist Church, c. 1920. Construction of the church began in 1881 based on designs by architect David E. Dunham. The church tower was 12 feet square and 100 feet high, and four Gothic windows were on each side. On October 13, 1895, the church was dedicated. Today the Lancaster Baptist Church is one of the most active community churches in the area. (M. Kingston.)

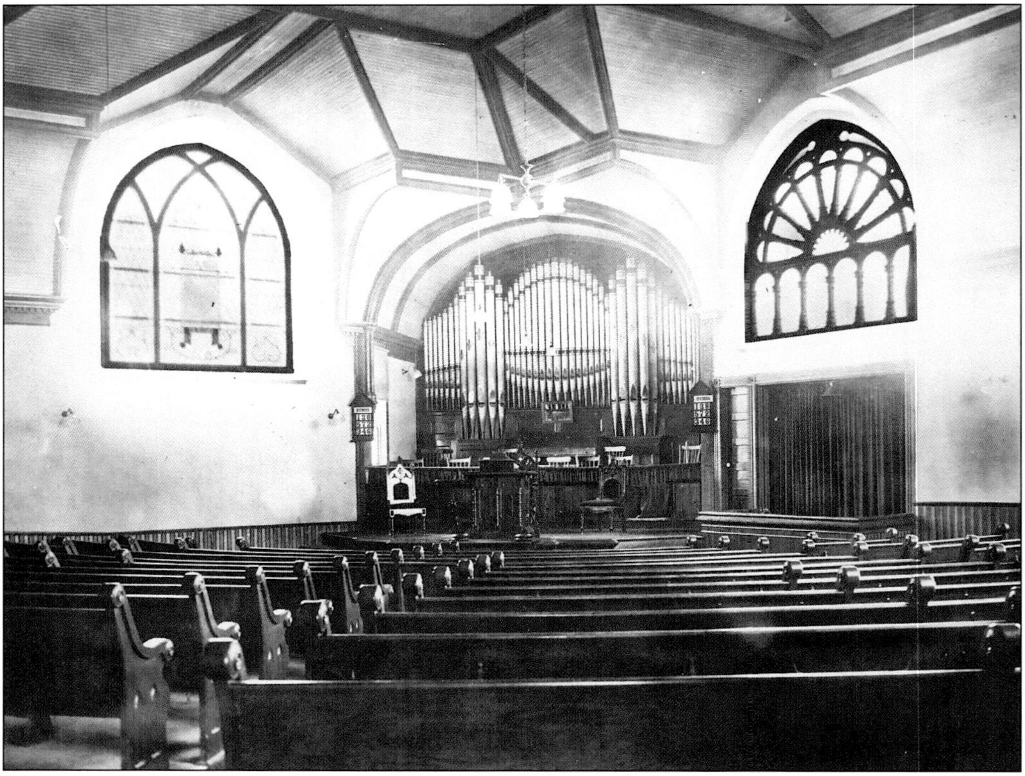

Fairville Baptist Church, c. 1910. "The church will be finished with ash and walnut, the principal arches, ceiling finish, etc. of stained pine . . . The chancel is to be fitted for accommodation of the choir. In front of the same, raised on a neat platform, will be the reading desk. A baptismal font screen, with an adjustable floor fitted on rollers, will be located on the platform". (Harris collection, PIRP #9407.)

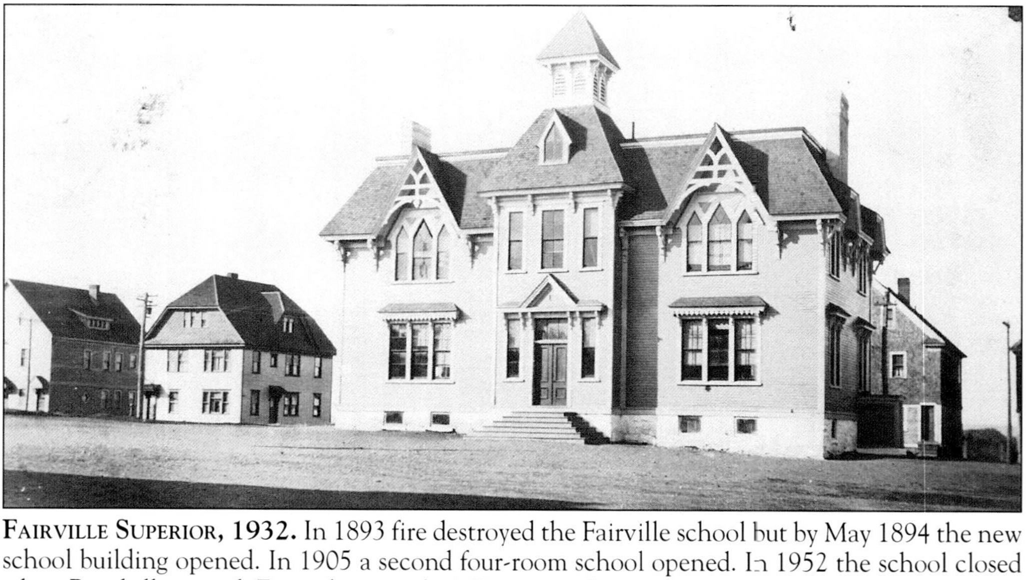

Fairville Superior, 1932. In 1893 fire destroyed the Fairville school but by May 1894 the new school building opened. In 1905 a second four-room school opened. In 1952 the school closed when Barnhill opened. From then until 1967, it served as Lancaster City Hall. Later it was the Motor Vehicle office and today it is a Co-Op housing complex. (Webb family.)

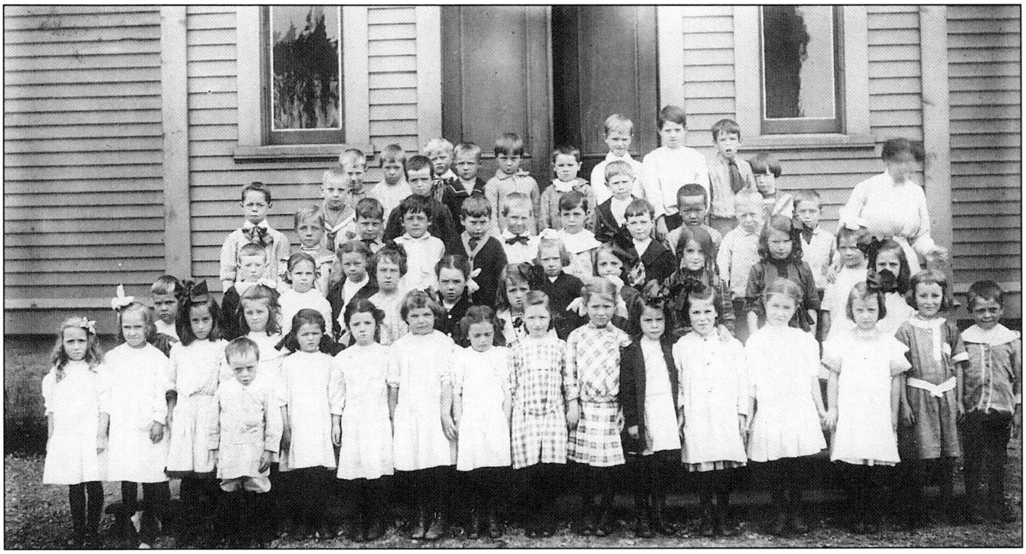

Fairville Superior, 1912. This is Miss O'Brien's grade one class. It appears as if every student followed their teachers advice and stood still for the photographer . . . that is everybody except the teacher! Do you recognize your parents or grandparents in this photo? (E. Boyd.)

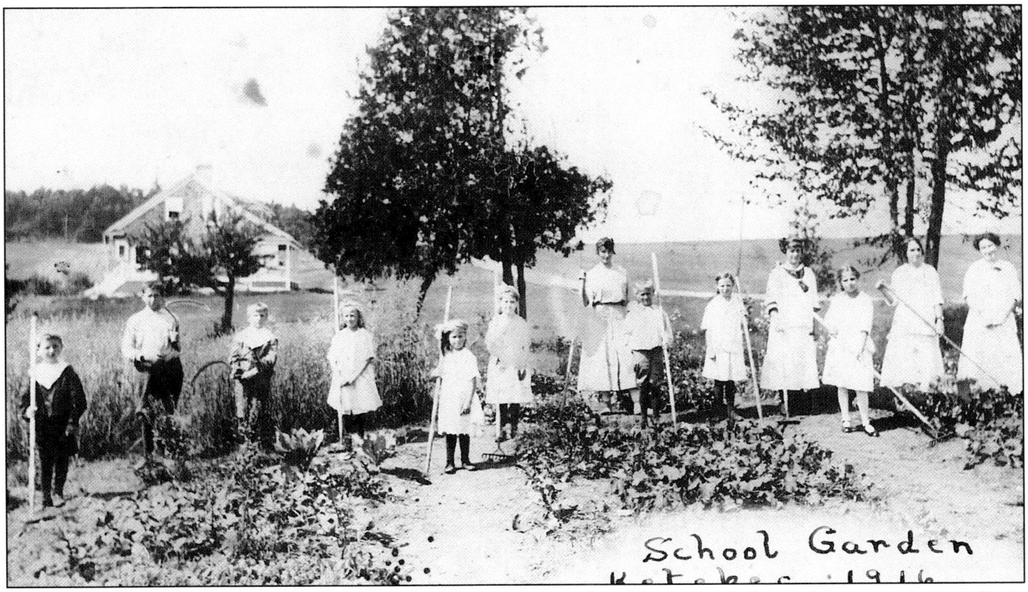

School Garden, 1916. Not only did students at the Ketepec School have to learn their three Rs, they also had to plant and grow their own vegetables. The only students identified are Milbey Vair, second from the left, and Eva Vair, fourth from the right. This school, built in the 1870s, was replaced with a three-room school in 1948. It closed in 1997. (M. Kingston.)

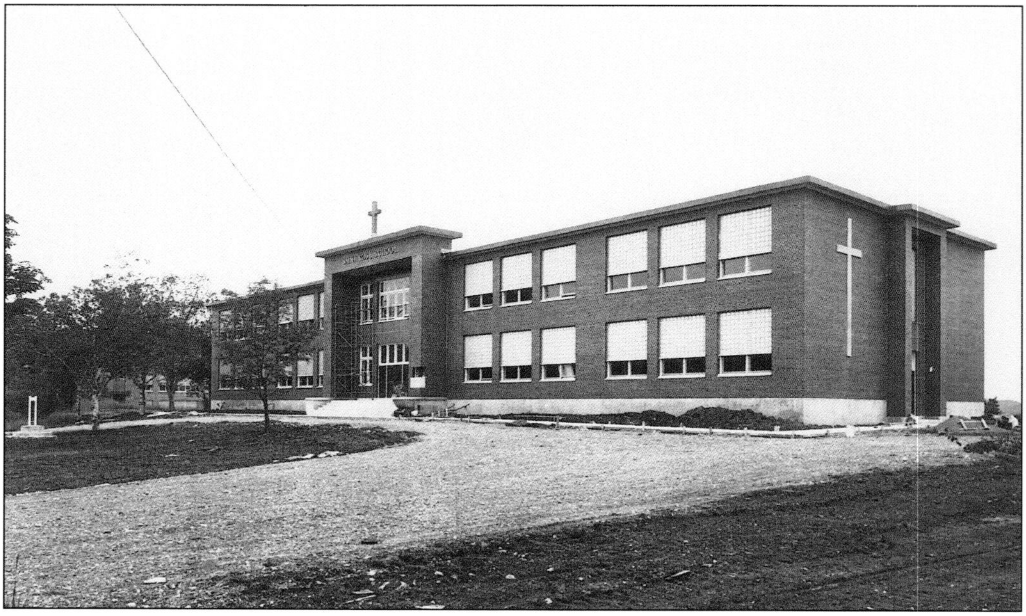

St. Rose, 1961. Situated on the former Ready property on Manawagonish Road, the current school was officially opened on May 1, 1961. It had over 320 students, 10 classrooms, and 14 staff. The Roman Catholic schools in Lancaster were established in the 1850s at Union Point, Spurr Cove (Milford), and the Short Ferry District (Pleasant Point). The nearby Barnhill Memorial School opened in 1953. (HSJ collection, PIRP #7028.)

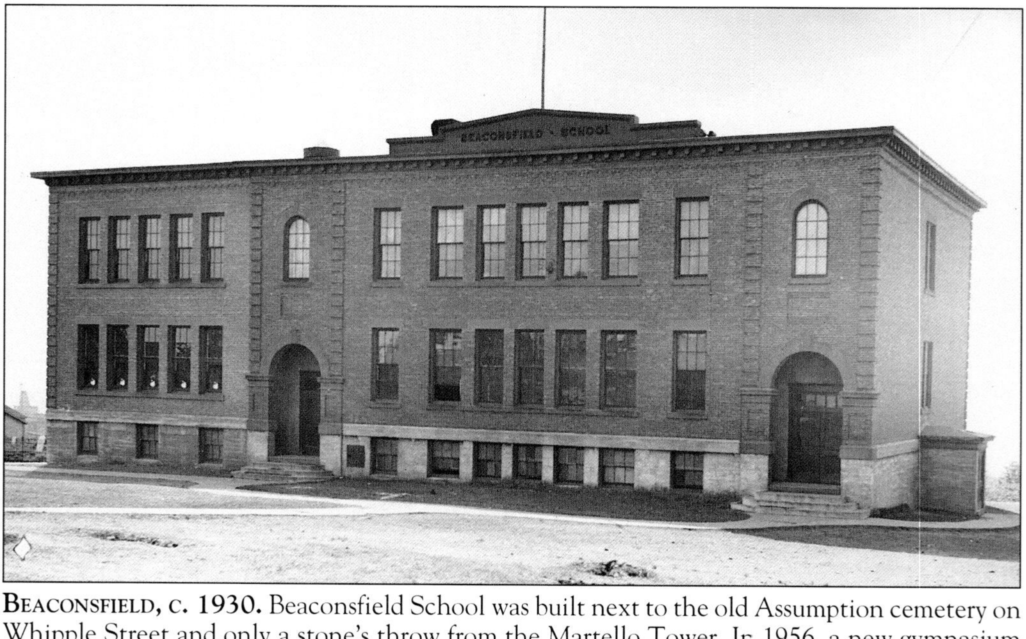

Beaconsfield, c. 1930. Beaconsfield School was built next to the old Assumption cemetery on Whipple Street and only a stone's throw from the Martello Tower. In 1956, a new gymnasium and six new classrooms were added to this original building. The architect for the addition was Stanley W. Emmerson. (K. Steen.)

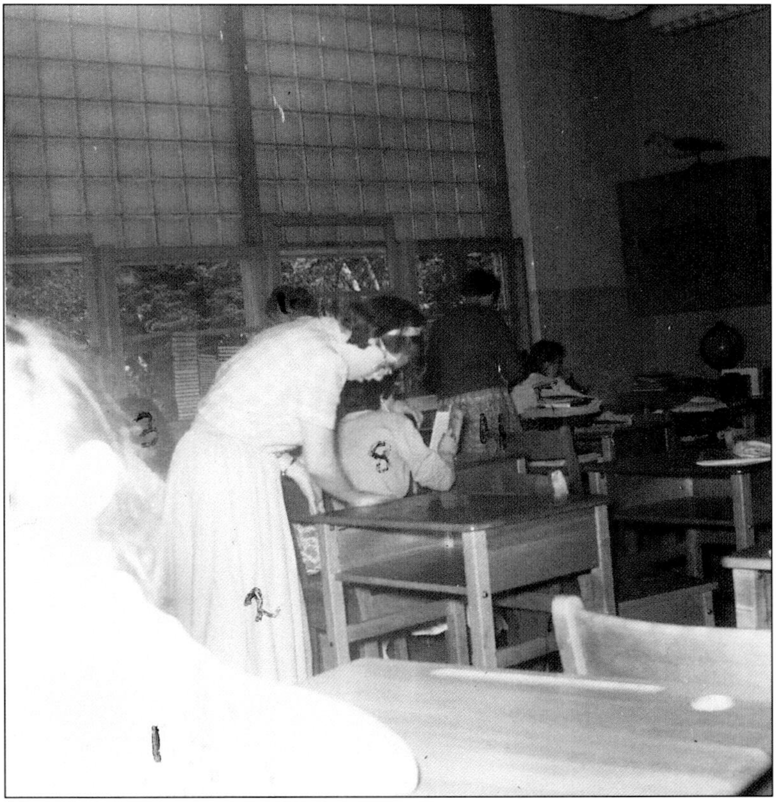

GRADE EIGHT, JUNE 26, 1958. Barnhill students of Irene Fraser are Sheila S. (#1), Jeanette Keirstead (#2), Susan Frost (#3), Gail Osborne (#4), Lillian Murphy (#5), Jean Melvin (#6), Sandra R. (#7), and ? (#8). (Canavan collection PIRP #9495.)

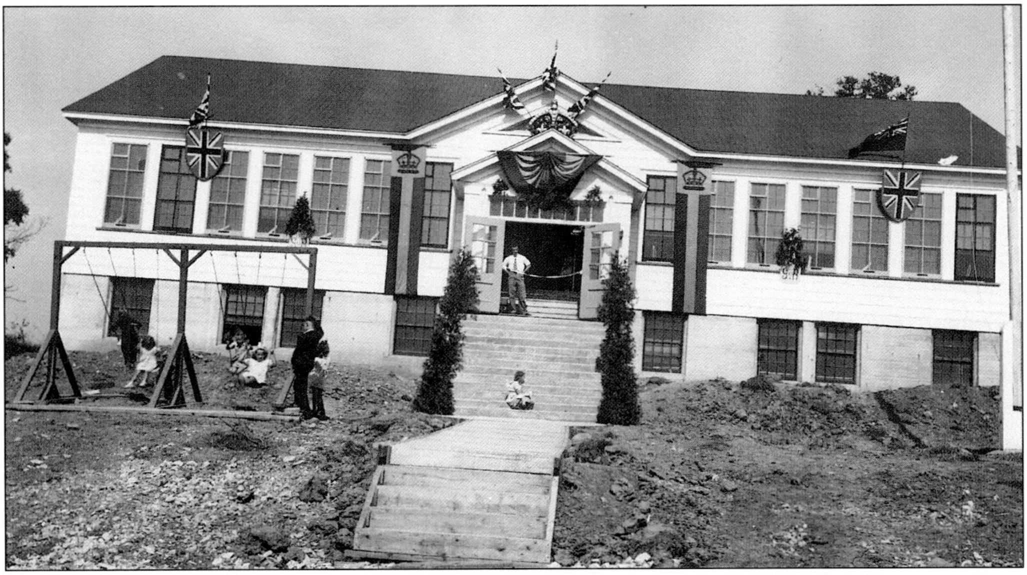

SCHOOL OPENING. The Dennis Morris Memorial School in Randolph officially opened on September 6, 1948. The land for the school was donated by the heirs of Dennis Morris, and the school architect was R.T. Steeves of Fredericton. The decorations on the school were under the direction of policeman Albert Perry. The original staff consisted of Ronald Graham, principal and grades seven and eight, Bertha Vautour, intermediate grades, and Carol Harris, primary grades. (Harris family.)

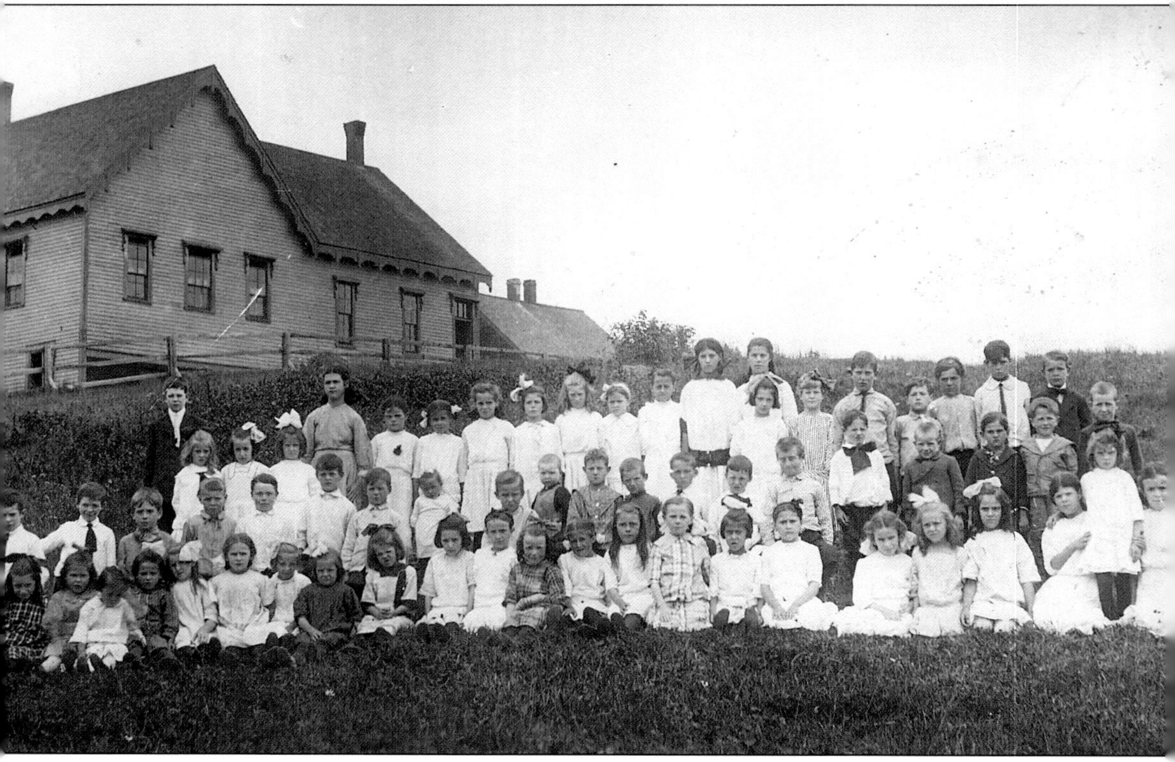

UNION POINT SCHOOL, 1915. This school was built before 1854 in the area of the current Irving Tissue Mill. In 1931, it became known as St. Rose School and continued as such until 1960. On March 6, 1961, the vacant school was destroyed by fire. The grade one, two, and three classes shown here were taught by Annie McElwaine; the students are, from left to right, as follows: (front row) Mary Mullaney, Nellie Martin, Annie Martin, Evelyn Martin, Mary Hurley, Anna Hurley, Gertrude Savage, Margaret McGovern, ? Kelly, unidentified, Celina Brideau, Dorothy Gifford, Edith Williams, Lillian Wallace, Helen McPhee, Anna Paul, Mary Brideau, ? Crowley, Alice Wallace, unidentified, Eva DesRoches, Lydia DesRoche (standing), and Hazel Palmer; (middle row) Joseph Delaney, Dominic Mullaney, Fred Casey, Gregory McManus, Charles Murphy, Peter DesRoche, ? Rogers, unidentified, James Morris, William Ferguson, unidentified, Ted McGovern, Harry ?, Clement O'Connor, Charles Savage, James McMullin, Dan Mullin, Edward Elward, Stanley McPhee, and John Mullin; (back row) Clement Shannon, Ena Donovan, Elsie Crowley, Florence O'Neill, Josephine Delaney, Letitia Walton, Rita Fitzgerald, Mary ?, unidentified, Alfred Perry, unidentified, Henry DesRoche, and Eldon Palmer. (M. Bernard.)

Three

Police and Fire Services

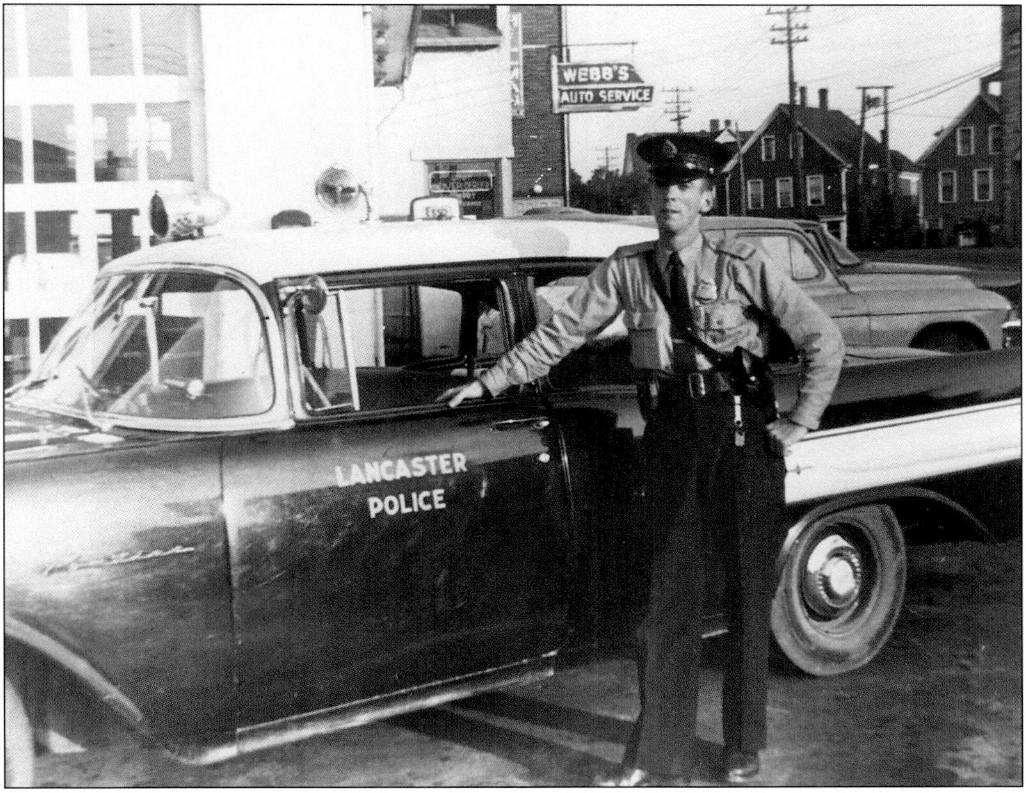

On Duty, c. 1958. Constable Harold Mayes joined the Lancaster Police Department in 1957. Harold said that his department "had a good working relationship with the Saint John Police Department." In 1960, he joined the staff of the NB Motor Vehicle Board, from which he retired in 1983. While he was known as a "holy terror" as a driver examiner, he states that it was the numerous traffic accidents he saw as a policeman that influenced the high standards he set for new drivers. Harold was also a member of the Beaconsfield Fire Department for 22 years. He is outside Webb's Service Station on Church Avenue. (Mayes collection, PIRP #7652.)

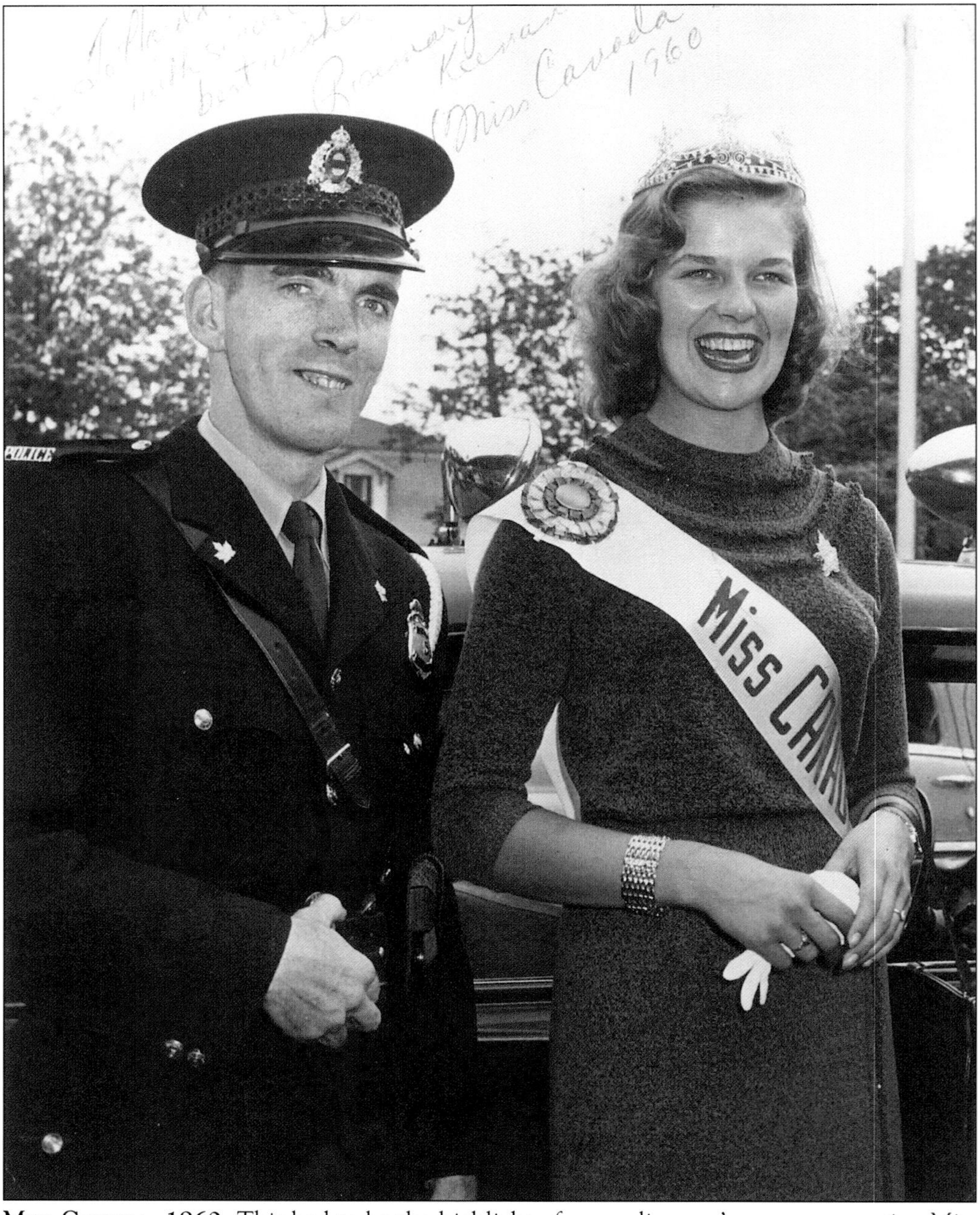

Miss Canada, 1960. This had to be the highlight of any policeman's career—escorting Miss Canada for the day. In this case, Miss Canada, Rosemary Keenan, just happened to be from Saint John. Apparently, a Saint John police officer was to meet Mayes at the Reversing Falls bridge so the exchange of responsibilities could take place. However, the Saint John police officer was unavailable so Harold took her around Saint John. (Mayes collection, PIRP #7660.)

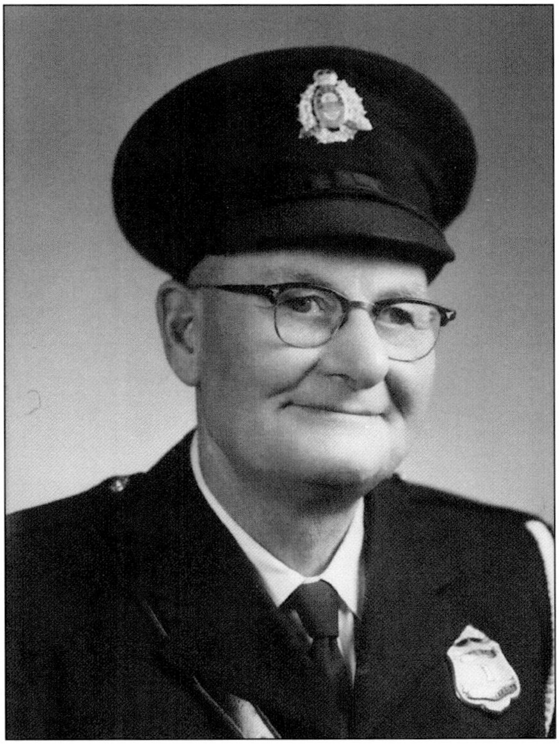

Policeman #1, 1965. Constable Charles McCormack, of Milford, was a Lancaster police officer for over 30 years, retiring on July 1, 1965. A note that accompanied this photo states, "I had some pictures taken for Police Dept. we all had them taken for office so I got 3 extras taken . . ." He retired a few months after this photo was taken. Charles was described as "a super person to work with." He died in 1969. (E. Boyd.)

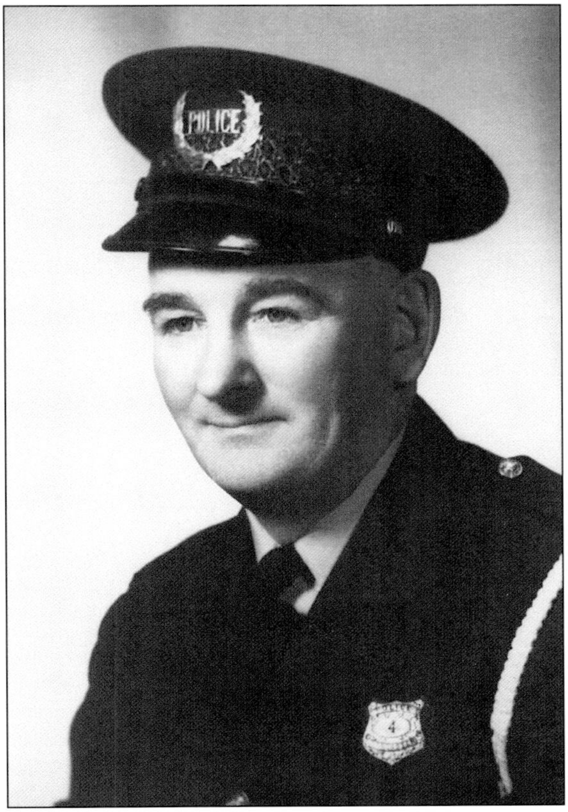

Lancaster Police Officer #4, c. 1960. Staff Sgt. Albert F. Perry joined the force on November 8, 1945, and was promoted to sergeant in 1953. He was secretary-treasurer of the Lancaster Police Association before retiring in 1966. He was always handing out candy to the kids; known as a "good community man," he was "always helping somebody." Albert was also known for his athletic abilities, being involved with baseball, sculling, speed skating, and boxing, and he was also involved in the design and promotion of the Lancaster Centennial Arena. (Perry collection, PIRP #9461.)

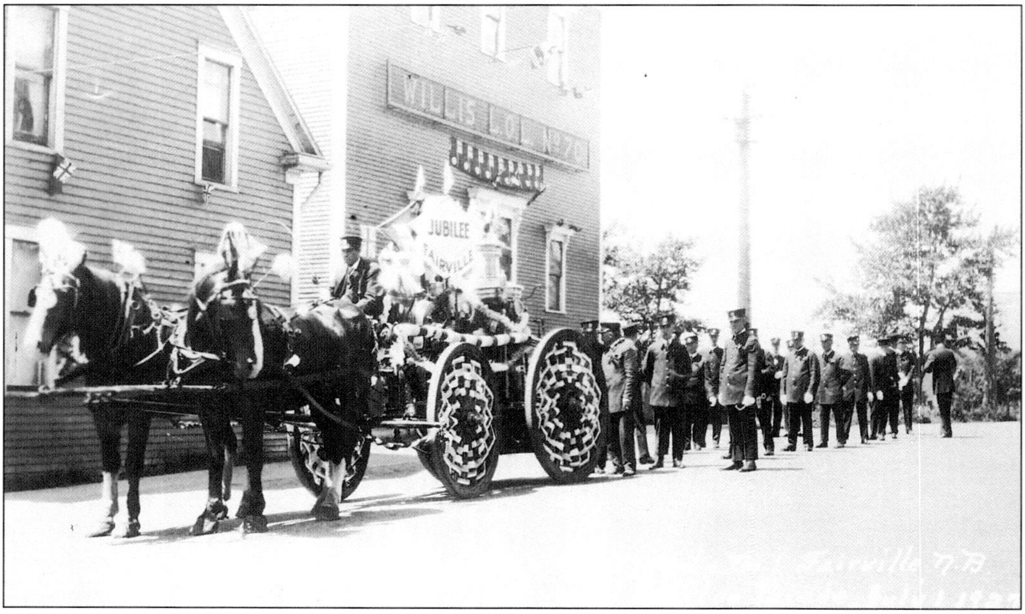

DIAMOND JUBILEE, JULY 1, 1927. The men of #1 station on Church Avenue have gaily decorated their steamer wagon and horses to celebrate Canada's birthday. In the rear is Willis Lodge #70, Loyal Orange Lodge. Other opportunities for such public demonstrations as this were the annual fireman's tournaments. The last Maritime tournament hosted by Lancaster was in July 1963. The event included the selection of a Miss Fireman, a ball, parade, banquet, street dance, and their infamous "Shirt Tail Parade". (E. Boyd.)

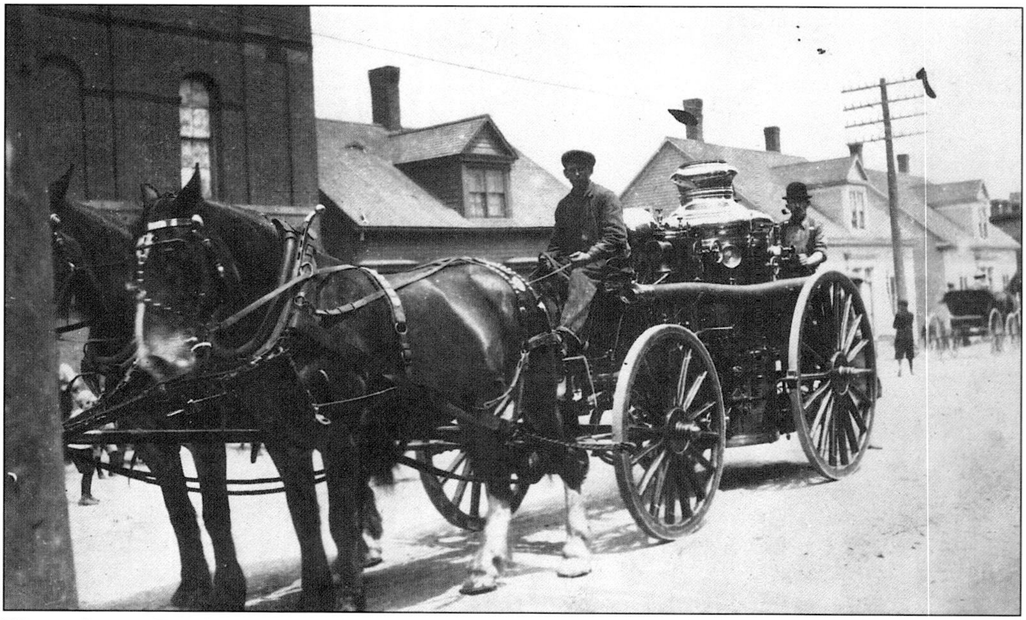

WHERE'S THE FIRE? C. 1906. The Fairville Fire Department pumper appears outside the Ready (Moosehead) Brewery. It is believed that this is the pumper that was sold to the Yarmouth Fire Fighters Museum in the 1970s. (McKinnon collection, PIRP #9385.)

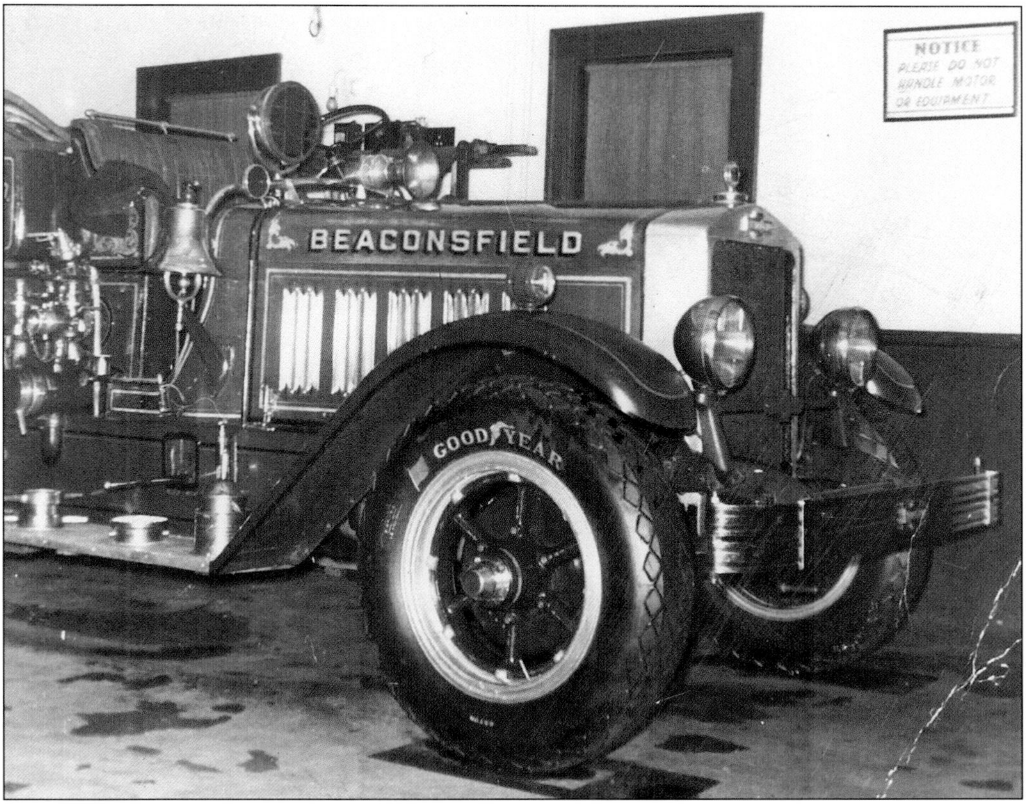

Names No More! The Beaconsfield Fire Department disappeared with amalgamation into Lancaster in 1953, and the Lancaster Fire Department disappeared with amalgamation into Saint John in 1967. Edmund Reid is at the front right, and Fred Brownell is behind the driver's wheel. W.P. Golding is to the right of Brownell. Note the decorative names painted on the hoods of the trucks. Fire vehicles have a long tradition of decorative embellishments. (E. Reid collection, PIRP #7893, #7891.)

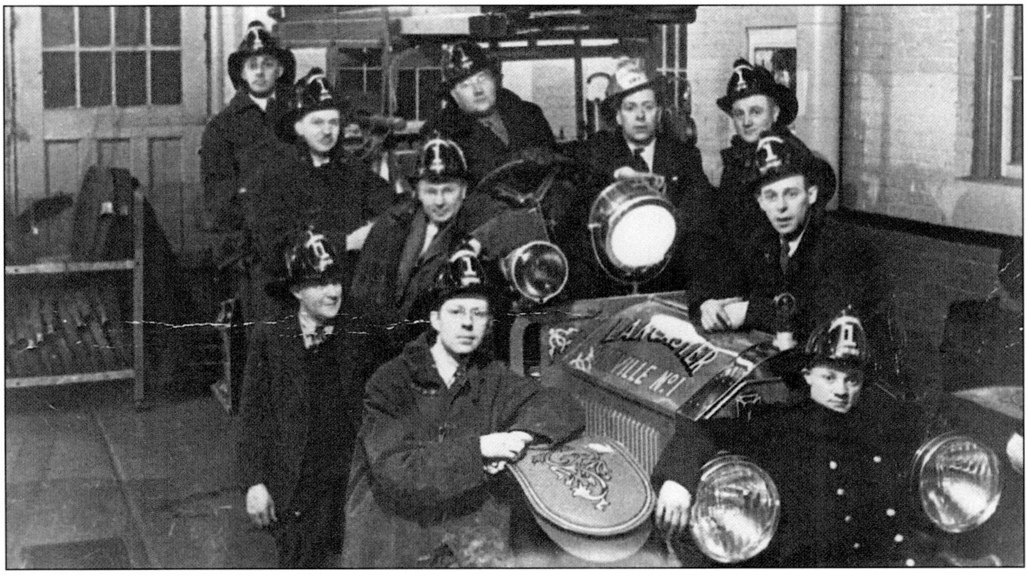

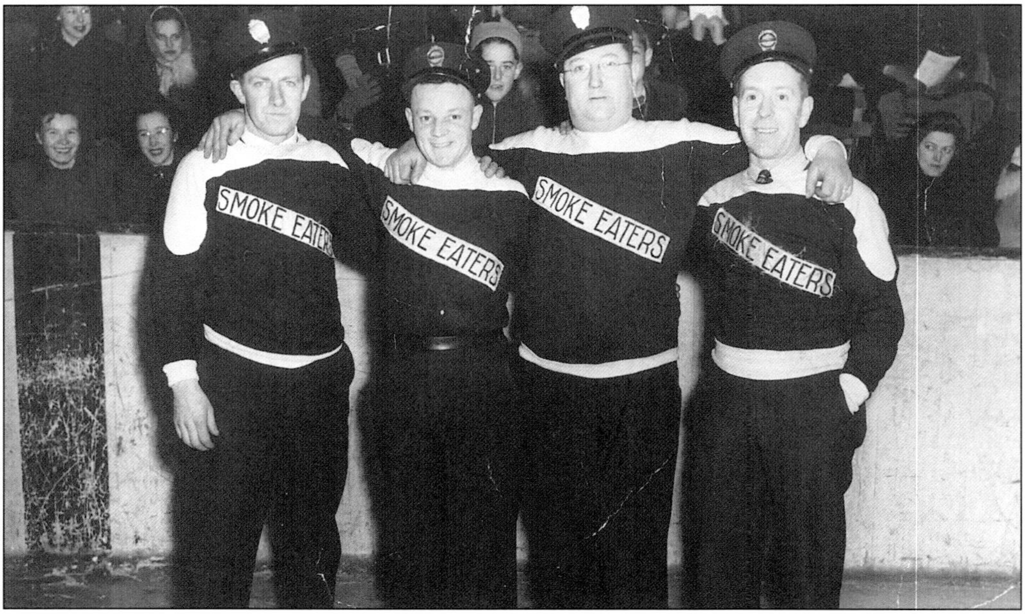

Smoke Eaters! c. 1960. With the name Smoke Eaters, and ice, these men kept the audience entertained during hockey games. Shown here, from left to right, are Tommy Butler, Edmund J. Reid, Fred Brownell, and P. Henderson. Reid retired in 1972 with the rank of lieutenant after 30 years of service with the Lancaster and Saint John Fire Departments. (E. Reid collection, PIRP #7896.)

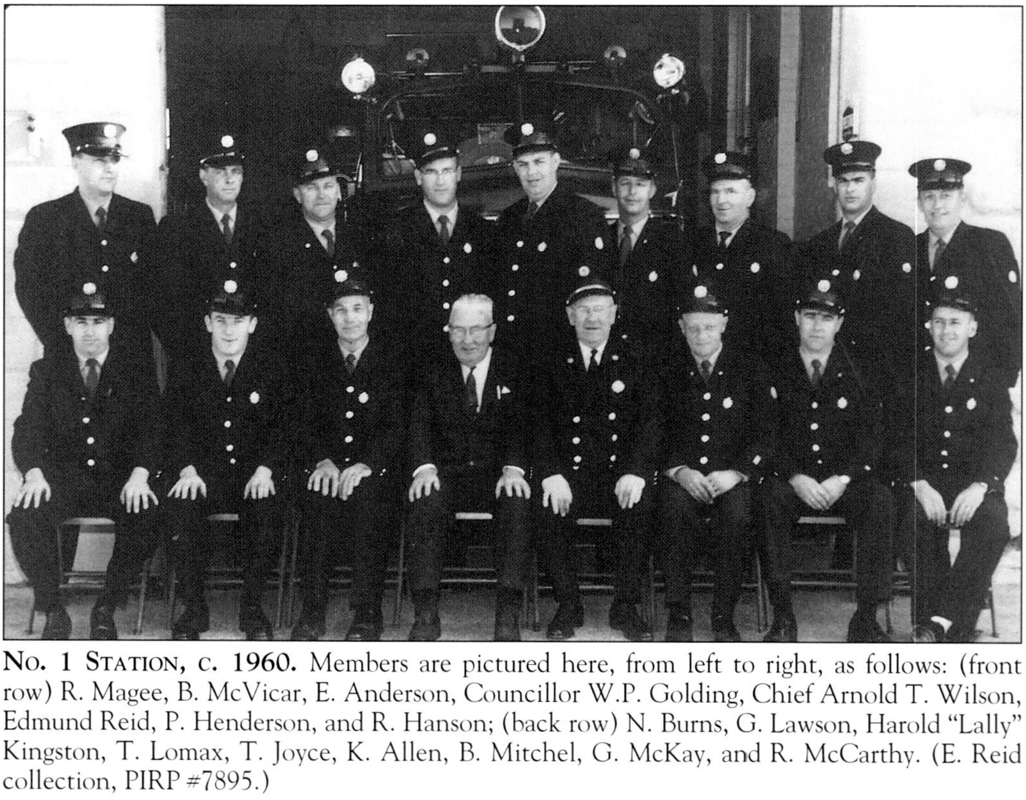

No. 1 Station, c. 1960. Members are pictured here, from left to right, as follows: (front row) R. Magee, B. McVicar, E. Anderson, Councillor W.P. Golding, Chief Arnold T. Wilson, Edmund Reid, P. Henderson, and R. Hanson; (back row) N. Burns, G. Lawson, Harold "Lally" Kingston, T. Lomax, T. Joyce, K. Allen, B. Mitchel, G. McKay, and R. McCarthy. (E. Reid collection, PIRP #7895.)

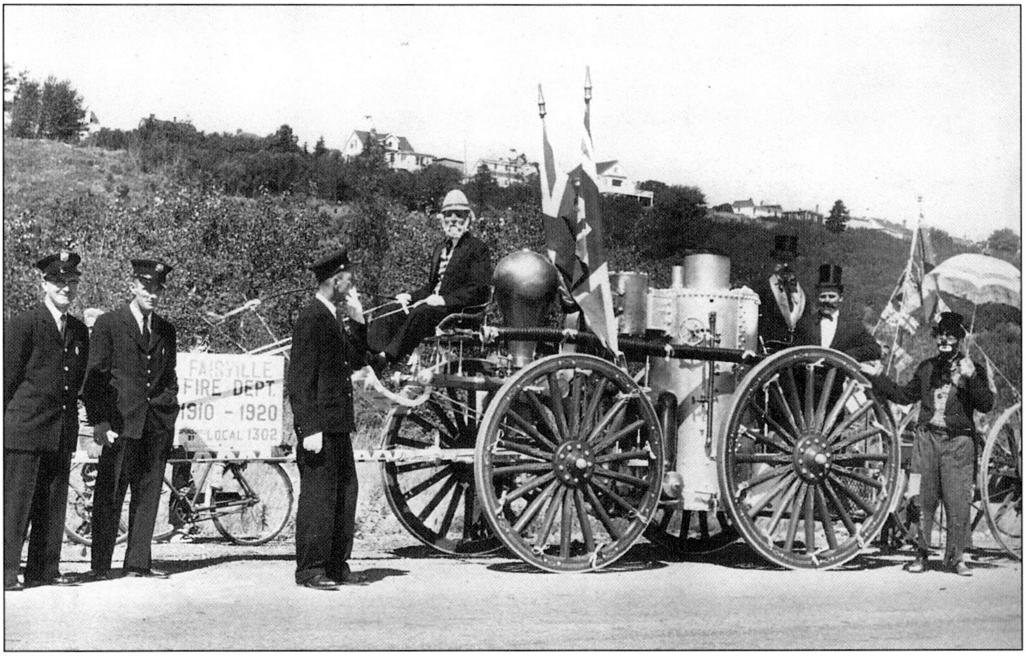

A Fireman's Parade! 1960. Nobody loved a parade more than a firefighter. This float represented the Fairville Fire Department between 1910 and 1920. Shown here, from left to right, are Harold "Lally" Kingston, Eddy Reid, Jerry Arseneau, driver Albert Perry, Dave Campbell, Pat Patterson, and an unidentified clown. (J. Arseneau collection, PIRP #7920.)

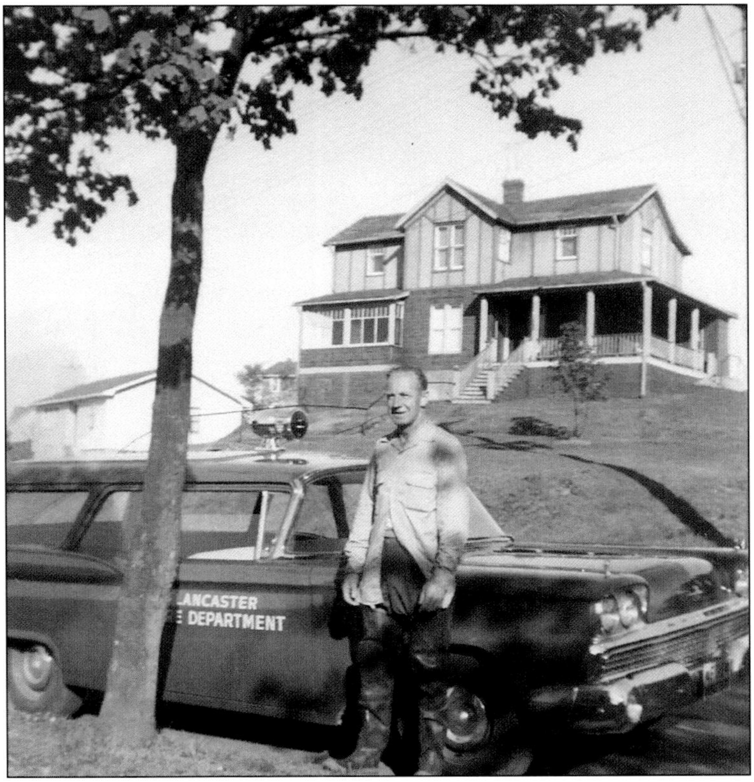

Ready When Needed! 1959. Tom Butler was a volunteer member of the Lancaster Fire Department for over 20 years. During an October 1956 fire, "Acting Fire Chief Thomas Butler had police ask Saint John Firefighters for aid . . . Chief Butler said that the blaze apparently originated in a bedroom in an apartment over the store of Lads and Lassies." (G. Butler.)

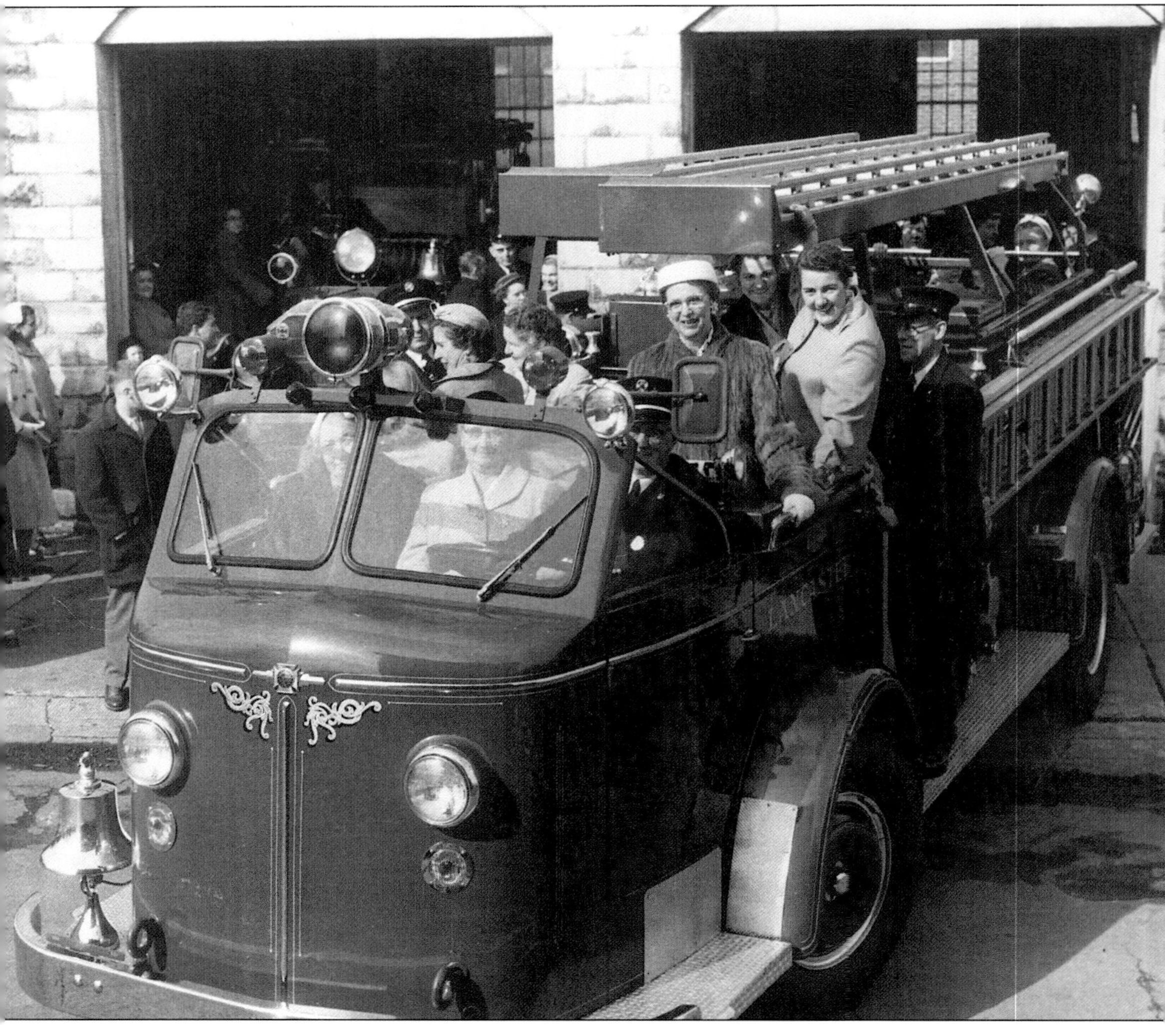

A Fire Call? c. 1955. This is obviously an open house at the station or else the recruiting drive was tremendously successful. The driver is Chief Earl Lawson, and at his right is his wife, Annie. Behind Chief Lawson is Mrs. Aubrey Sprague; to her left is Alice Patterson. Between these two ladies is Eva Nason. Standing on the side of the truck at the right is Aubrey Sprague. (McKinnon collection, PIRP #7919.)

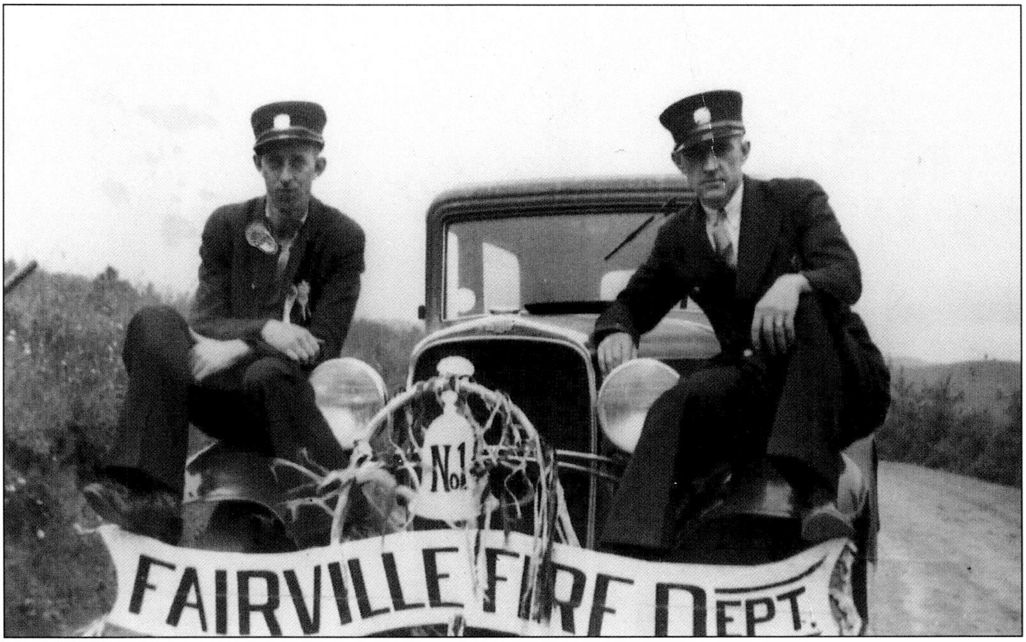

CHIEF'S CAR? c. 1930. If this car is decorated for a parade, where is the parade? From the background it looks as if this picture was taken in the middle of the country, and for 1930s Fairville, that could have been on Manawagonish Road. The firefighters are Silas Cheeseman (left) and Pat Patterson. (E. Reid collection, PIRP #7887.)

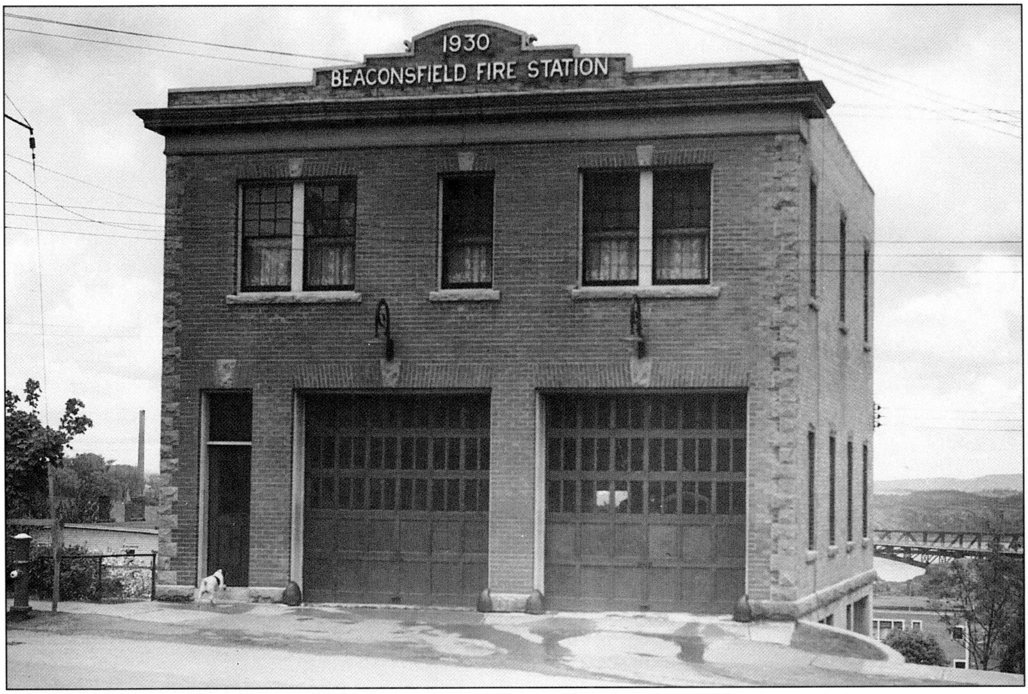

BEACONSFIELD STATION, c. 1935. The date stone tells when it was built, and the station served the Beaconsfield, Lancaster, and Saint John Departments until it was closed in the 1970s, when it was sold and converted into a house. (K. Steen.)

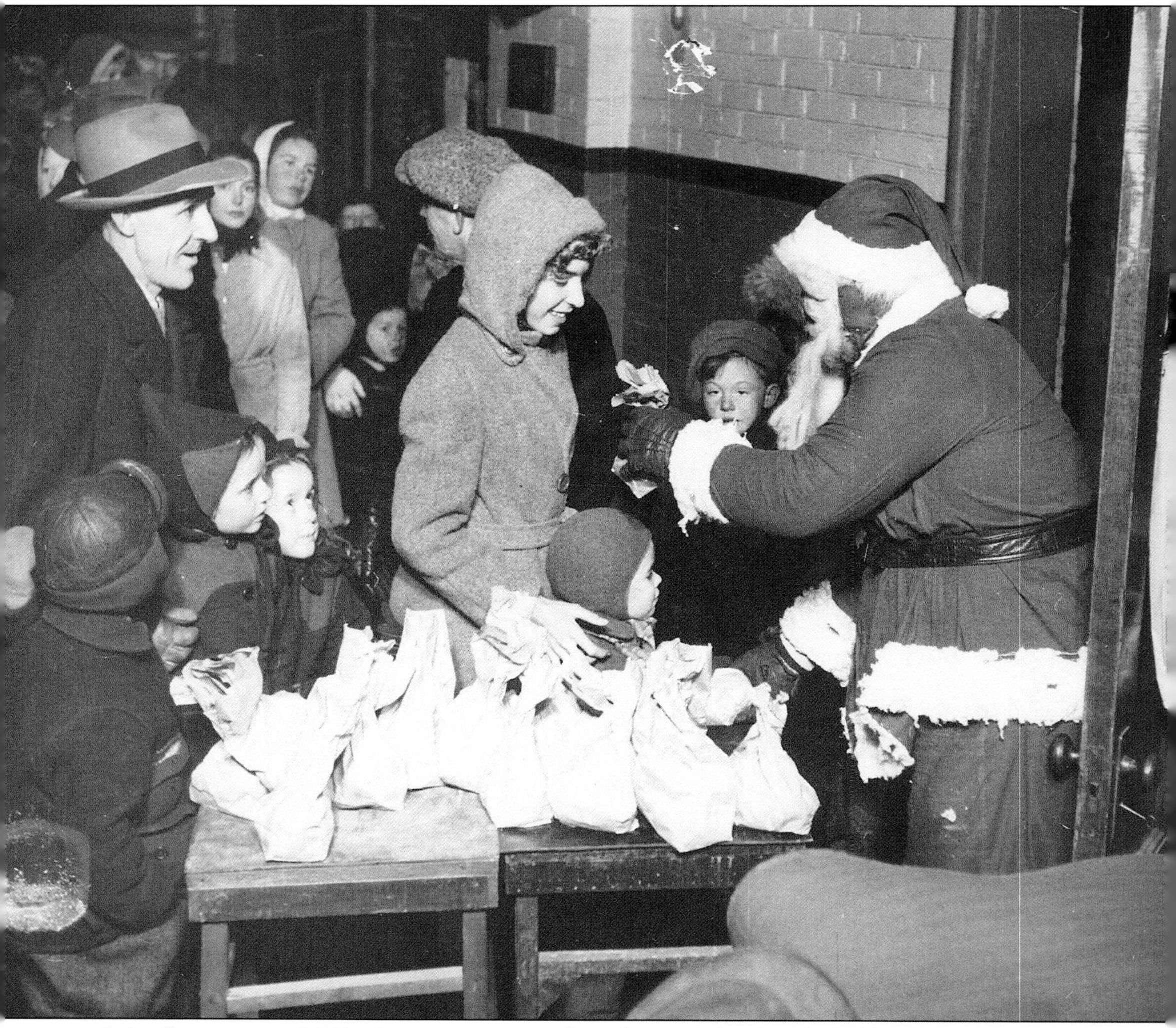

It's Santa, c. 1950. It was an annual tradition—the local children would come into No. 1 station at Christmas where they received a bag of goodies and chatted with Santa. For many years Santa was none other than Albert Perry. And who is the lucky girl with Santa? She's Penny Hovey, daughter of firefighter Chris Hovey. Do you recognize anybody else? (P. Hovey.)

Four

Royal Visits

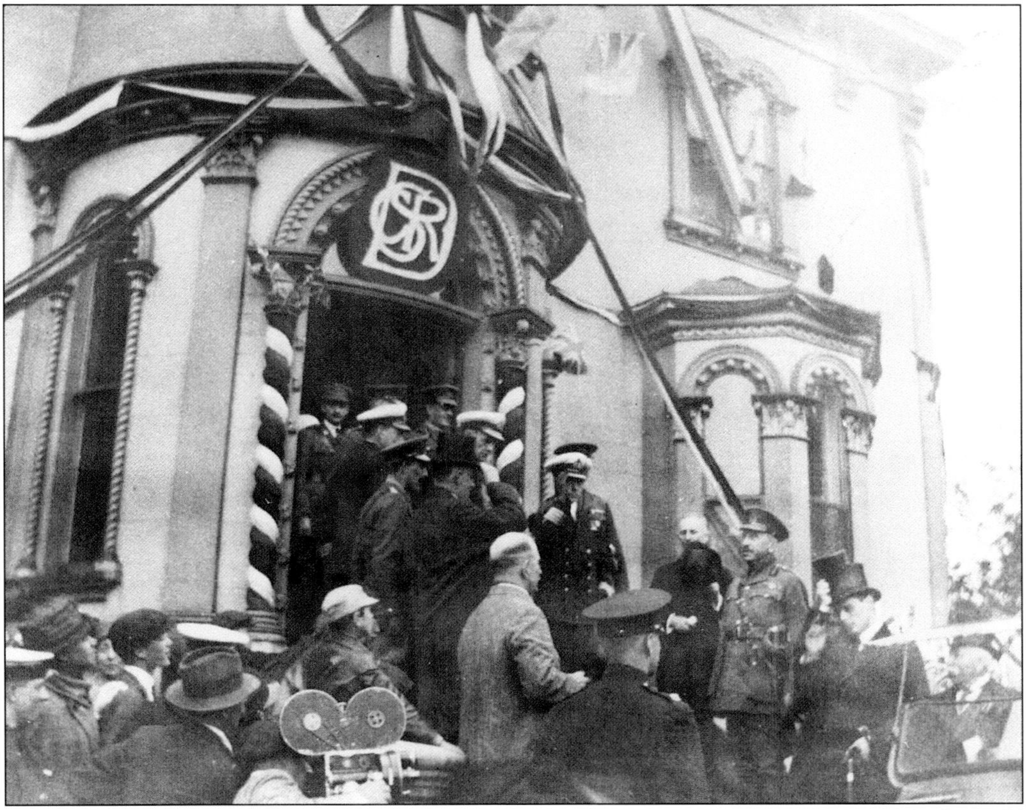

Jewett's Castle, August 1919. During the Joy Day celebration marking the end of World War I, HRH the Prince of Wales (centre.) visited the wounded soldiers at the military hospital. Note the movie cameraman at the bottom left. There were over a dozen movies shot of this visit, but only a few minutes of footage survive. The Prince later abdicated his throne for the "woman he loved". (Morrison collection, PIRP #4847.)

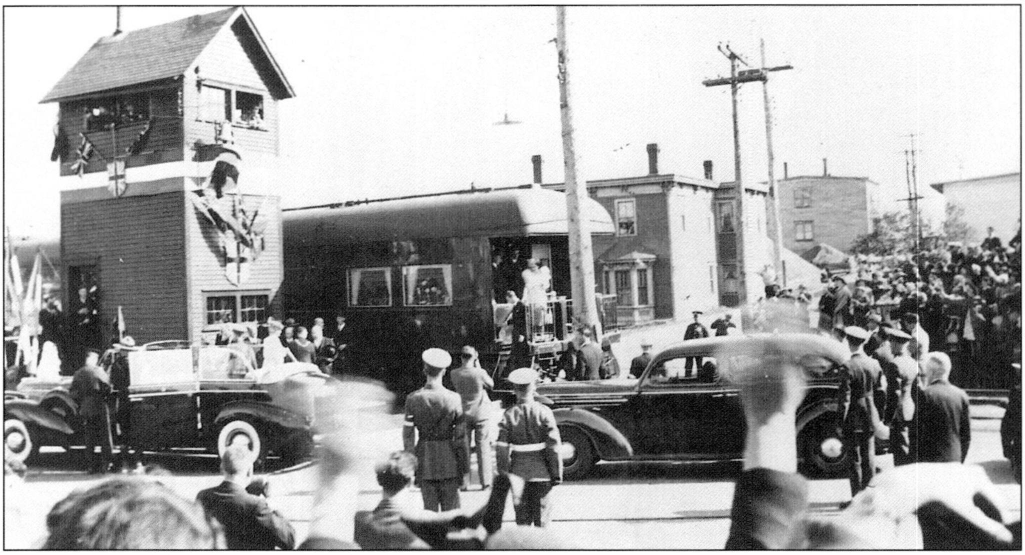

Royal Visit, 1939. On June 13, King George and Queen Elizabeth became the first reigning monarchs to visit Saint John. They were met just outside the Fairville station, and the car route through Fairville was lined by thousands of eager and proud Canadians. (Chittick collection, PIRP #7952.)

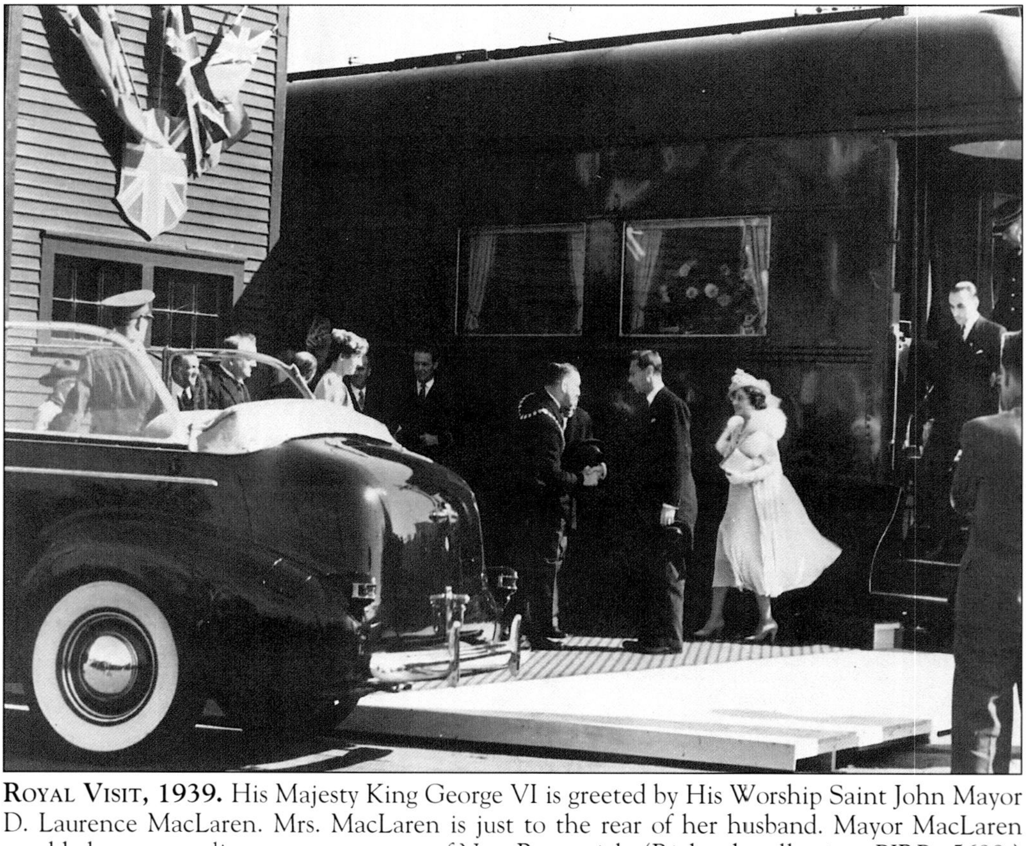

Royal Visit, 1939. His Majesty King George VI is greeted by His Worship Saint John Mayor D. Laurence MacLaren. Mrs. MacLaren is just to the rear of her husband. Mayor MacLaren would also serve as lieutenant governor of New Brunswick. (Richards collection, PIRP #5698.)

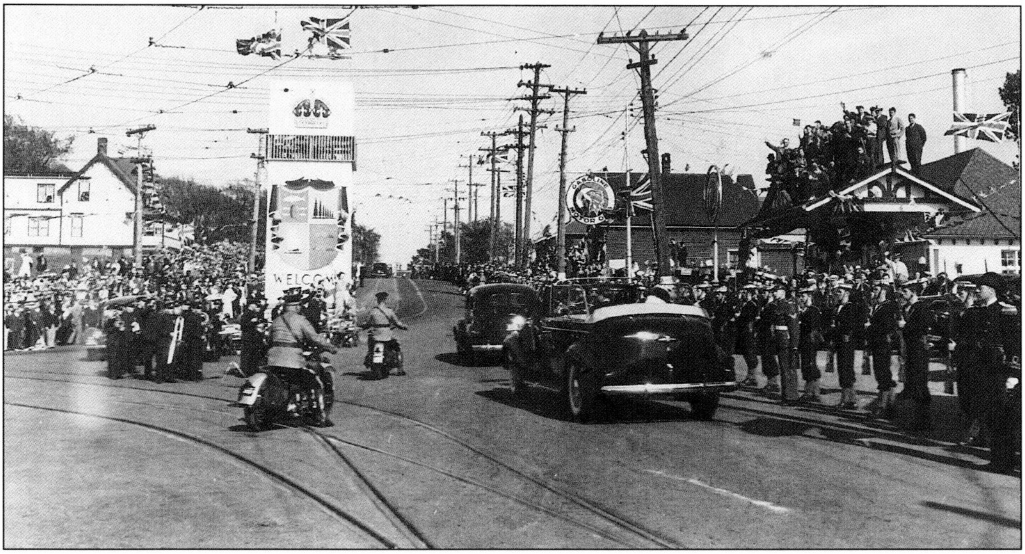

SIMMS CORNER, 1939. With Their Majesties in the rear car, the motorcade starts down Lancaster Avenue. Members of the Carleton Cornet Band are at the left, and as can been seen at the right, every available roof space was used to get a better glimpse of the King and Queen. (Richards collection, PIRP #5699.)

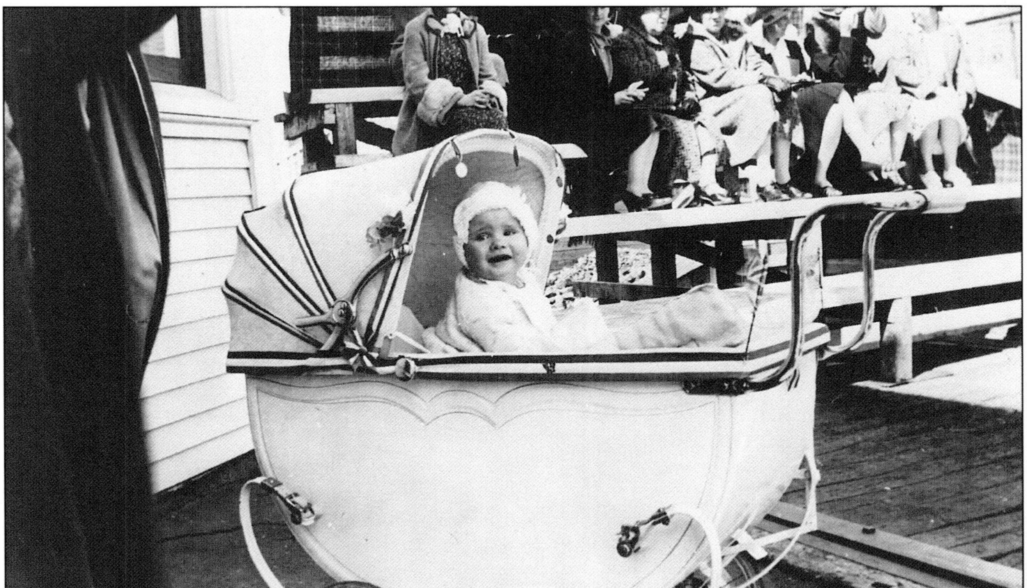

ISN'T SHE CUTE! 1939. The Chittick and Nelson families had their own bleachers set up in front of C.R. Nelson's coal office at Simms Corner. Heather Chittick was all ready for the occasion. Note the commemorative medals hanging off the top of her carriage. (Chittick collection, PIRP #7955.)

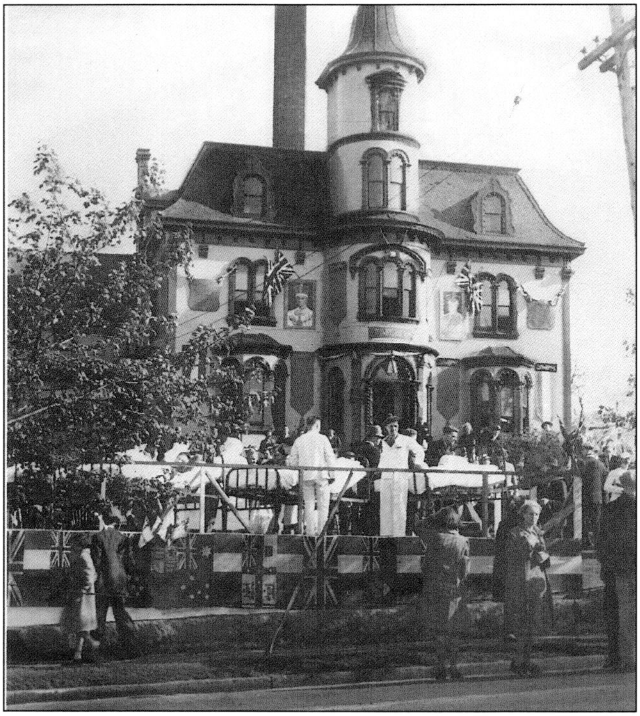

DVA Hospital, 1939. On June 13, dozens of veterans were moved out of the hospital and onto the lawn, so they could be greeted by Their Majesties. A faux pas by tour organizers saw the King and Queen drive by without stopping. When the mistake was realized the King and Queen were furious, but time constraints did not allow for them to return to the hospital. (Hatchette collection, PIRP #4564.)

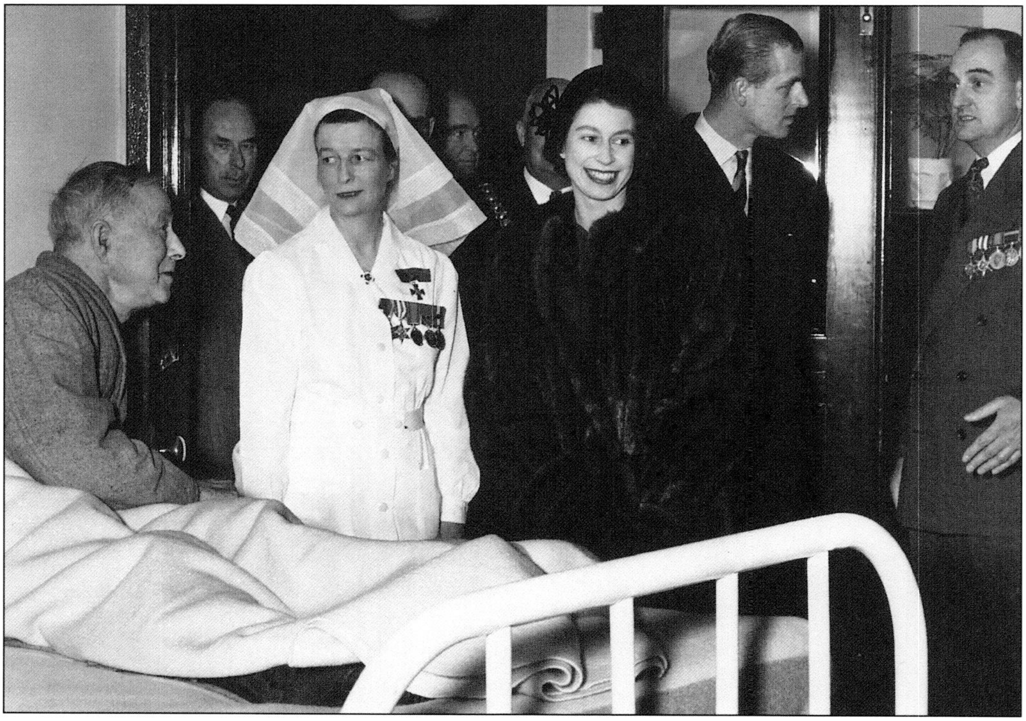

A Princess Visits, 1951. On November 6, 1951, Princess Elizabeth and Prince Philip visited the Lancaster DVA hospital to make amends for the mistake of the 1939 tour. The patient is Private Albert Angel, a World War I veteran from Wales; Matron Sarah Miles is also shown. (Richards collection, PIRP #5719.)

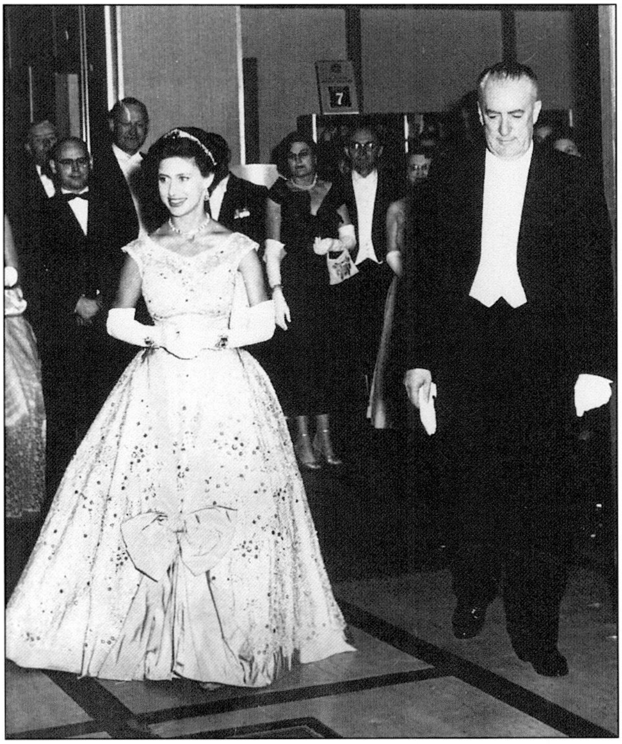

Another Princess, c. 1955. Princess Margaret visited Lancaster shortly after amalgamation. With the Princess is Lieutenant Governor O'Brien. In the rear with glasses is Mayor Parker D. Mitchell, and to his left is his wife, Ethel Chittick. (Chittick collection, PIRP #7940.)

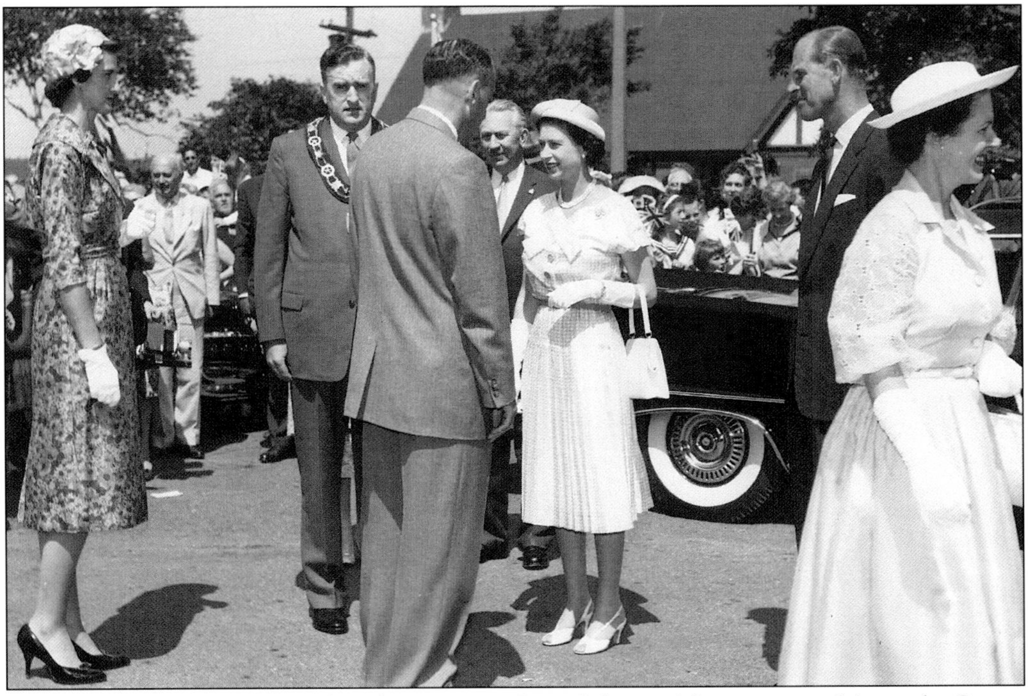

The Queen, July 1959. In her first visit to Saint John and Lancaster as Monarch, Queen Elizabeth ensured that the veterans at the DVA were an important part of her itinerary. At the left is Mayor Bert Huestis and Mrs. Huestis. The Red Cross Lodge is seen in the rear. (HSJ collection, PIRP #9085.)

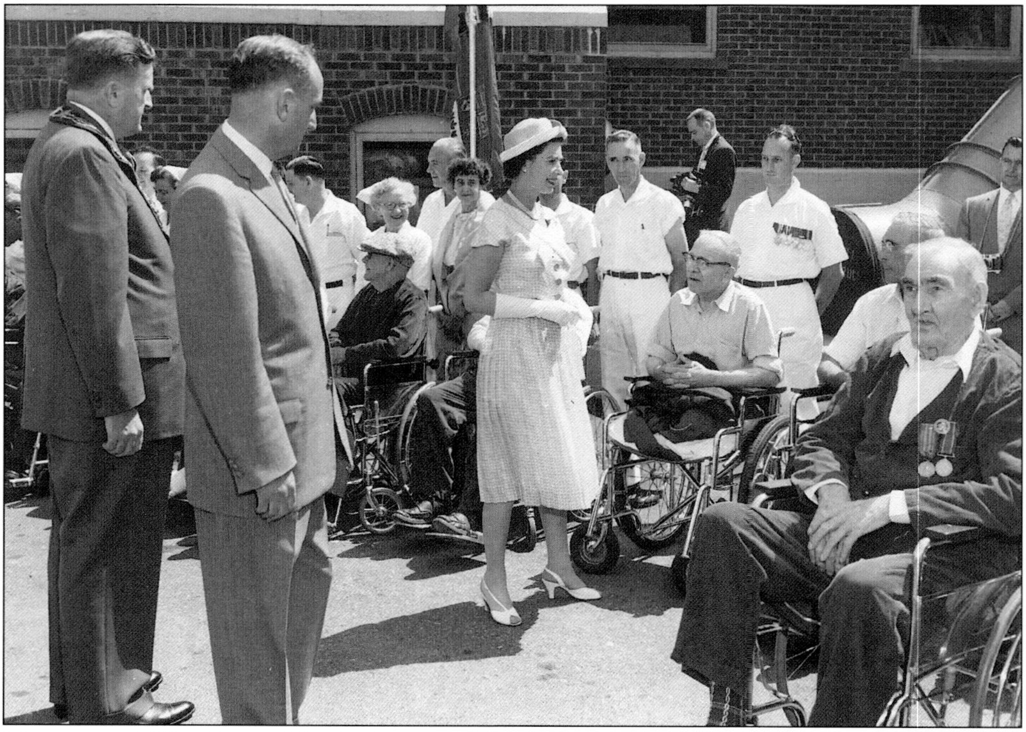

VETERANS, 1959. Queen Elizabeth and Prince Phillip spent a great deal of time meeting and speaking with the veterans at the DVA hospital. The veterans were from the South African War, and World Wars I and II. Do you recognize the photographer at the rear in the top photograph? As seen by the crowds in the photo below, this Royal visit was a popular event. (HSJ collection, PIRP # 9088, #9087.)

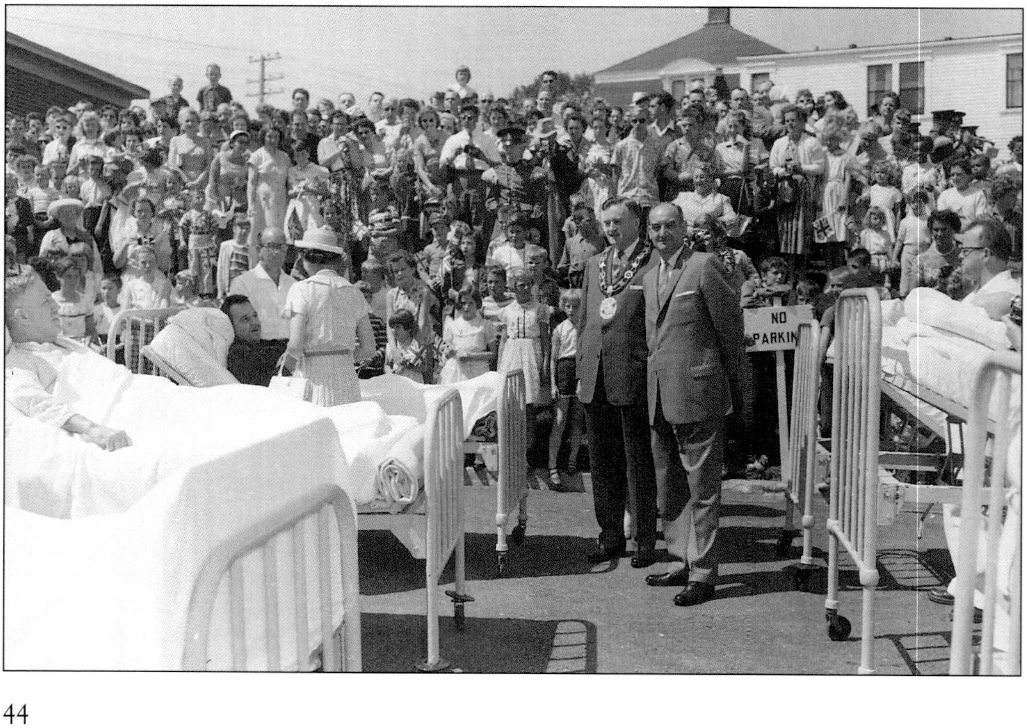

Five

Incorporation

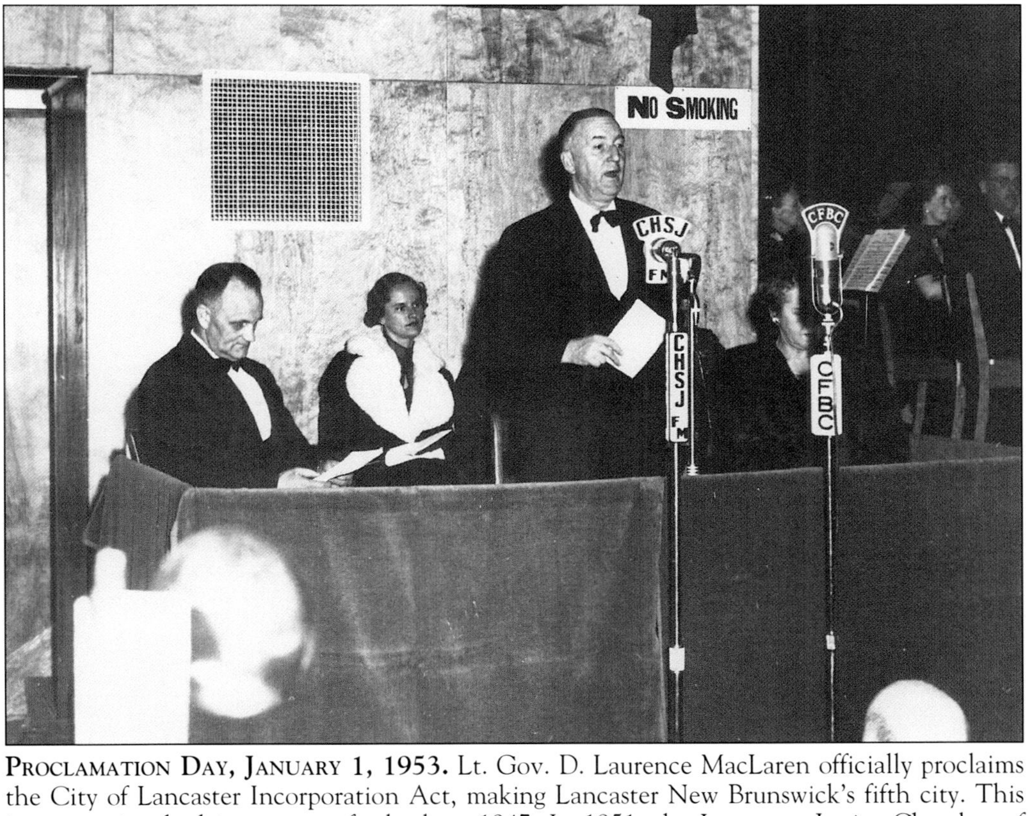

Proclamation Day, January 1, 1953. Lt. Gov. D. Laurence MacLaren officially proclaims the City of Lancaster Incorporation Act, making Lancaster New Brunswick's fifth city. This incorporation had its roots as far back as 1947. In 1951, the Lancaster Junior Chamber of Commerce established the Dexter Committee, under chair Val Dexter, to study the Limerick Report, also known as the Lancaster Survey Committee report, concerning the municipal make-up of the Parish of Lancaster. The incorporation absorbed the communities of Fairville, Randolph, Beaconsfield, Milford, Quinton Heights, Ridgewood Heights, Fundy Heights, and Dominion Park. (HSJ collection, PIRP #6024.)

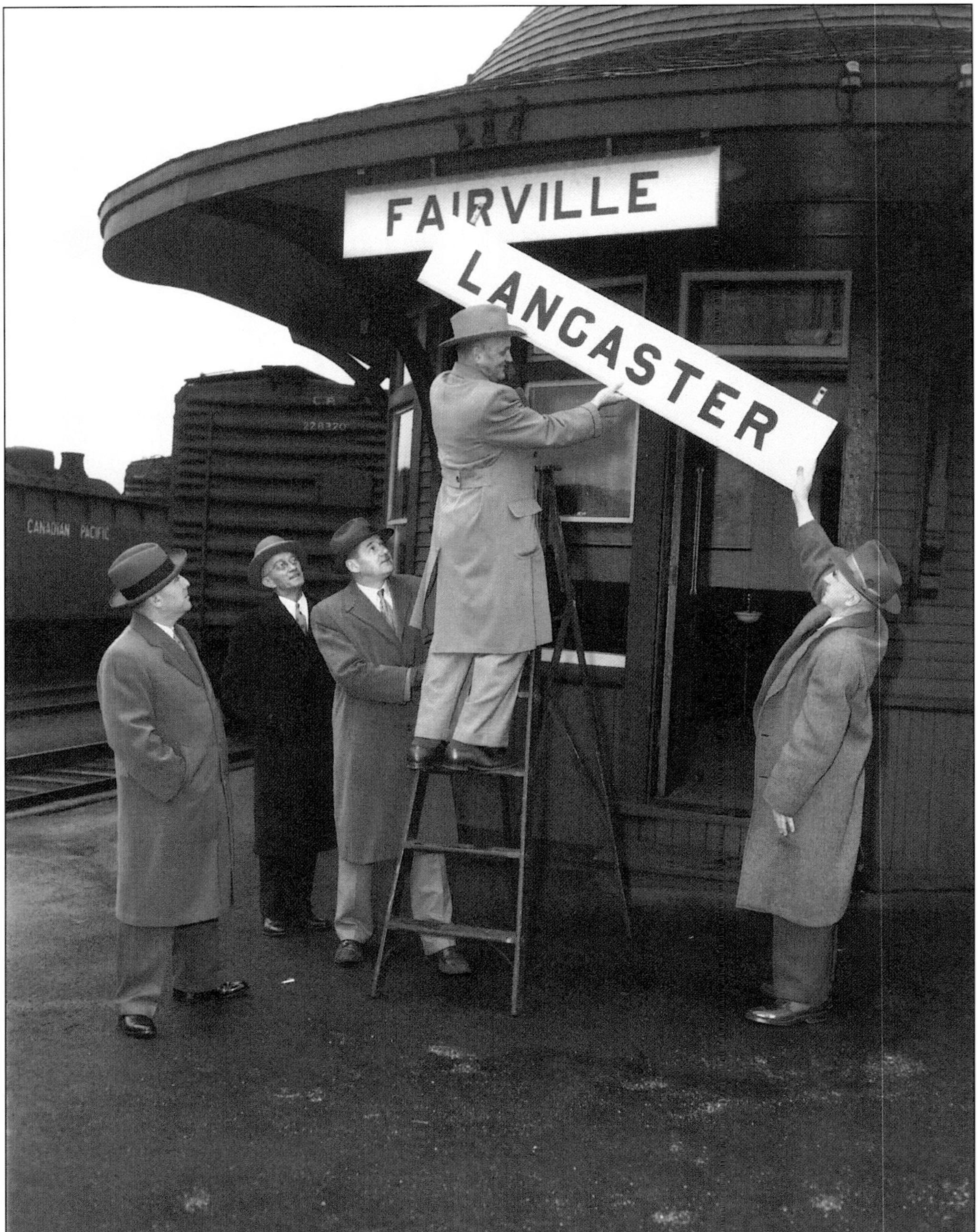

Name Change, 1953. Perhaps the most visually dramatic change with incorporation was the renaming of the Fairville train station behind Moosehead Breweries to the Lancaster train station. The Lancaster sign was still on the station just before it was demolished. It is now undoubtedly in some train collector's basement! (HSJ collection, PIRP #1247.)

CITY CREST, JUNE 23, 1954. During the first anniversary celebrations of the City of Lancaster, Mayor Tom Horsler unveiled the City of Lancaster crest. At left is Dr. George McBeath from the New Brunswick Museum, and Frances Ruddock, who painted the crest. (HSJ collection, PIRP #7807.)

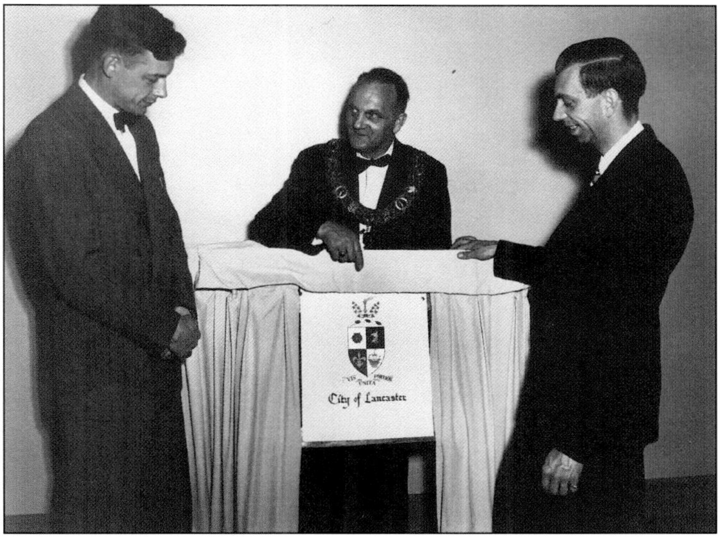

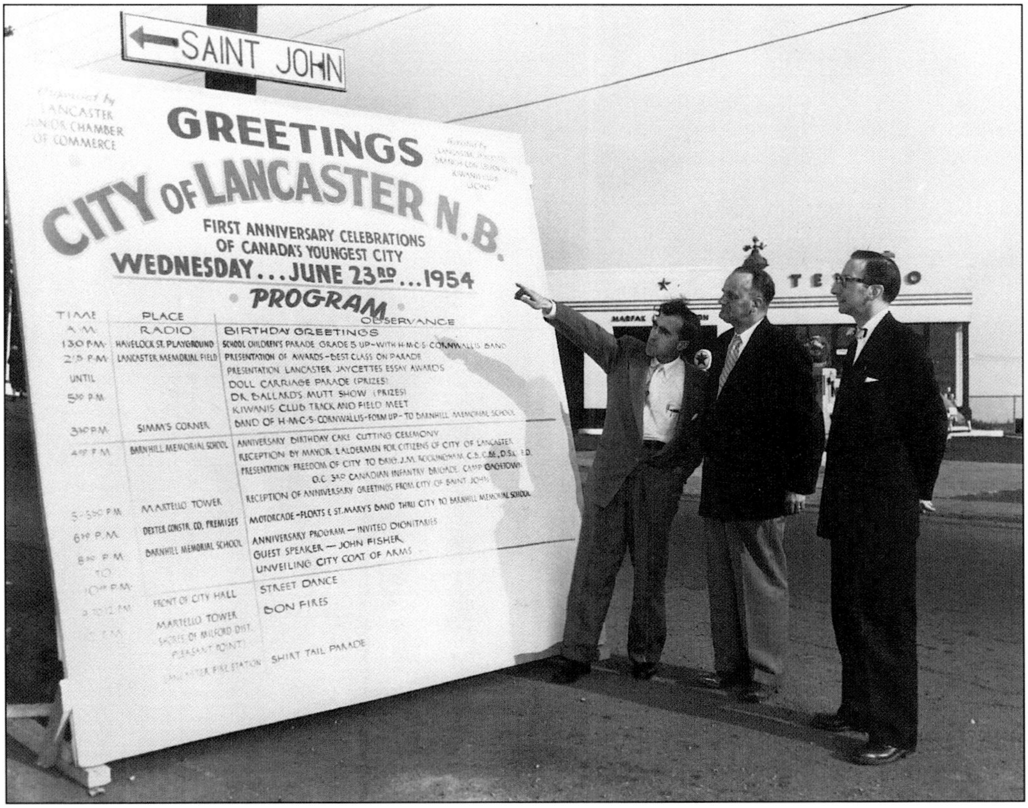

FIRST BIRTHDAY CELEBRATION, JUNE 23, 1954. Tom McCarthy points out the day's planned events with Mayor Tom Horsler and City Solicitor Lyman Purnell. The day-long event was sponsored by the Lancaster Junior Chamber of Commerce, assisted by the Lancaster Jaycettes, Branch #69, Canadian Legion, and the Kiwanis and Lions Clubs. Events took place at Havelock Street playground, Lancaster Memorial Field, Simms Corner, Barnhill Memorial School, Martello Tower, Dexter Construction, Lancaster City Hall, Pleasant Point, and Fire Station No. 1. (HSJ collection, #7813.)

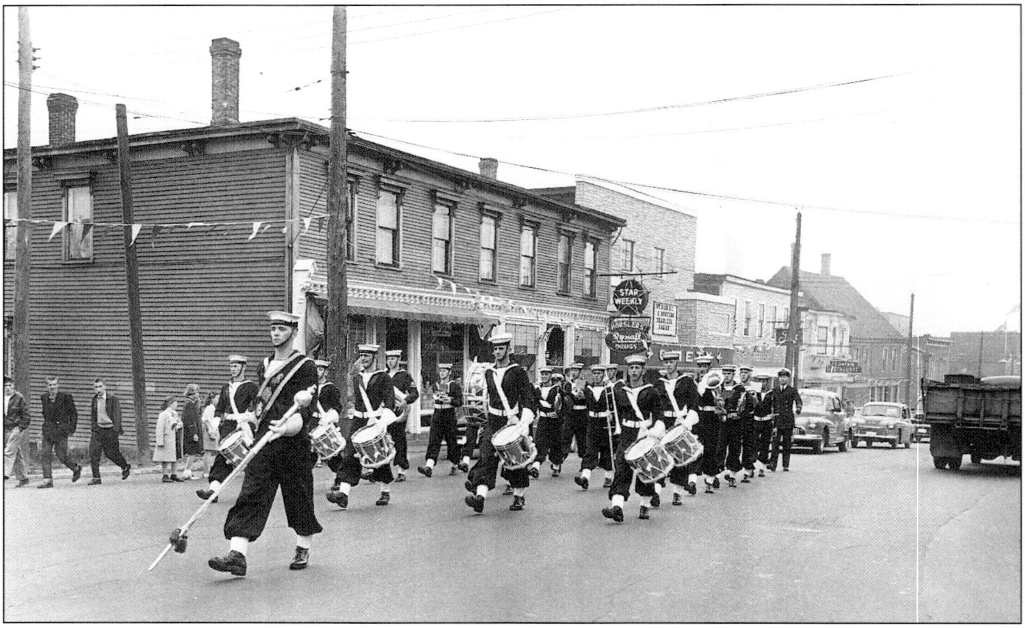

NAVY BAND, 1954. At 3:30 p.m. on June 23, the band of HMCS Cornwallis paraded from Simms Corner to Barnhill Memorial School. Earlier in the day, they had paraded the grade five and up schoolchildren at Havelock Street playground. In the background, one can see Horsler's drugstore, the Gaiety, Horsler's gift shop, and the Fountain Restaurant. (HSJ collection, PIRP #4447.)

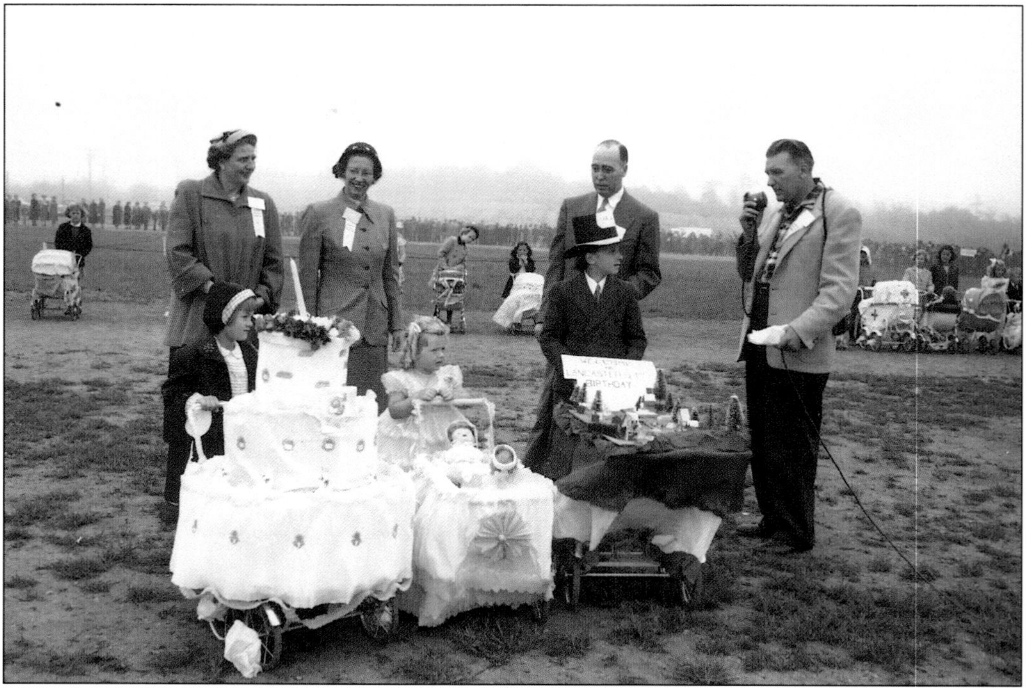

DOLL CARRIAGES, 1954. At the Lancaster Memorial Field prizes were awarded for the best doll carriages on parade. The carriage on the left is of a birthday cake, the centre is of two dolls, and the right is a diorama of Lancaster. (HSJ collection, PIRP #7815.)

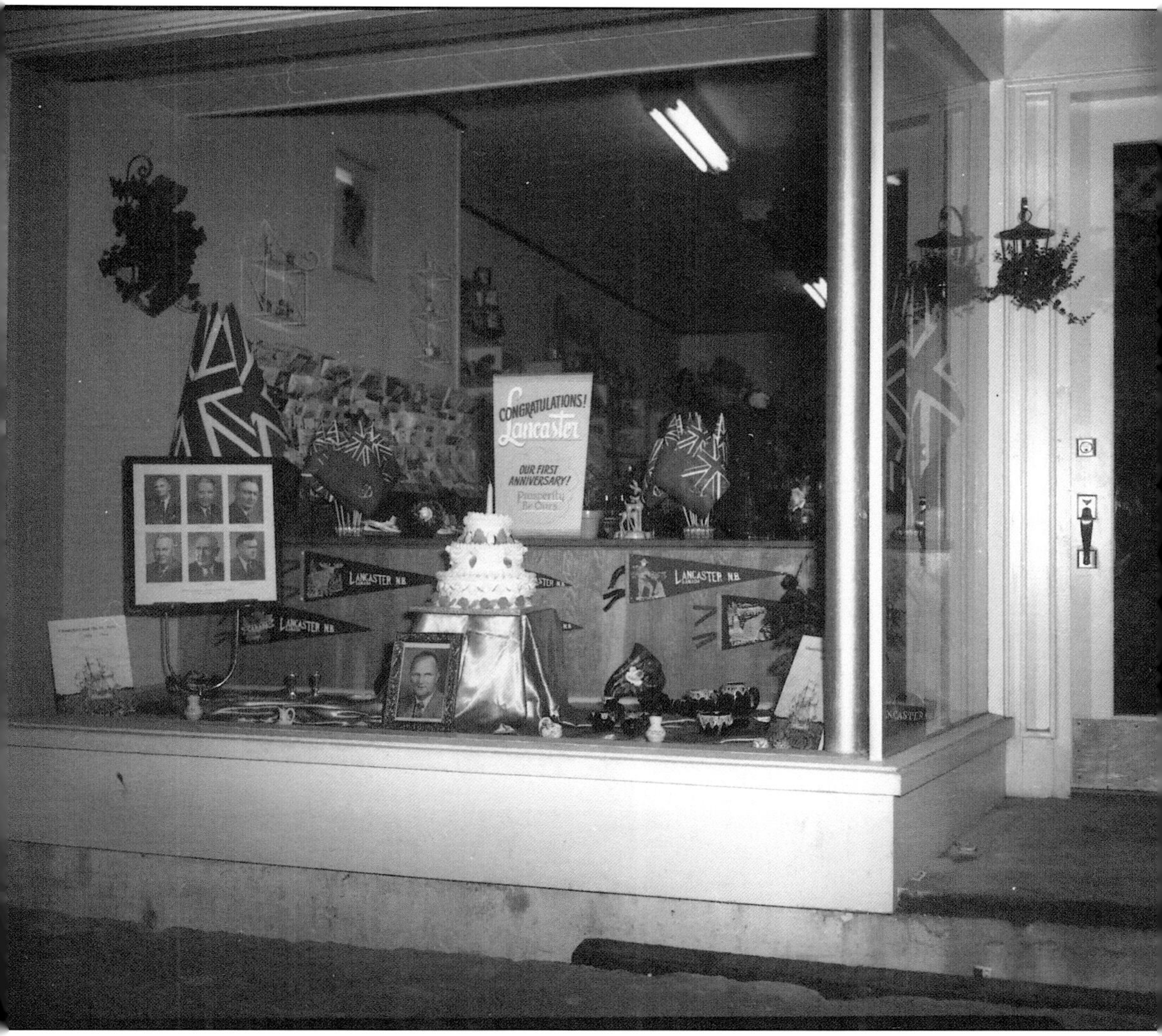

WINDOW DISPLAY, 1954. This is probably Horsler's gift shop next to the Gaiety theatre. The window sign proudly boasts "Our First Anniversary—Prosperity Be Ours". In the window are several Lancaster souvenirs, including three different banners, a child's hat, and at least three different types of souvenir china. The photograph in the display is of the first common council. (HSJ collection, PIRP #7814.)

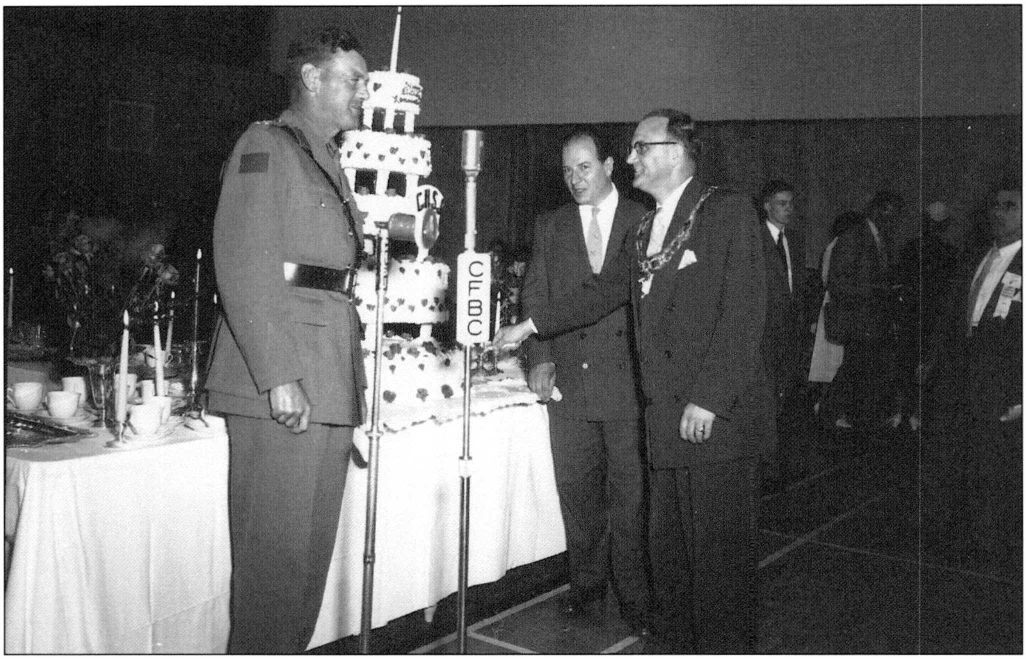

CAKE CUTTING, 1954. Mayor Tom Horsler cuts the anniversary birthday cake with Brig. J.M. Rockingham and John Fisher, "Mr. Canada", observing. At the extreme right is Tom McCarthy, chairman of the anniversary program and president of the Lancaster Junior Chamber of Commerce. Below, Brigadier Rockingham gives a piece of cake to Catherine, daughter of James Brittain of Ridgewood Heights. (HSJ collection, PIRP #7820, #7822.)

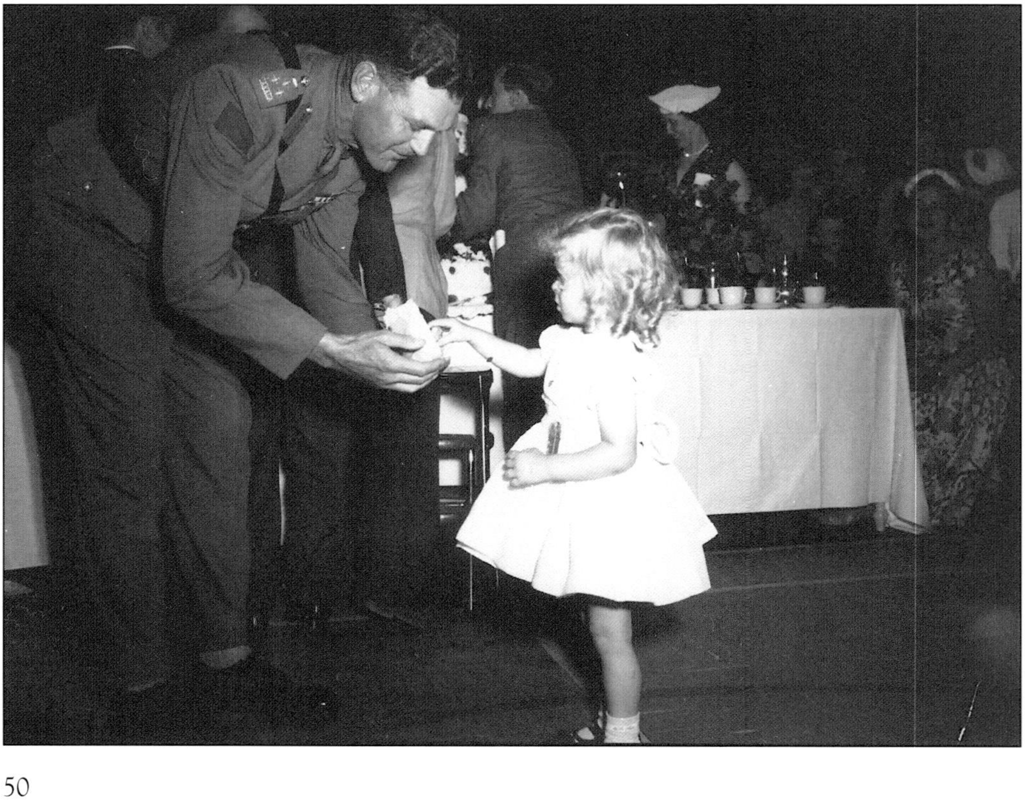

Six

Citizens of Lancaster

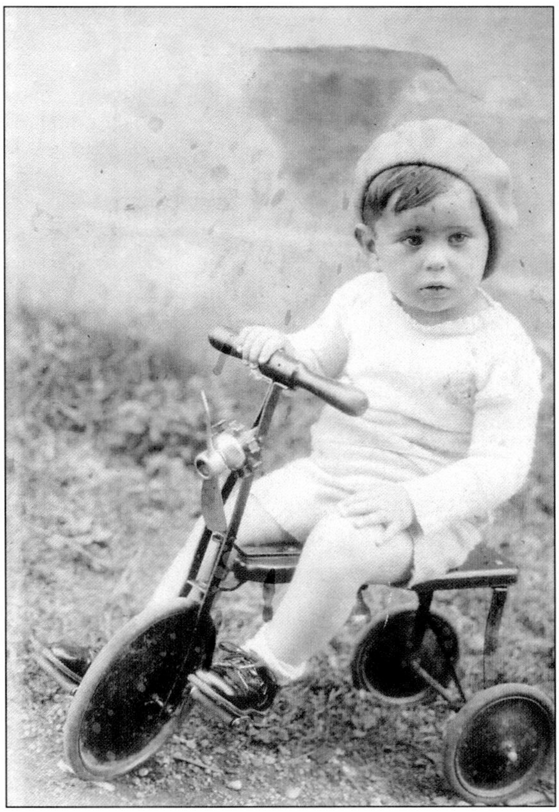

Trike or Aeroplane? 1932. Byard Herrington really must have flown on his tricycle. Note the aircraft engine and propeller under the handle. Born in 1930, Byard attended Fairville Superior as well as a school in New York. He worked as an electrician at the pulp mill and at the Kimberly Clark tissue plant. Children like Byard, and those like his parents and grandparents, served their communities well over the two centuries of Lancaster's existence. Regardless of the business name, or the sports team or the event, it was the people of Lancaster who made it the special community it was then, and continues to be today as part of Saint John. (Mrs. B. Herrington.)

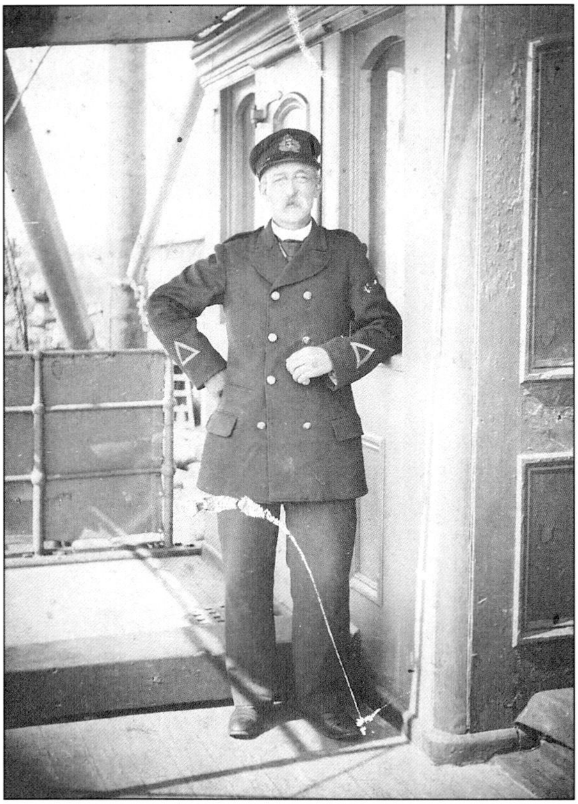

MASTER MARINER, C. 1890. A seafaring way of life was natural for many of the boys and men of Lancaster. While some served on the high seas, others worked the riverboats and steamers within New Brunswick. Capt. George Fitzgerald, a well-known family name in Lancaster, followed his father, James, as a master mariner. (M. Bernard.)

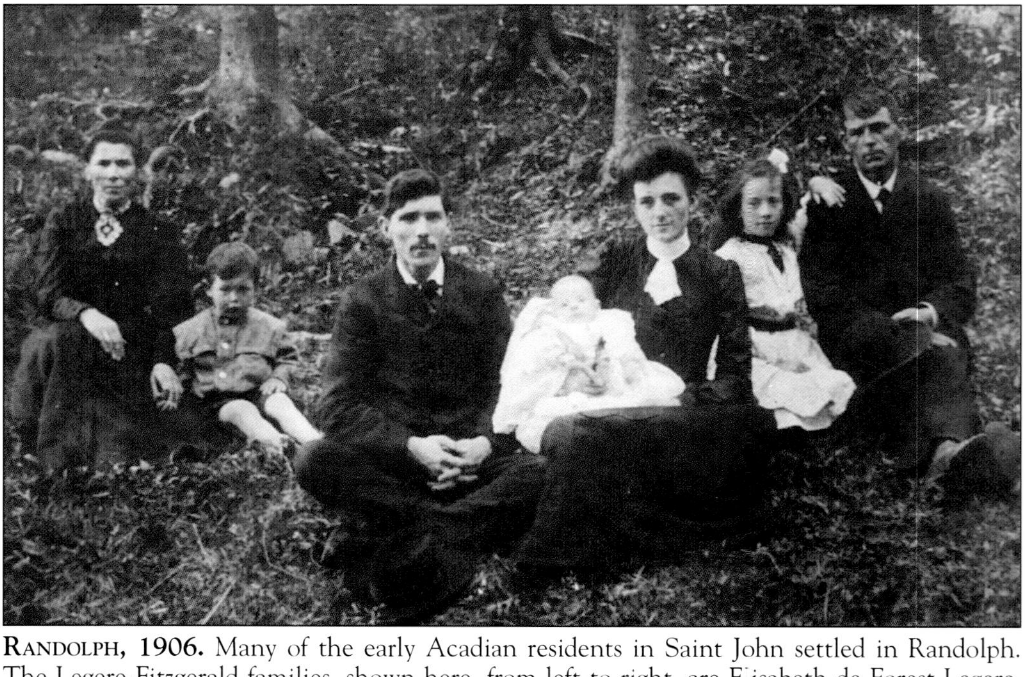

RANDOLPH, 1906. Many of the early Acadian residents in Saint John settled in Randolph. The Legere-Fitzgerald families, shown here, from left to right, are Elisabeth de Forest Legere, grand-mere, Stanley Fitzgerald, Edmund Fitzgerald, George Legere, Lena Legere, Gertie Legere Thibideau, and Simon Legere. (M. Bernard.)

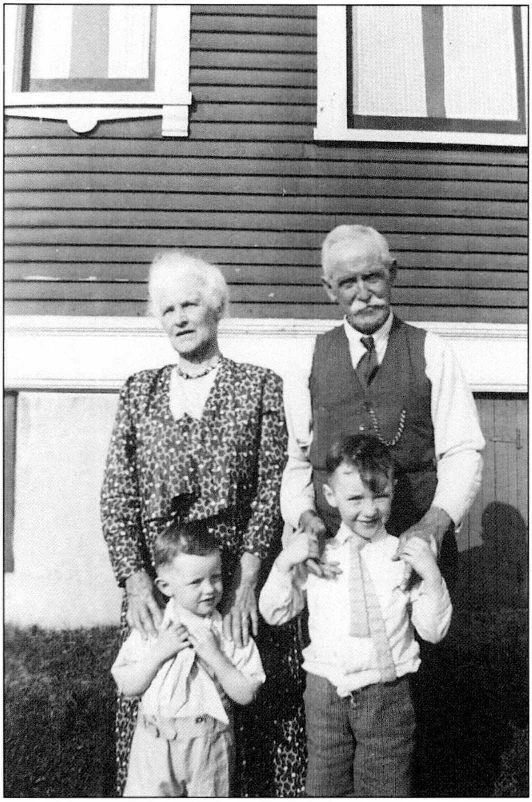

Maternal Grandparents, c. 1931. Ellen and Daniel Murphy are shown here with grandsons Fred and Joe Hazel. Daniel was a blacksmith and then later became assistant collector of customs at the port. Fred became editor-in-chief of the Evening Times Globe. Joe became a radiologist in Montreal. (F. Hazel.)

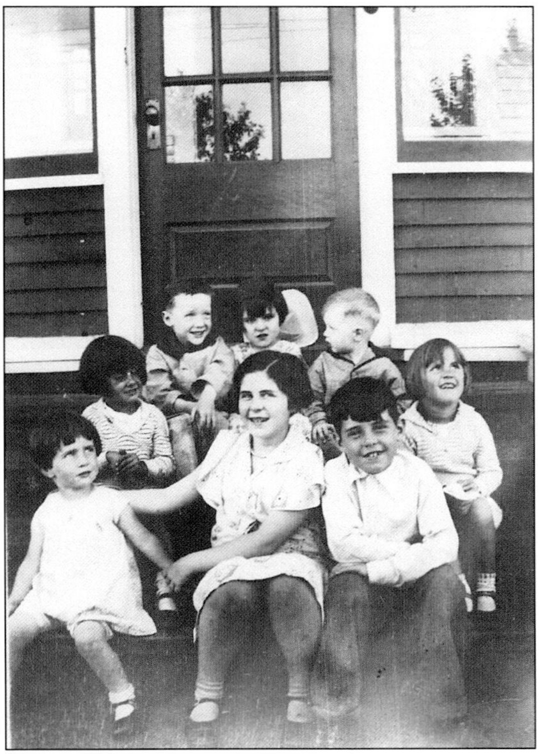

Hazel-Murphy Clan, August 19, 1931. Pictured are Marion (2yrs, 7mos), Fred (2yrs, 8mos), Mary (4yrs, 3mos), Joseph (5yrs, 5mos), Joan (4yrs, 4mos), Frances (5yrs, 11mos), Kevin (8yrs, 9mos), and Dorothy (10yrs, 5mos). (F. Hazel.)

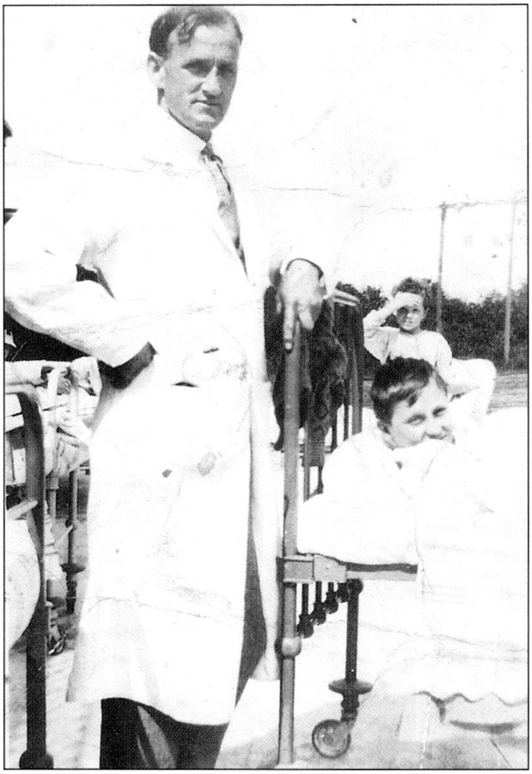

Prominent Citizen. Hartley Green served both Lancaster and Saint John as a member of the common council and several other community organizations and commissions. He was a prominent businessman, an active sports promoter, a Mason, and a 43-year member of the Luxor Temple. At left, Hartley is shown while a patient at the old TB hospital. Below, Hartley (at the right) is holding his daughter Carol at his farm in Lorneville, *c.* 1944. He died in 1994. (Green family.)

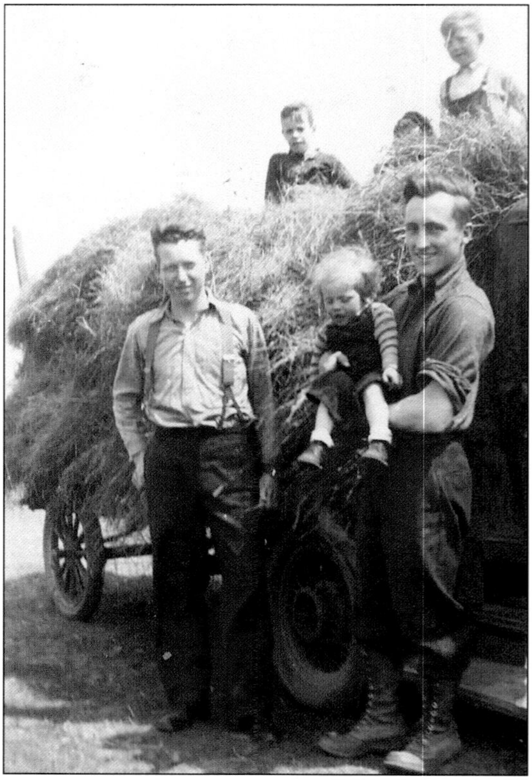

SLEDDING WHEREVER THERE IS SNOW! c. 1930. Jean, daughter of coal merchant Frank Hamm, is obviously enjoying the season's snowfall. For many children in Carleton and Lancaster, recreational areas also served as business or work areas. Behind Jean can be seen signs for the Cunard and Anchor-Donaldson shipping lines. (Hamm collection, PIRP #9500.)

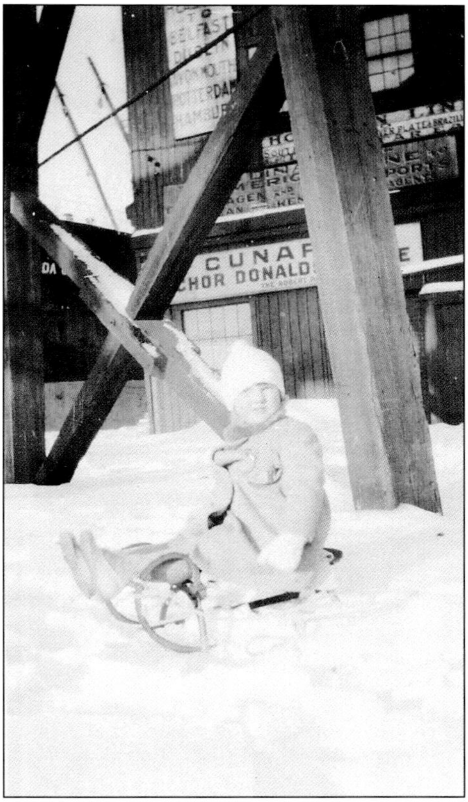

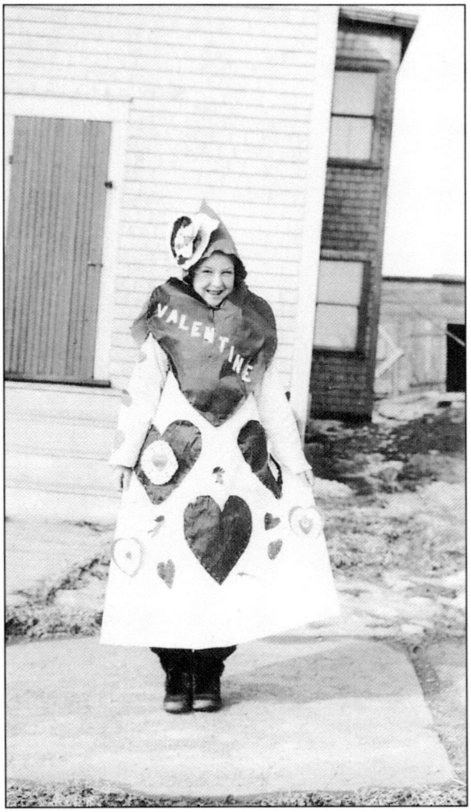

BE MY VALENTINE, c. 1935. With a costume like this, Carol Harris, daughter of Ida and William Harris on Ready Street, probably had a few valentine suitors lined up. (Harris family.)

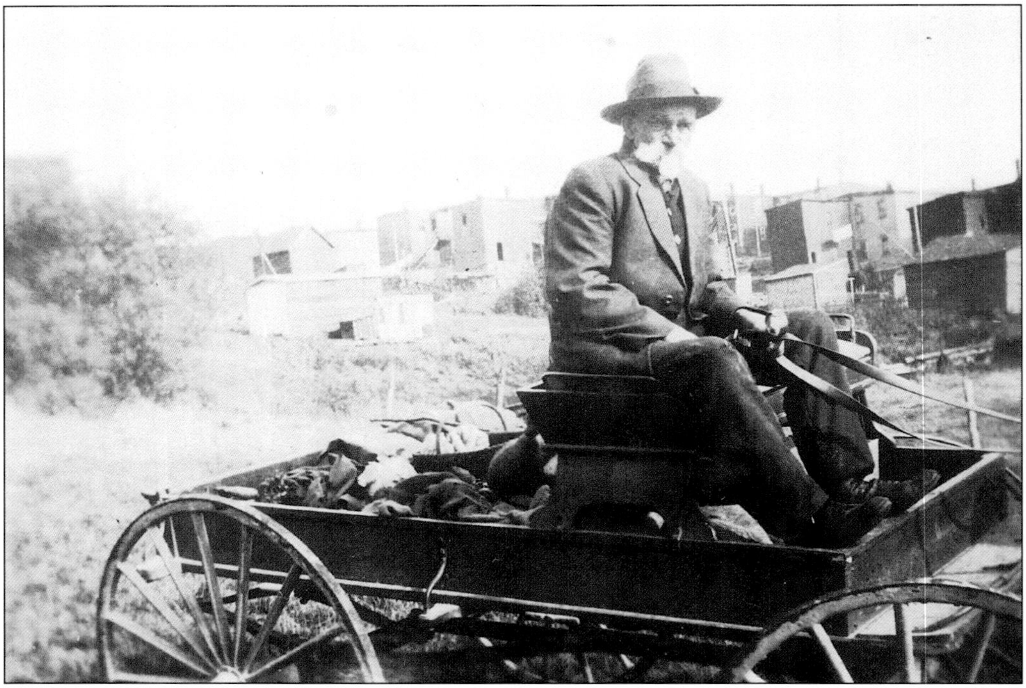

Delivery on Time! c. 1900. While few may think of Manawagonish Road as a farmer's area, men like George Harris worked the land his entire life, taking their produce into Lancaster. Today there is only one farm left on the avenue, and that shortly will be turned into another housing development. (M. Kingston.)

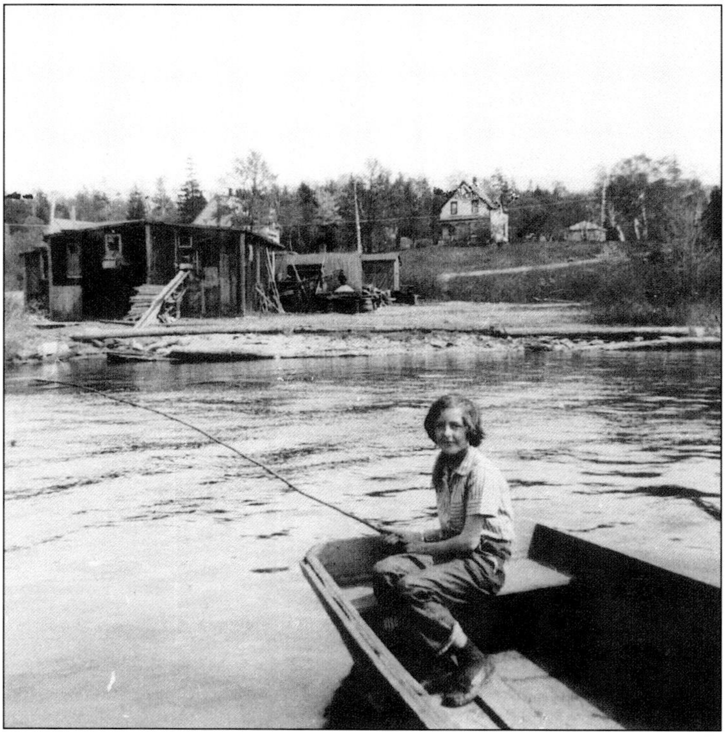

Are the Fish Biting? Elaine March in the summer of 1953 or 1954 probably didn't catch many fish, but this photograph also captured the Sterling P. Lodge & Son Sawmill at left and the Miller house in the rear. The mill made apple and fish barrels. (M. Bernard.)

St. John River Skating, 1951. Margery Fitzgerald is shown here with her grandfather James Fitzgerald. Margery wrote "my first skates were red and I loved them." (M. (Fitzgerald) Bernard.)

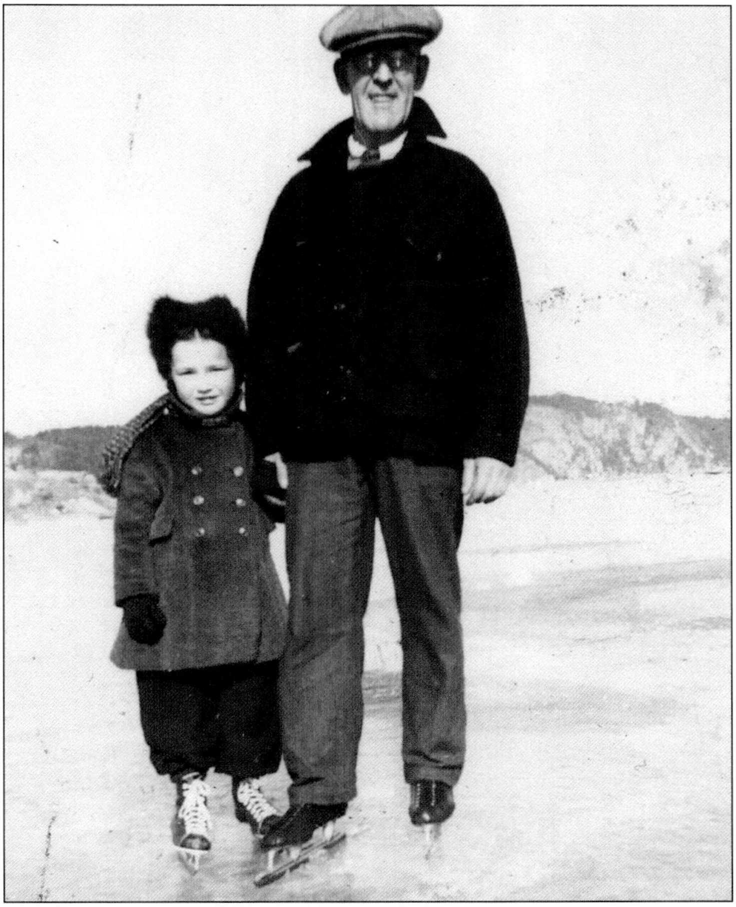

Santa's Knee, Christmas, 1959. Christmas without a visit to Santa at MRA's on King Street was just not Christmas. Patti Green and all her sisters made sure that they sat on Santa's knee and told him what they wanted for Christmas. (Green family.)

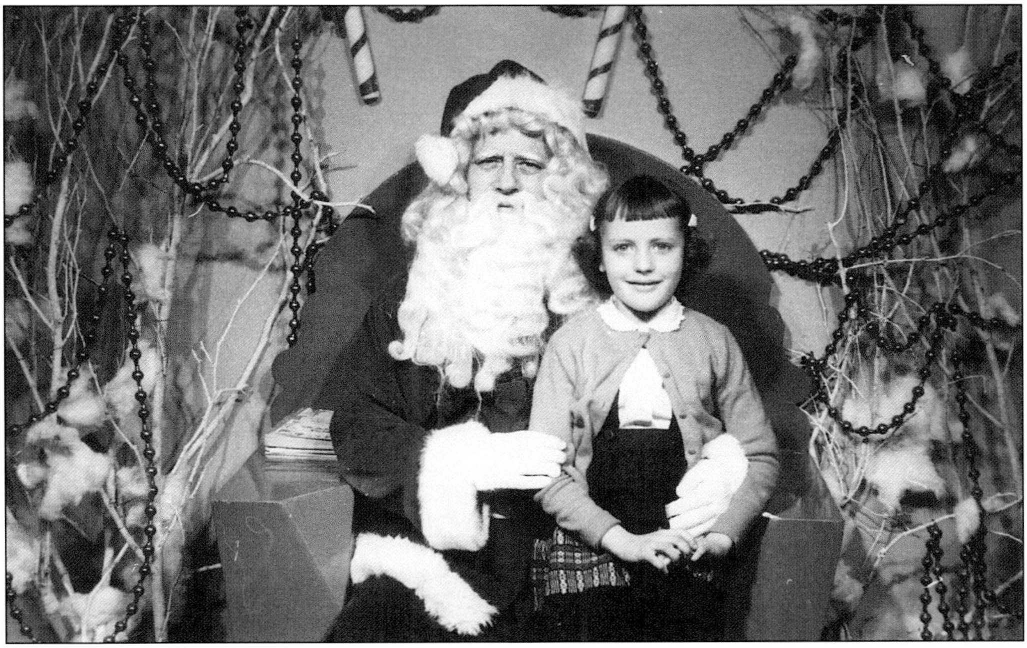

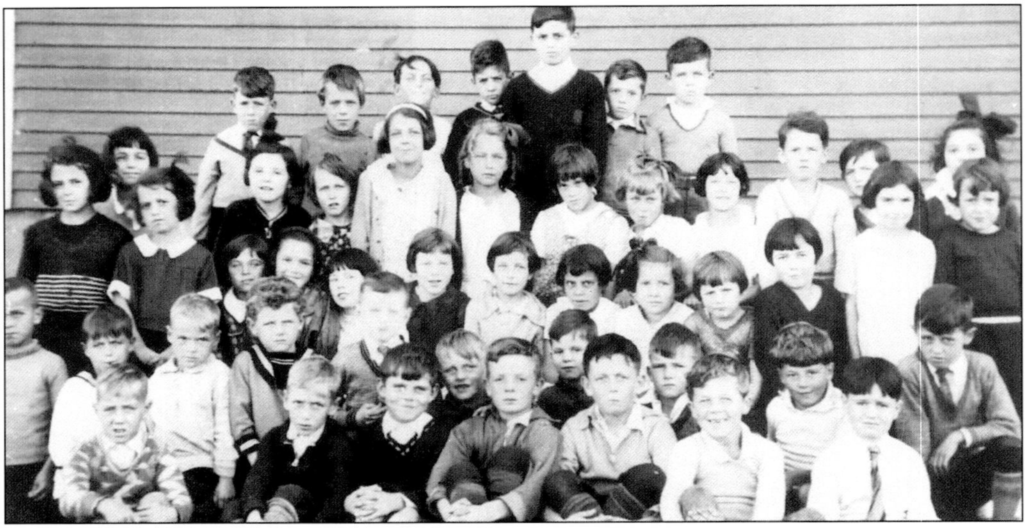

St. Rose's School, c. 1935. Classmates are shown here, from left to right, as follows: (first row) Fred Hanlon, Frank Hooley, Fred Kelly, Gordon Reid, Ronald "Buck" Logue, Nick Dobblstyne, and Francis Doyle; (second row) "Lally" Harold Kingston, Art Mullin, Willie McGovern, Ron Horgan, Fred Hazel, unidentified, Pat Duffy, Michael Kennedy, Joey Dobblstyne, and George Jenkins; (third row) unidentified, unidentified, Mary Keleher, unidentified, unidentified, Madeline McGill, Audrey Fenton, unidentified, Theresa Fenton, Helen Duplisea, Lorna Malloy, Marie ?, Connie Conlon, Margie O'Keefe, and Mary Reid; (fourth row) Gloria Gould, Mary Carton, Theresa Mullin, Lena Paré, Gabriel Brouche, unidentified, unidentified, Kay Mullin, Kay O'Keefe, Mary Bradbin, Eileen Bradbin, and Suzanne Brouche; (back row) Eugene "Pat" Graham, Raymond "Mucky" Kingston, Francis Keleher, Vinnie Joyce, George Thiberge, Marcel Thiberge, and Joe Horgan. (F. Hazel.)

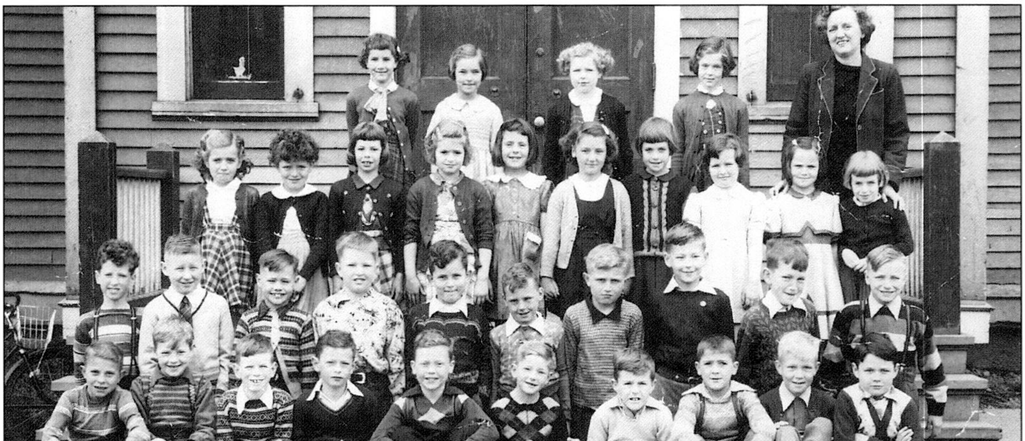

Fairville Superior, Grade 2, 1952–53. Classmates pictured here, from left to right, are as follows: (front row) unidentified, unidentified, Charlie Sancton, Billy Spragg, Billy Green, Richard McColgan, ? Fox, unidentified, Billy Hooper, and Cecil Brownell; (second row) unidentified, Daryle Neve, John Cunningham, Joseph Batten, Wayne Hovey, unidentified, Denis Luck, Jimmy Irving, Benny Tibbett, and unidentified; (third row) Mary Allingham, Penny Nason, Susan Frost, Tracy Lee Belyea, Gail Osborne, Frances English, Jean Melvin, Carol Green, Judy Taylor, and Jane Watters; (back row) Caroline Earle, Catherine McIntrye, Carol Bryant, and Marilyn Elkin. (Penny Hovey.)

Ice Fishing, c. 1950. Robert Lodge (left) and Frederick "Telly" Wallace built this windbreak out of poles and burlap to protect themselves from the wind blowing down the broad expanse of the river. There is one fish next to Robert's left foot. Must have been a poor day for fish! (Lodge family.)

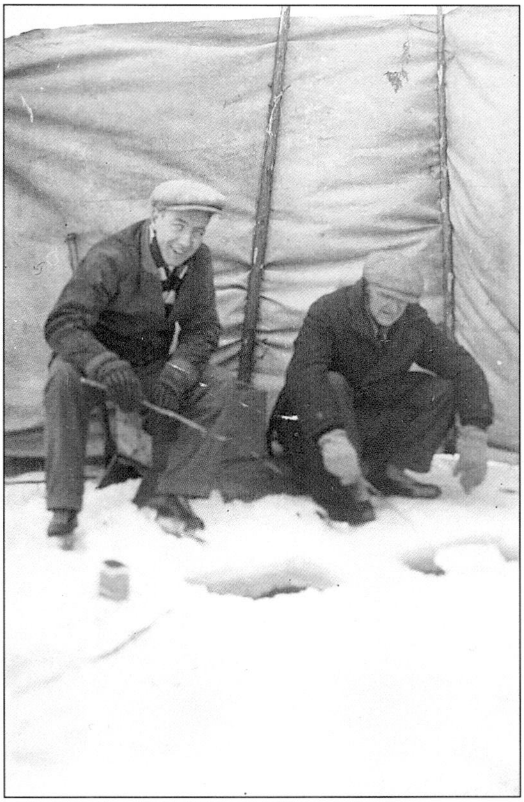

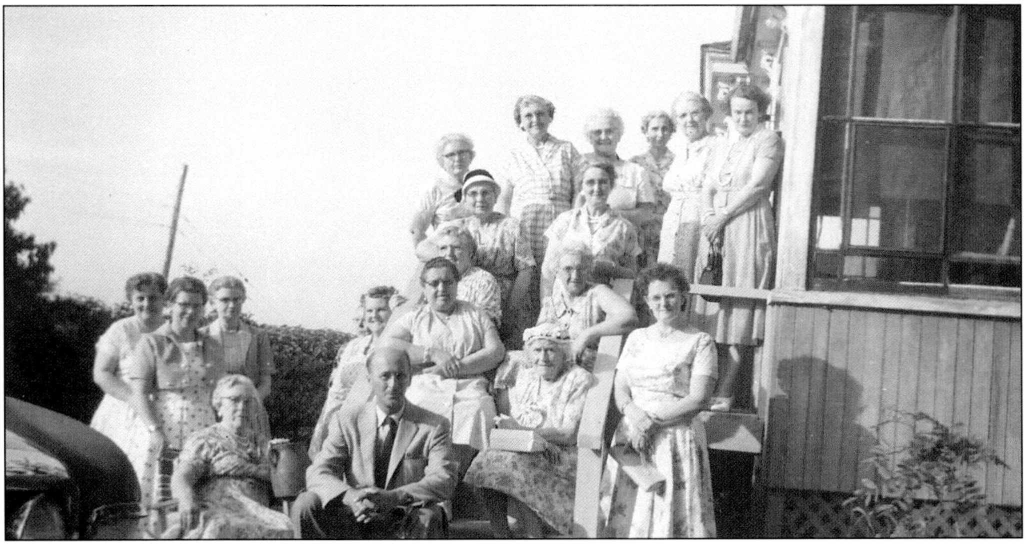

Summer Picnic, August 1958. These women are members and guests of the Senior Women's Missionary Society of Lancaster Baptist Church. The picnic was held at the home of Mrs. Ella Arbo at 151 Milford Road. The ladies posing here, from left to right, are Ruth Lodge, Doris Lodge, Esther Smith, Edna Dykeman, unidentified, Evelyn Mowry, Reverend Hartlin, Sadie Keating, Bertha Watters, Agnes Reid, Ida Harris, Caroline Harris, Ella Arbo, Pearl Atherton, Ethel Whipple, Mrs. Hartlin, Dorothy Logon, Louise Clark, and Muriel Jones. (Lodge family.)

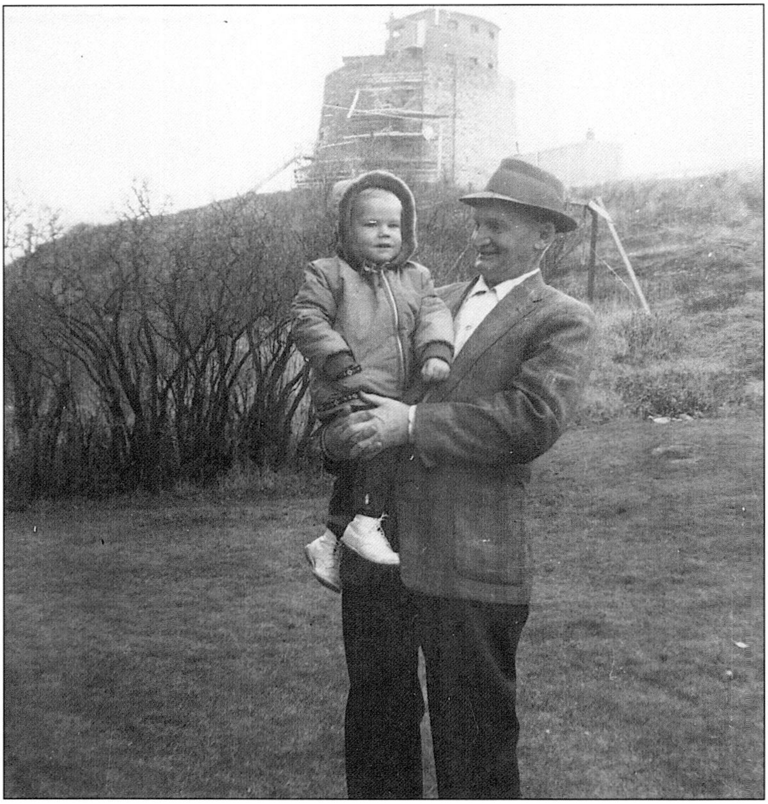

Grandfather and Son, 1960. Hilton Walton is holding his grandson, Paul Belyea, in the backyard of his house at the corner of Lancaster Avenue and Fundy Drive, with repairs underway on Martello Tower. Hilton was a district manager for the Power Commission on Manawagonish Road. (L. Rolston.)

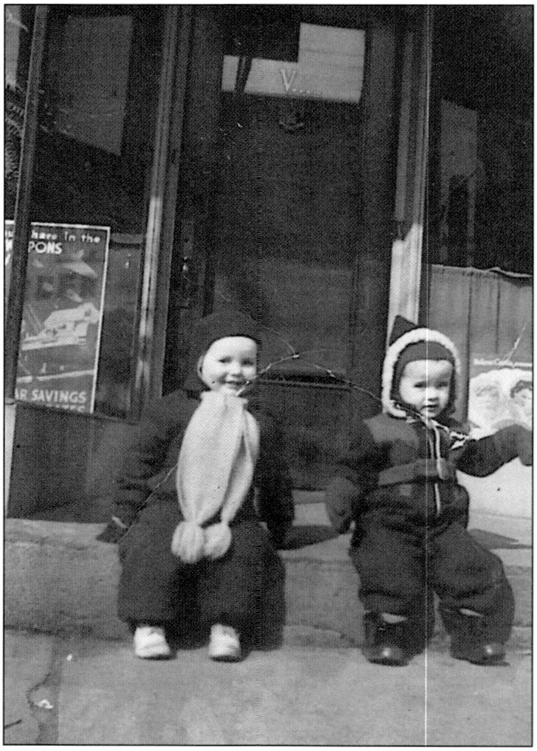

Wartime Photo, c. 1944. Norm Garey and Frank Haggarty are on the steps of the Palms Restaurant. There is a War Savings Bond poster in the window and the letter "V" for victory on the door. (N. Garey.)

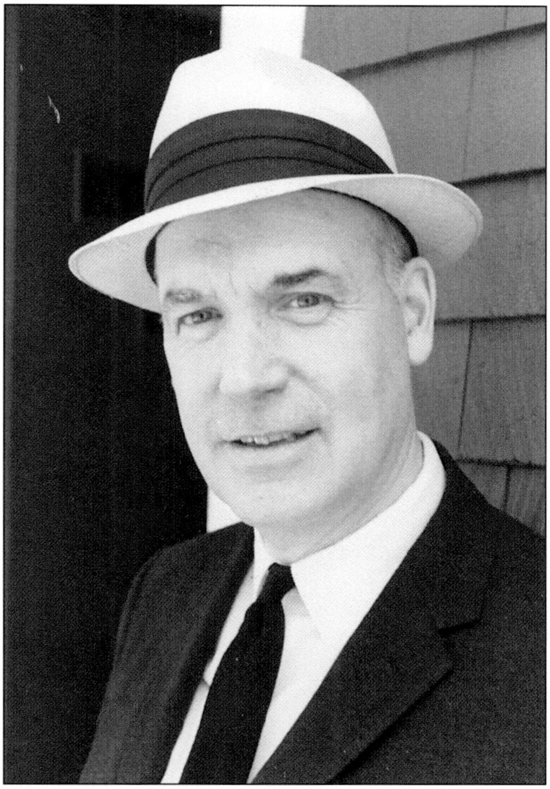

Mayor of Murphyville, 1961. "There is a strong possibility that Lou Murphy is a living saint among us". These kind words summed up Lou's enormous contribution to his community. A school trustee as well as a municipal and provincial politician, Lou was the stalwart champion on moral and ethical issues facing his constituents. His Thunder Hill creation, begun in 1966, continues to sparkle, like the "twinkle in his eyes" at Christmas time. Lou is holding his nephew Don's daughter, Laura Coholan; her sister Sheila is at her right and their cousin, Karen Gallant, is to her left. (Top photograph courtesy of B. McHarg; bottom photograph courtesy of Don Coholan.)

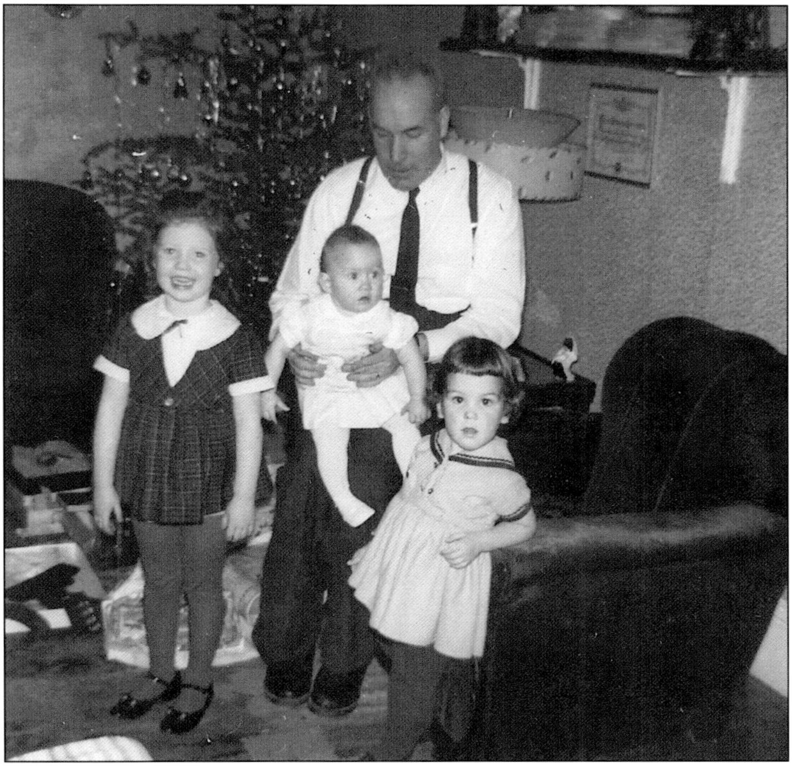

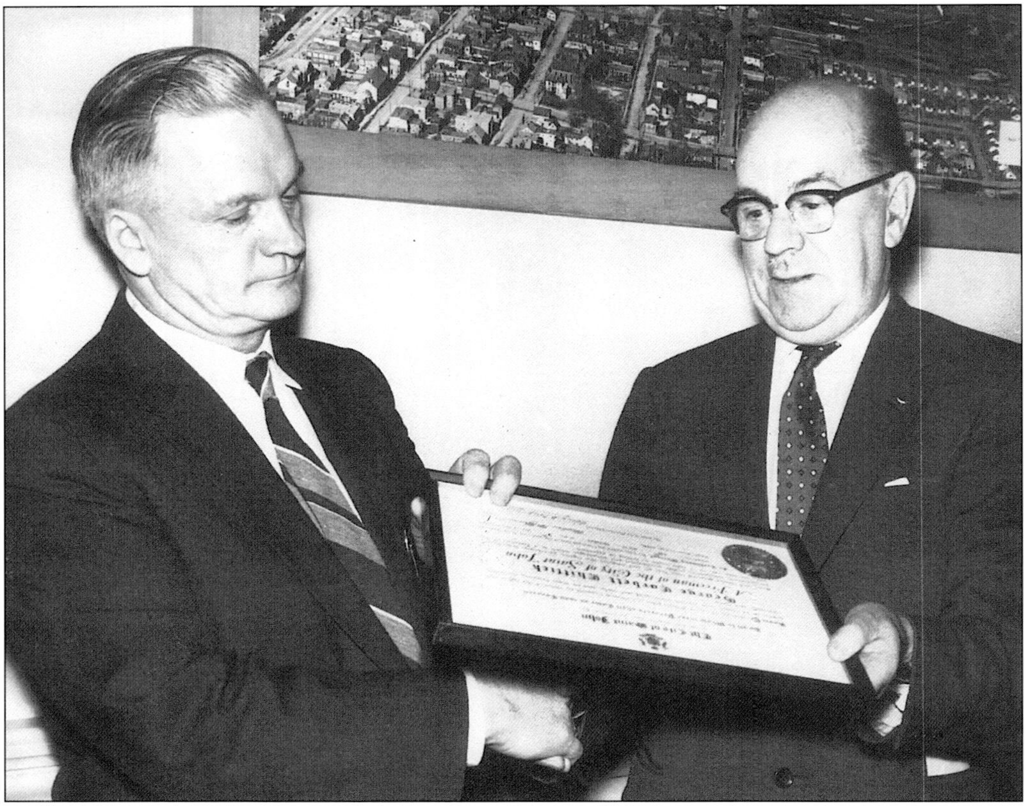

Freedom of the City, October 28, 1958. George Chittick, a resident of Lancaster, received Saint John's highest award "for the courage and resource he showed in directing the rescue of a city fireman (John Kyle.) trapped for four and a half hours below a collapsed wall at the tragic fire on Main Street". The presentation was made by Saint John Mayor W.W. Macaulay. (Chittick family.)

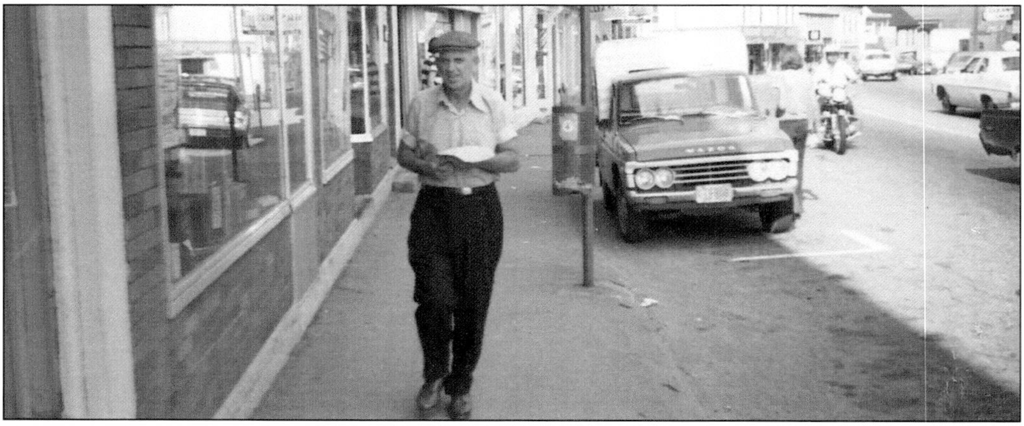

Fairville's Unofficial Mayor, c. 1975. In 1991, Louis Murphy and his nephew, Don Coholan, erected a plaque in memory of Paul. Located across from Moosehead Breweries, it reads: "Dedicated to the Glory of God and In Loving Memory of PAUL PHILLIPS 1930–1991. He personified friendliness, kindness, and a servant to all. Fairville, later known as Lancaster, was home to him, and to the people he was their "Unofficial Mayor". No happy time that passes is ever really gone If it leaves a lovely memory for looking back upon"! (K. Steen.)

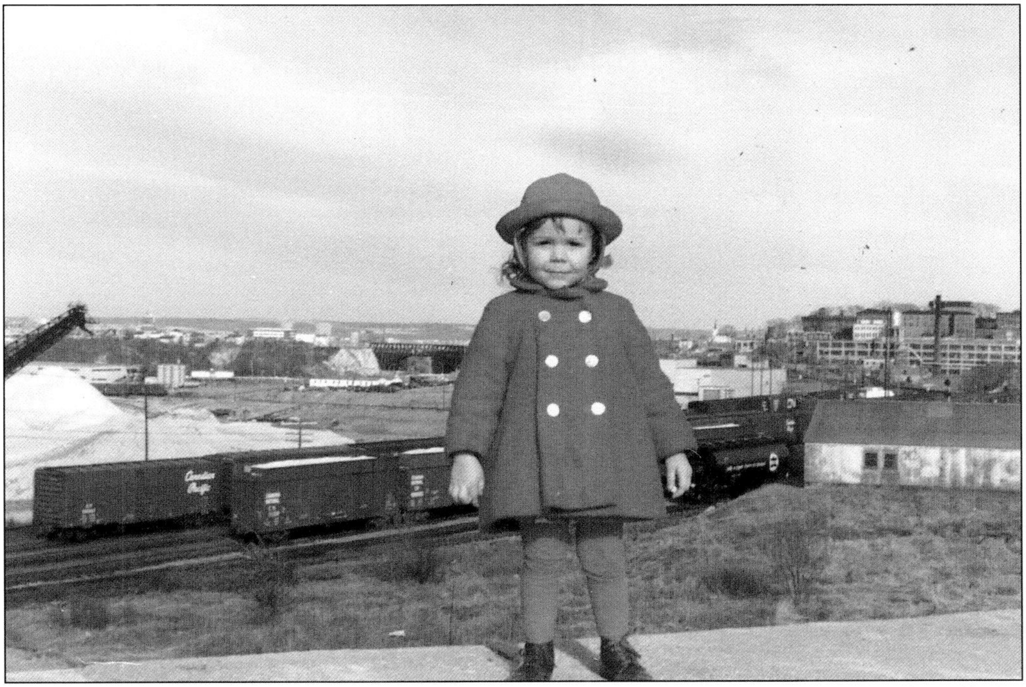

I'M CUTE!!! c. 1967. Carmella, daughter of Louis and Winnifred Poirier, has the pulp mill, the CPR rail yard, Simms and Centracare (at the right), and Douglas Avenue in the background. Louis and his family lived on Main Street across from the post office. (Poirier family.)

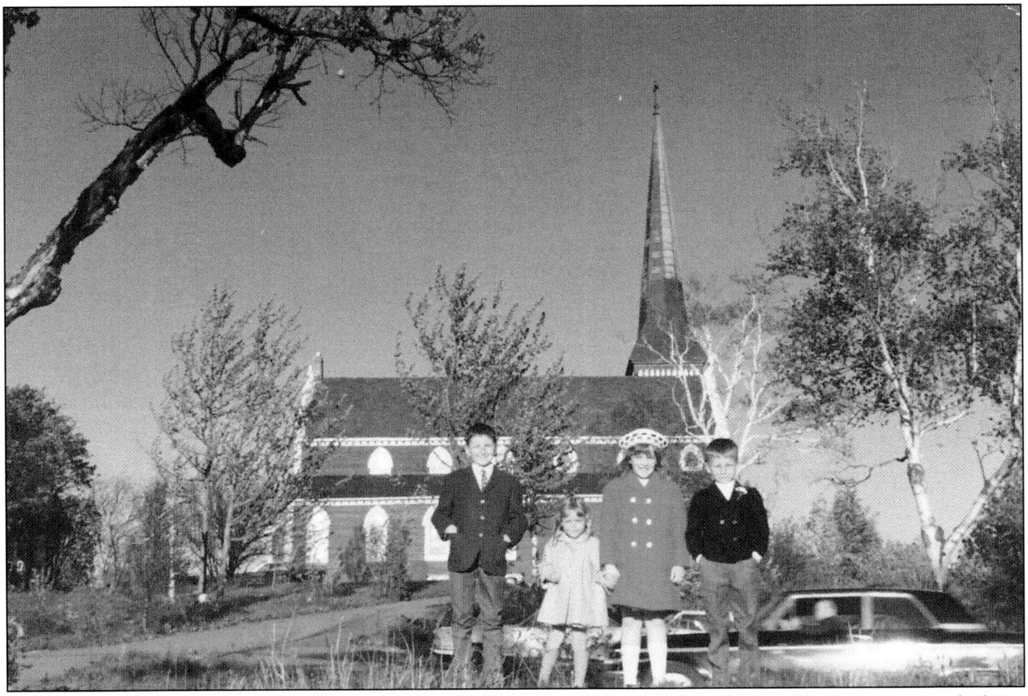

A BARBER'S FAMILY, c. 1967. Rudy, Carmella, Rose Marie "Nuni", and Paul just attended St. Rose's Church, seen in the background. Although Louis is often remembered for his barbering skills, his wife, Winnifred, was a popular seamstress! (Poirier family.)

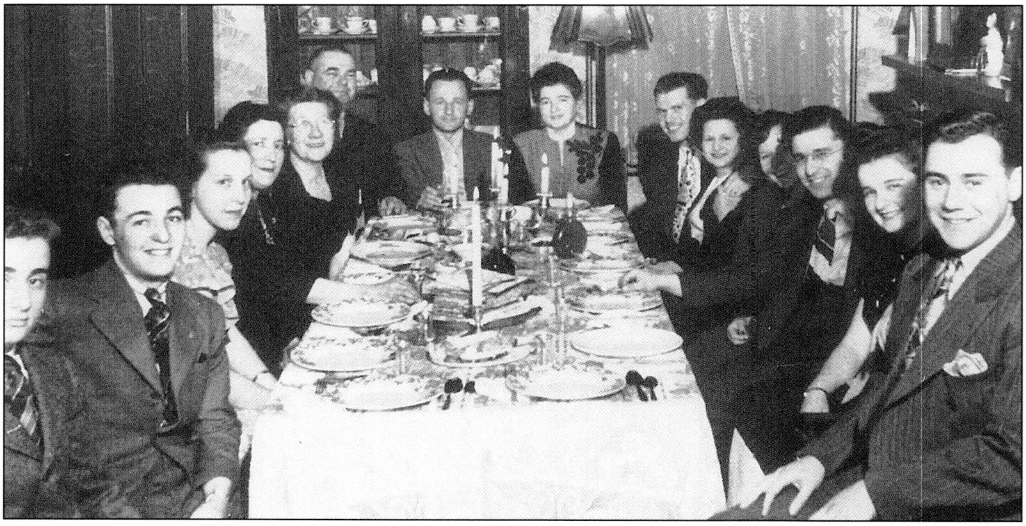

SEDAR, C. 1942. Lancaster had a small but vibrant Jewish community. Members are shown here, from left to right, as follows: (left row) Sam Koven, Joe Koven, Jean Sereisky, Sara Zides, Minnie Sereisky, Max Sereisky, Morris Koven, and Rose Koven; (right row) Lloyd Epstein, Muriel Epstein, Mildred Boxer of New York, Jerry Koven (later owner of the Fairville Department Store), Honey Koven, and Murray Zides (who later became Commissionaire of Planning for Saint John). (Saint John Jewish Historical Museum.)

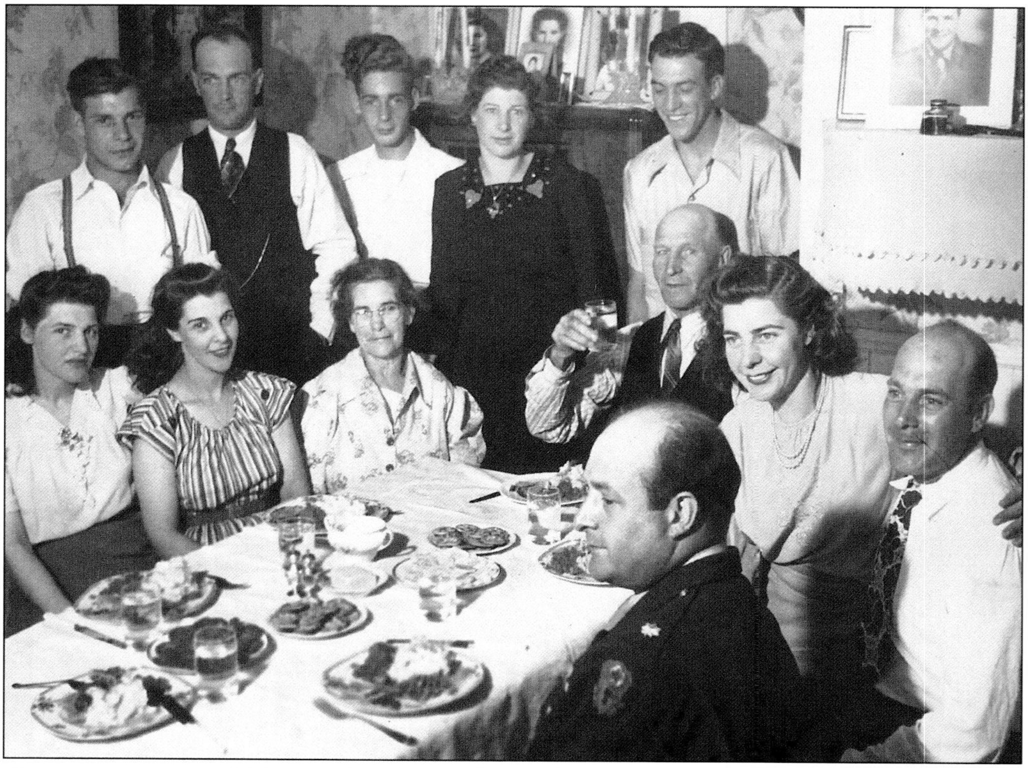

GOGAN FAMILY, C. 1946. Standing, from left to right at the rear, are Edgar, Bill, Albert, Lena, and Leo. Seated at the table are Mary, Dorothy, Natalie, Paul, Zelda, Ernie, and Frank. Frank served in the American Armed Forces. (Perry family.)

Seven

Domestic Architecture

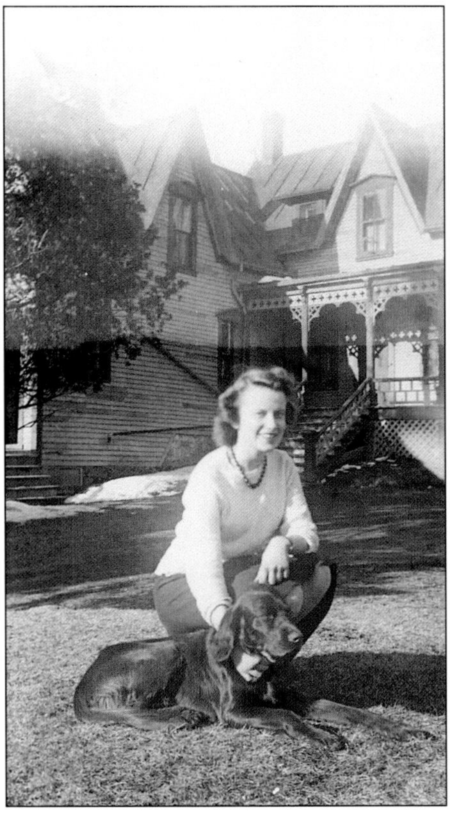

Randolph Home, 1943. Margaret Fitzrandolph poses with her dog in front of her Carpenter Gothic house. Margaret attended Saint John High School. The domestic architecture of Saint John West today covers the entire architectural heritage of the province. The earliest is the Georgian home of Jonathan Sewall, *c.* 1790. In Lancaster we had the Greek Revival home of Samuel McCormick, just recently demolished. There are Carpenter Gothic homes as shown here, Italianate-style like Albert Perry's home on Greenhead Road, and Queen Anne homes with Arts and Crafts influences such as the Tippet-built homes on Manawagonish Road and Lancaster Avenue. Then there are homes such as the Harris home on Manawagonish Road, which is described as Maritime Vernacular because it has no readily identifiable features of other styles. Although not shown within the pages of this book, there are a host of modern styles such as the post-war construction in Greendale and the new subdivision on the old Provincial Hospital Annex on Sand Cove Road. (M. McManus.)

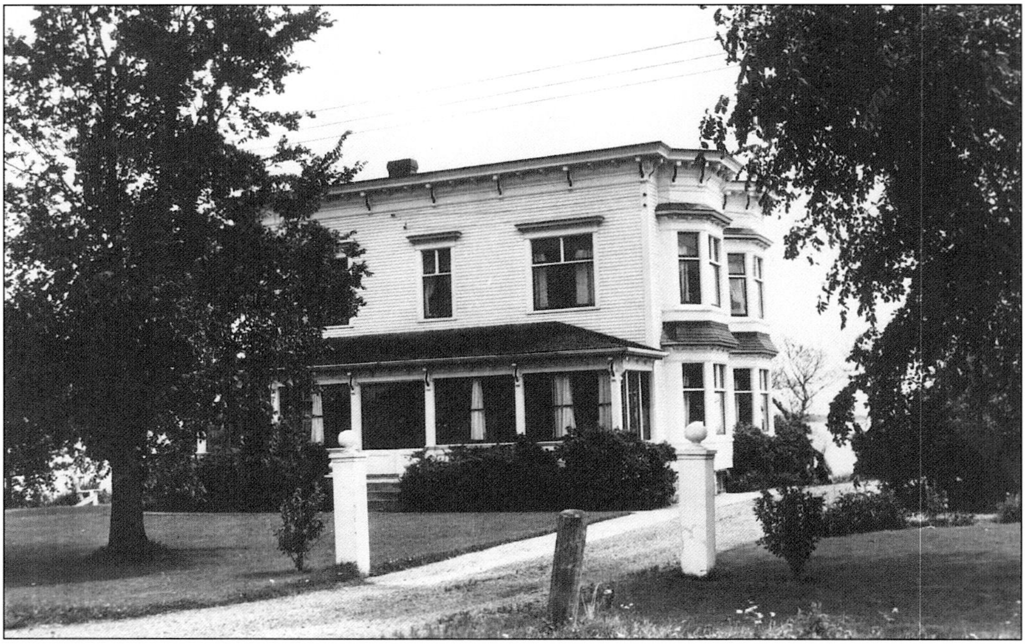

Glebe Farm, c. 1950. This was the home for George Chittick's family on Sand Cove Road. It had formerly been the Manchester Dairy property. With some minor changes to the building, it is now the Inn-on-the-Cove, one of the more popular tourist accommodations in Saint John. (Chittick collection, PIRP #7941.)

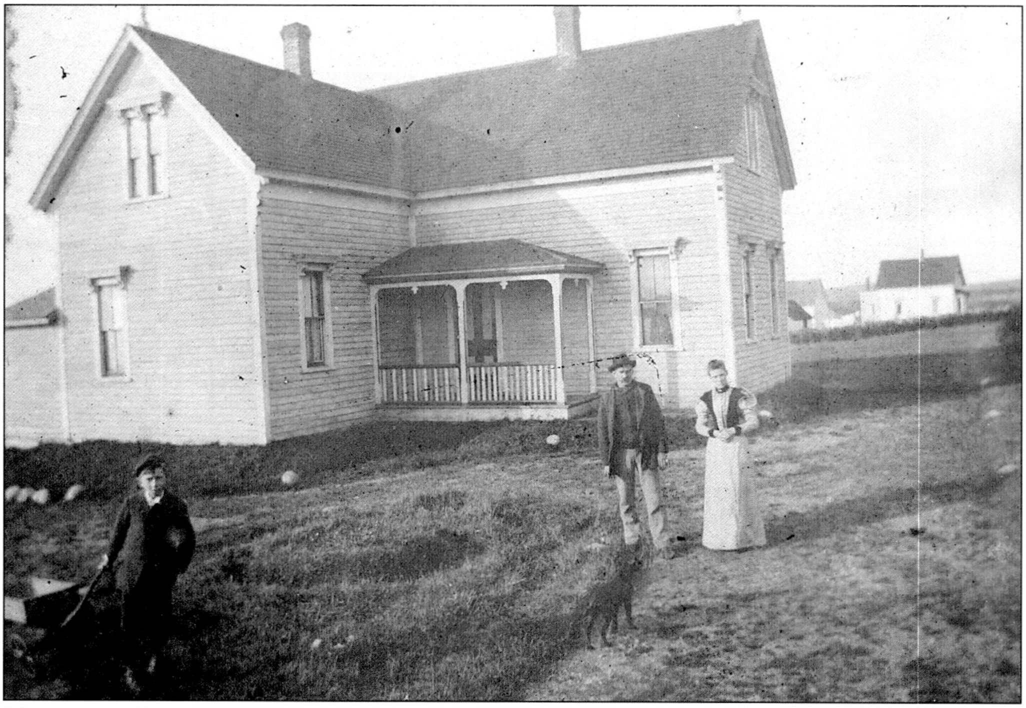

Mahogany Road Home, c. 1900. George and Margaret Harris lived in this house for most of their lives. The house still stands on Manawagonish Road, although there have been some changes to the building. (M. Kingston.)

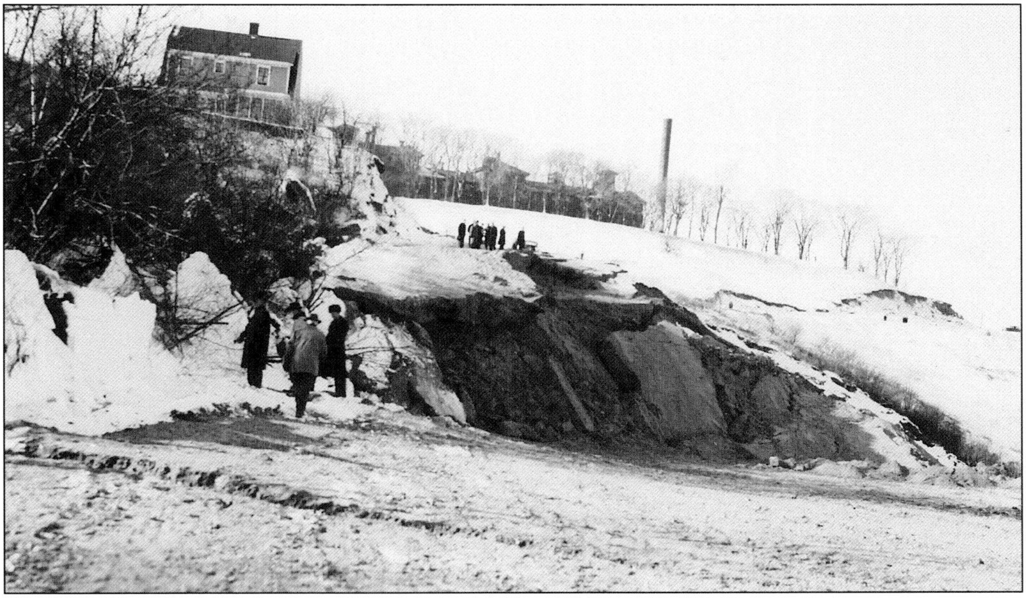

LANDSLIDE, 1949. While the city was having a road built beside the Reversing Falls Tourist Bureau, a massive landslide took away a large portion of the backyards of these properties on Lancaster Avenue. George Chittick, who was called in to inspect the properties, recorded this information on the back of the bottom photo: "Land subsidence rear of house Art Ready lived in within 8 ft of rear of bldg. I dropped a tape over side 43 ft. perpendicular." (Chittick family.)

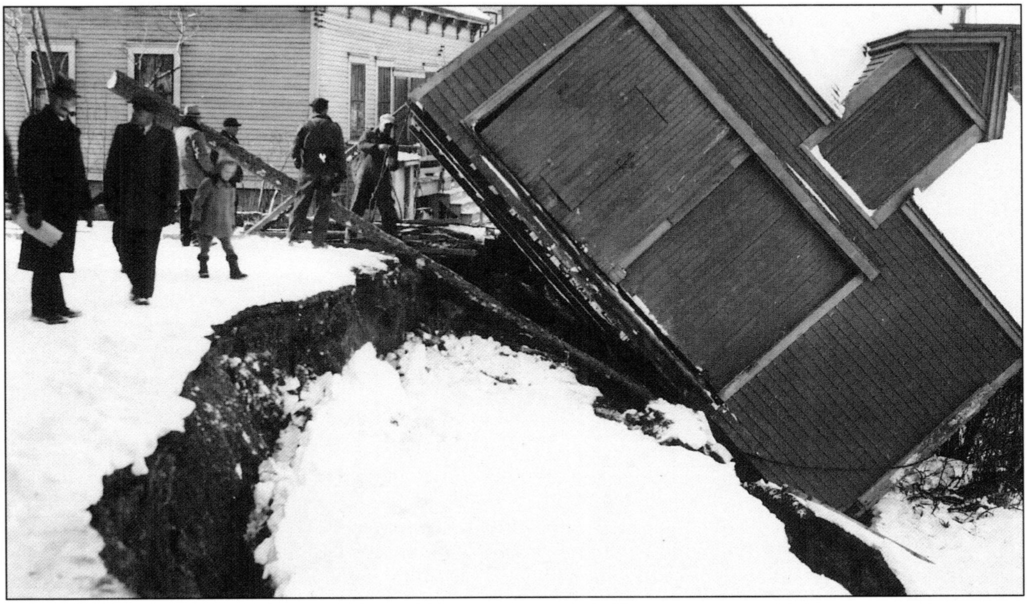

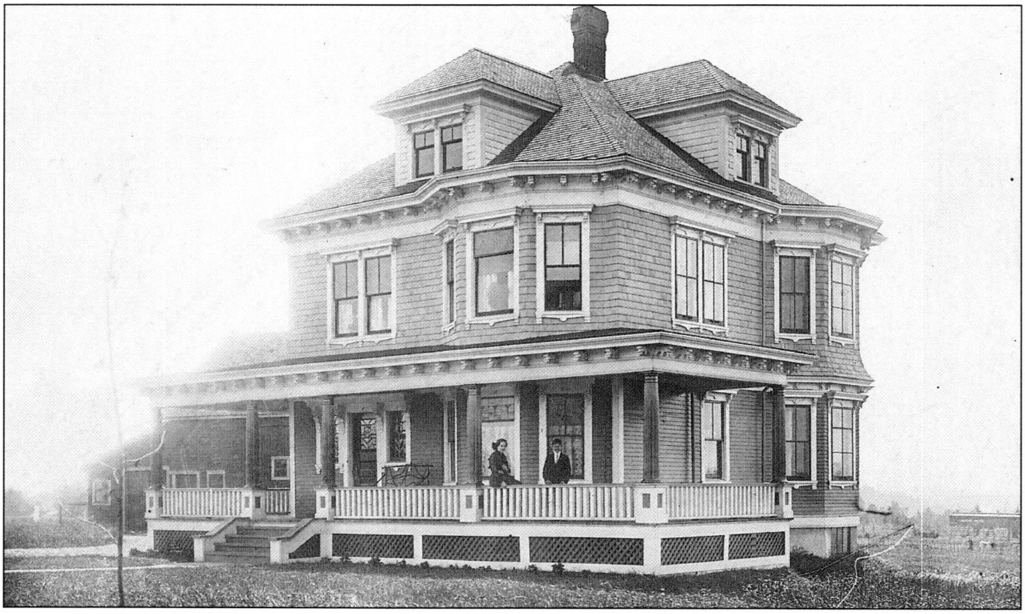

Murphy Homestead, c. 1910. Ellen and Daniel Murphy lived here for most of their adult lives. Daniel later became assistant collector of customs at the port. This house is still in its original location at 670 Sand Cove Road, although the porch has been removed and the original siding has been replaced with vinyl. (F. Hazel.)

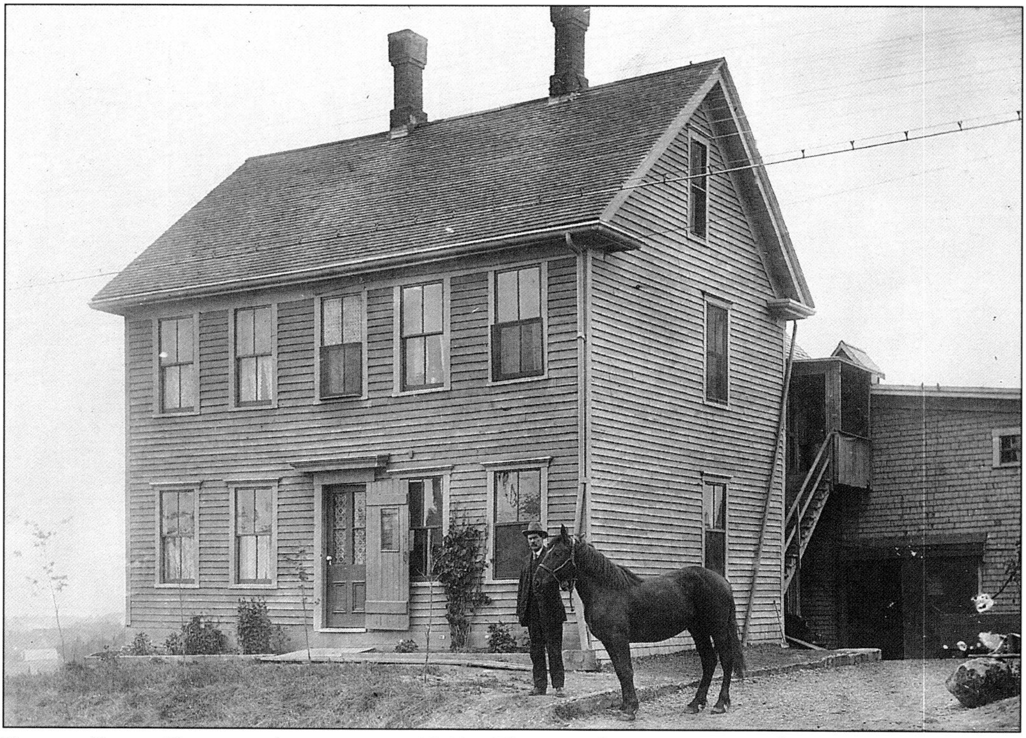

Eighty-Four Church Avenue, c. 1910. This was home to Samuel McCormick and his brother Fred and sister-in-law Elizabeth. Fred's three daughters owned it until the 1970s. The house was demolished in the mid-1990s. (E. Boyd.)

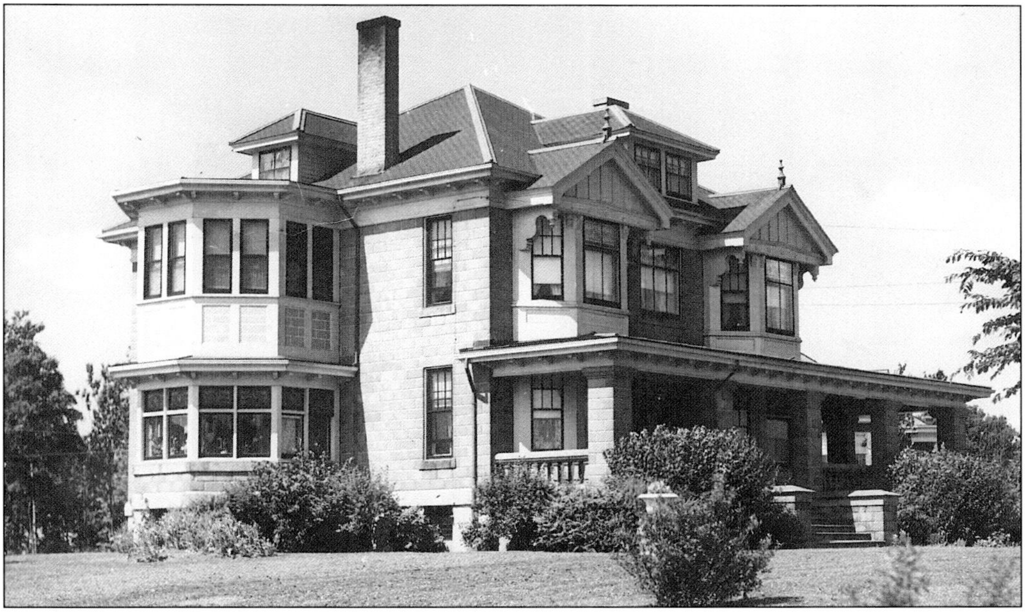

TIPPETT HOME, C. 1925. In the 1920s there were several homes built of this concrete block to simulate stone. The Queen Anne-style home at 824 Manawagonish Road was built by Harry Tippett and his partner, Murray K. Long, of Maritime Construction Ltd., for J.L. O'Brien, a manager at NB Breweries Ltd. Harry's son James now lives in the house. (K. Steen.)

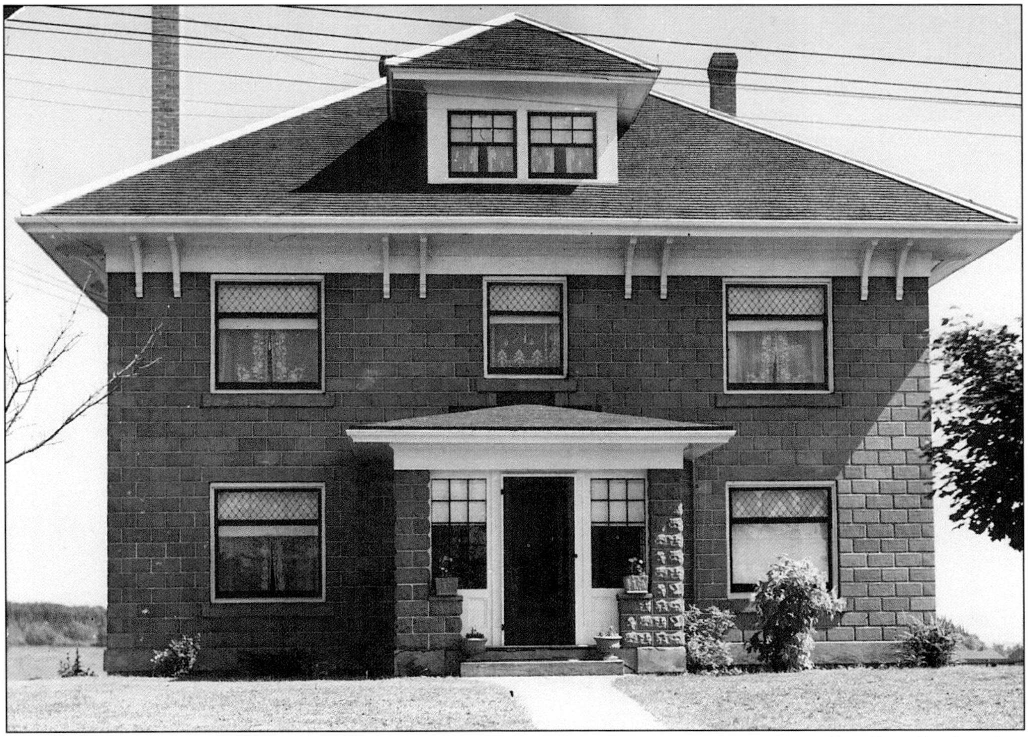

ANOTHER TIPPETT-BUILT HOME! C. 1925. Maritime Construction Ltd. also built this home in the 1920s at 851 Manawagonish Road for Harry Tippett's mother-in-law, Isabelle Lowell. (K. Steen.)

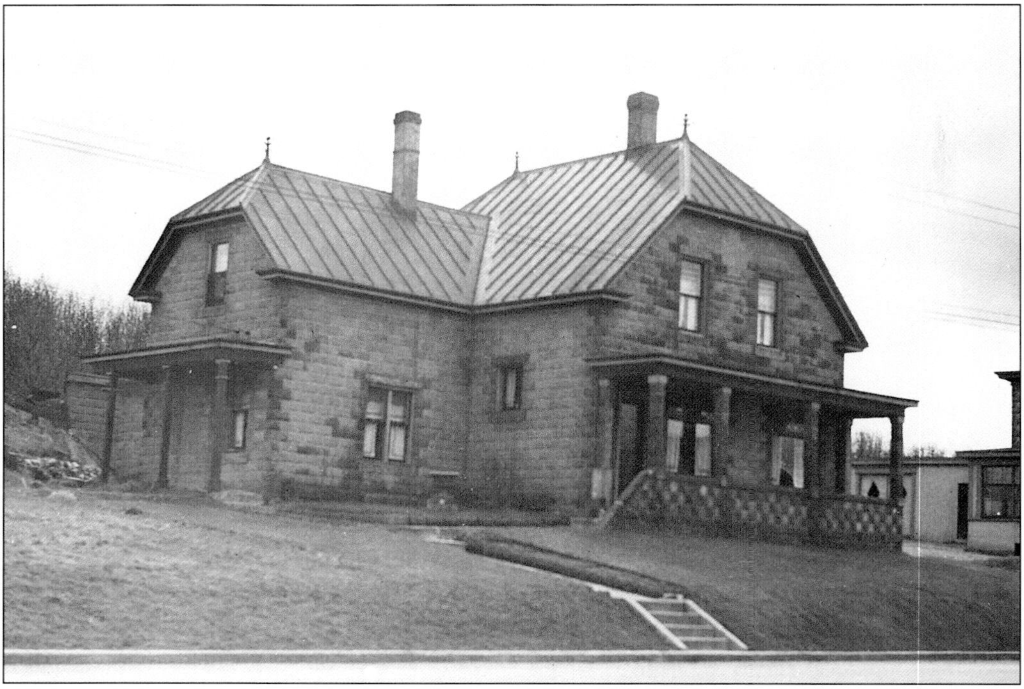

More Tippett Homes! c. 1925. The above home, at 548 Lancaster Avenue, was built for Murray K. Long, Tippett's partner in Maritime Construction Ltd. It was later home to Harry D. Hopkins, longtime Saint John common clerk. It has what is called a jerkins truncated metal roof. Below, 558 Lancaster Avenue was built for Charles R. Nelson, prominent Lancaster coal dealer. The construction of these homes was far from traditional, using concrete blocks to simulate stone. (K. Steen.)

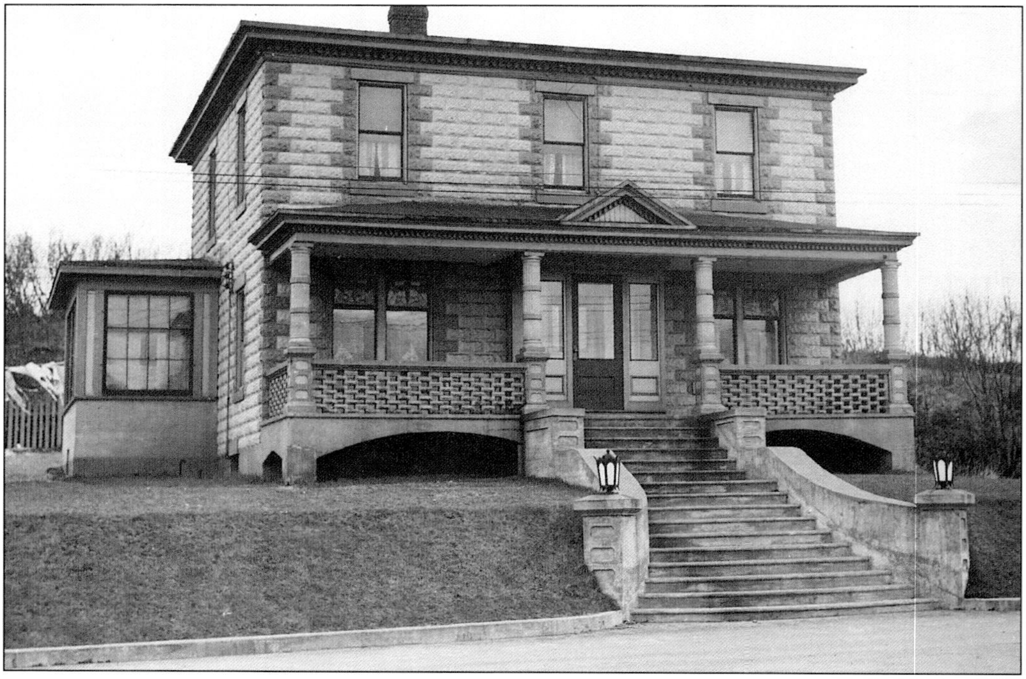

Eight

Recreation

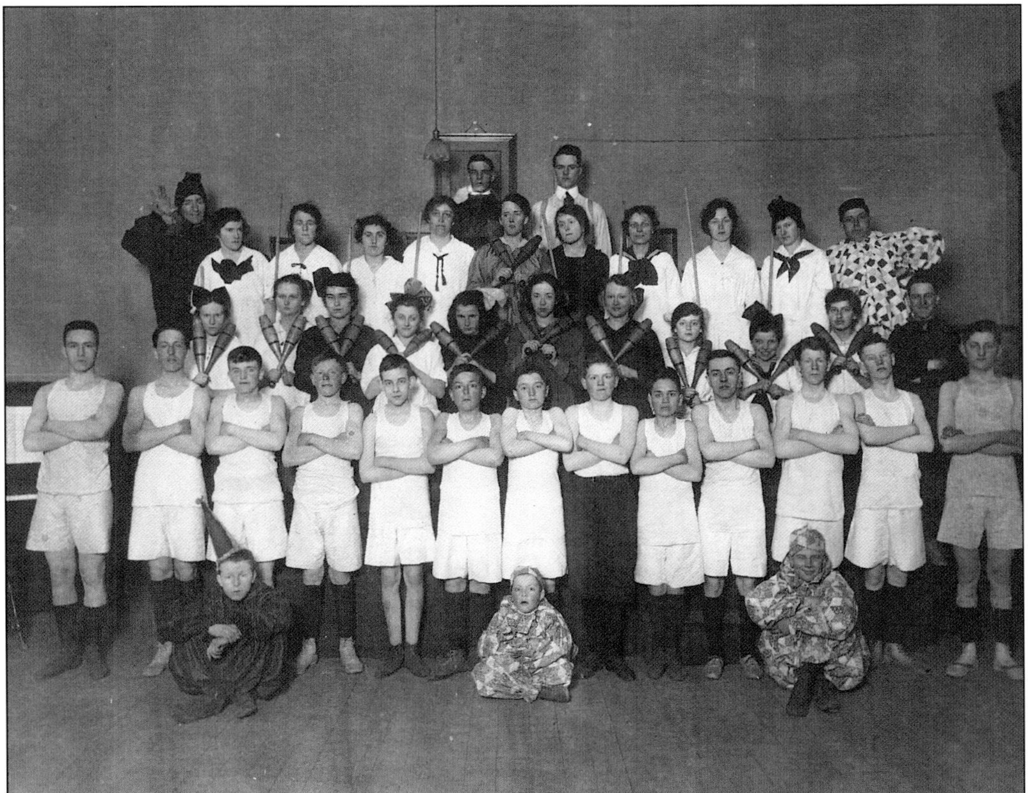

Gymnastics Club, c. 1916. Fairville Baptist Church had an active sports program for the youth of their church. Rev. P.R. Hayward, who came in May 1914, had a structure at the rear of the parsonage converted into a gymnasium. This gym was torn down in the early part of World War II. (Harris collection, PIRP #9406.)

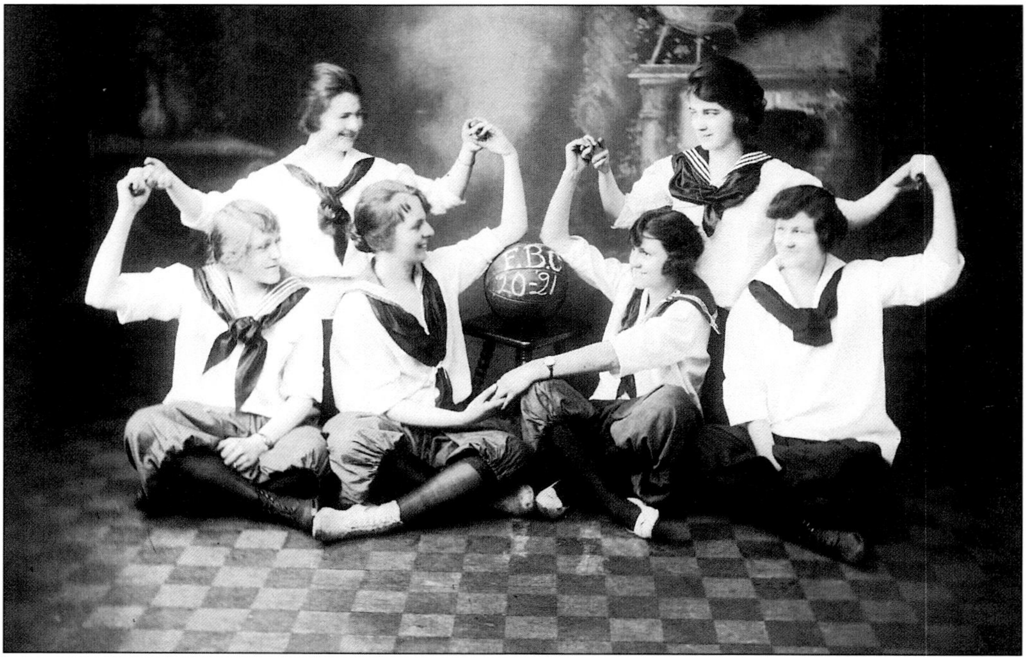

BASKETBALL CHAMPIONS, 1920–21. In addition to their gymnastics program, Fairville Baptist Church had at least one championship basketball team. The members were, from left to right, as follows: (front row) Helen Sime, Hattie Cheeseman, Ida Harris, and Myrtle (Fowler) Jenkins; (back row) Sadie (Stevens) Hobart and Lillian MacDonald. (Harris family.)

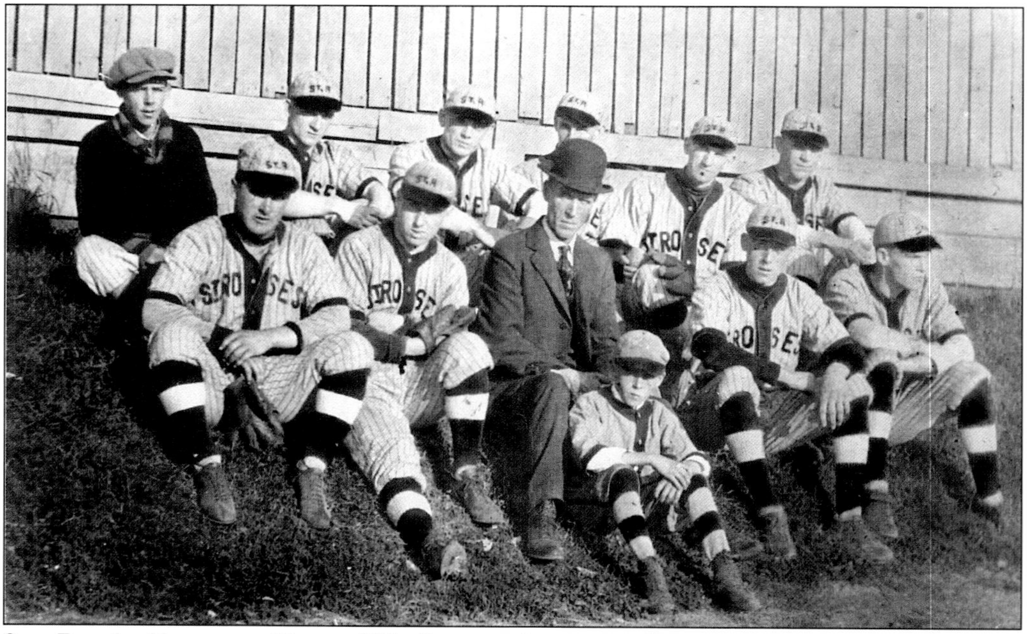

ST. ROSE'S BASEBALL TEAM, NB SENIOR AMATEUR CHAMPIONS, 1923. Members are shown here, from left to right, as follows: (front row) M. Fitzgerald and mascot; (middle row) W. Murphy, Haggie Conlon, J. Fitzgerald, F. Fitzgerald, and R. McMurray; (back row) R. Sherwood, F. Campbell, E. Dalton, Joe O'Toole, and E. Howard. M. McLaughlin is not pictured. (Buccaneers Pub collection, PIRP #9073.)

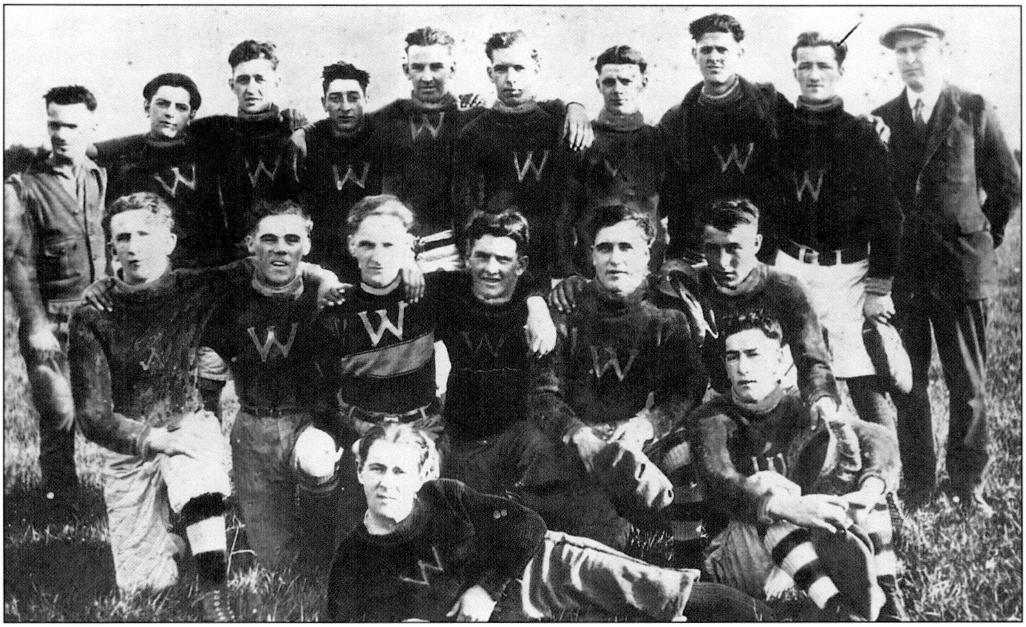

Fairville Wanderers Football Team, 1924. Members are, from left to right, as follows: (front row) John Garey and Louis Murphy; (middle row) Leonard Upton, Mike Crilley, Wilfred Hooley, Dan Murphy, Arthur Quigg, and Joe Chisholm; (back row) Timothy Hooley, Joe Doyle, James McCausland, Thomas Cranny, John Jayes, Curtis Gailey, Frank Logan, Robert DesRoches, George Reid, Arthur W. Cartin, and coach. (Buccaneers Pub collection, PIRP #9471.)

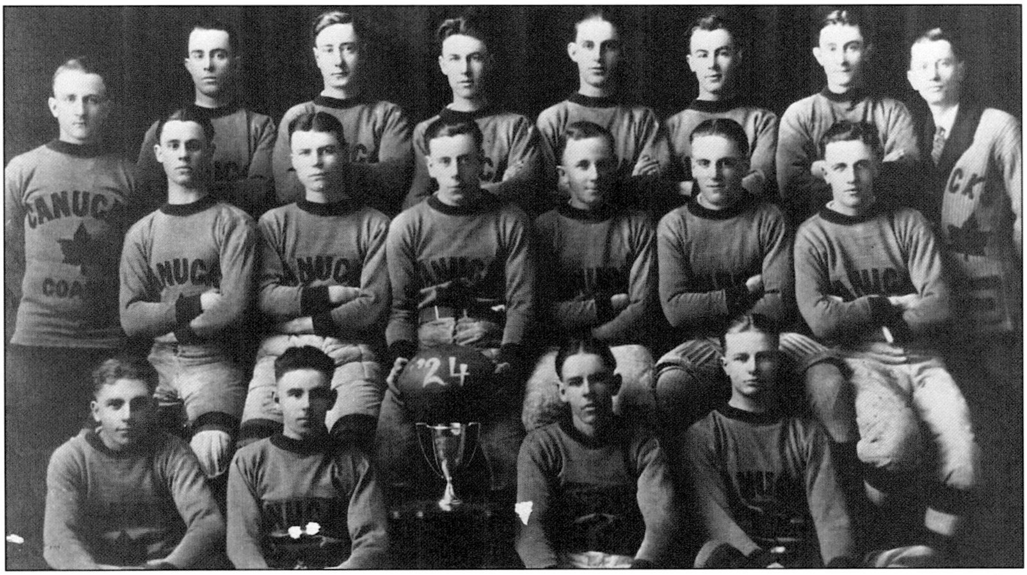

Canuck Football Team, 1924. The Canucks were the undefeated champions in Saint John that year. The team members were, from left to right, as follows: (front row) J.F. Casey, J.H. McManus, Ron A. Sherwood, and William J. McColgan; (middle row) Drew Mulcahy, Eddy C. Snodgrass, Fred T. Fritz, H. Peters, L.W. Bedford, and W. Arthur Miles; (back row) F.W. Timothy, S.E. Linton, Purdy M. Cougle, F.A. Baxter, F.J. Stear, L.C. Jones, Leslie G. Linton, and William H. Stinson. (Olsen collection, PIRP #7964.)

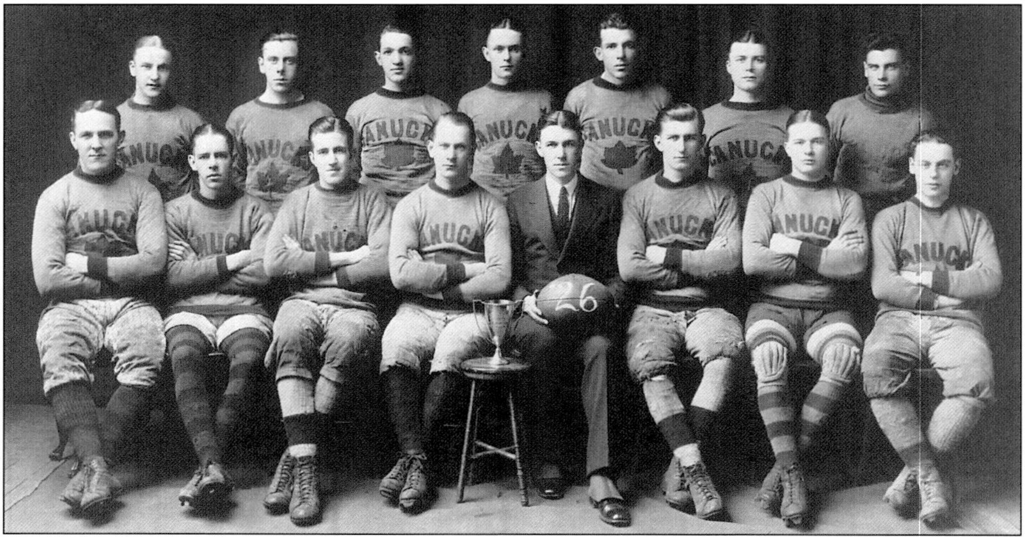

CANUCK FOOTBALL TEAM CHAMPIONS, 1926. Teammates are, from left to right, as follows: (front row) Newt Fanjoy, Ron Sherwood, quarterback, A. Merritt, Fred Duff, A. Baxter, quarterback, manager, R. Corbett, William McColgan Jr., and F. Jarvis; (back row) C. Merryweather, half-back, W. von Ritcher, full-back. On May 30, 1927, the team held a banquet in honour of Fred Duff and Marion Black's wedding the next day. Marion wrote a poem for the team, the last few stanzas being: "So to each and every good Canuck; We wish the very best of Luck; For boys with such sweet baby faces; Can not help but take first places . . . Now to them all . . . Congratulations; For they've lived up to all Expectations; And trust that in the coming year; They'll bring the trophy right back here." (Olsen collection, PIRP #7965.)

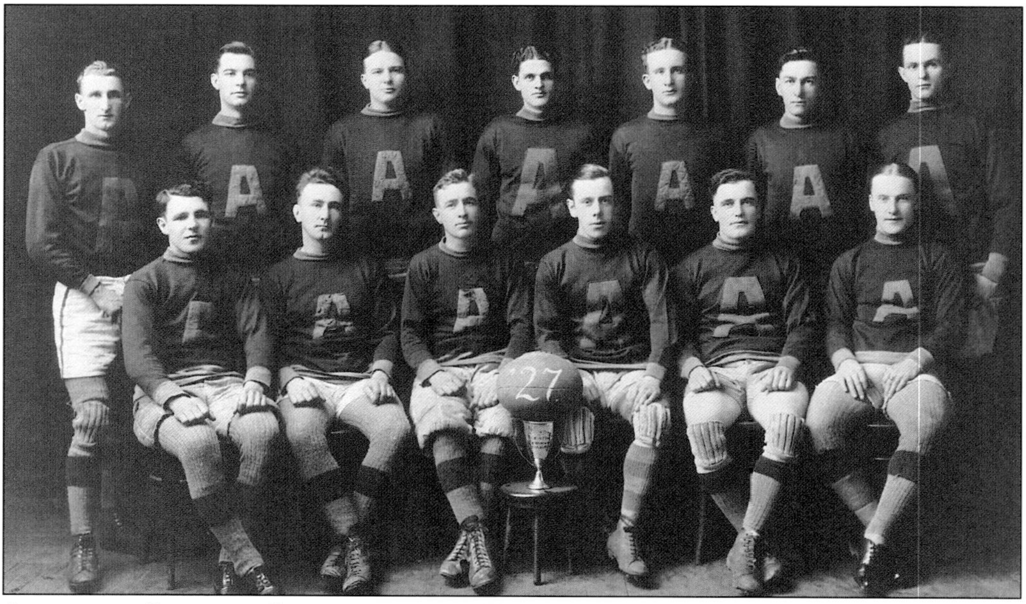

ARGONAUTS FOOTBALL CHAMPIONS, 1927. Teammates are pictured here, from left to right: (front row) J.O. O'Toole, half-back, W. Draft, half-back, William McColgan, half-back, D.P. Desroches, full-back, and L. Upton; (back row) G. McManus, E. O'Toole, F. Fox, manager, Fred Fritz, quarterback, captain, A. Quigg, quarterback, and C. Merryweather, half-back. (Olsen collection, PIRP #7966.)

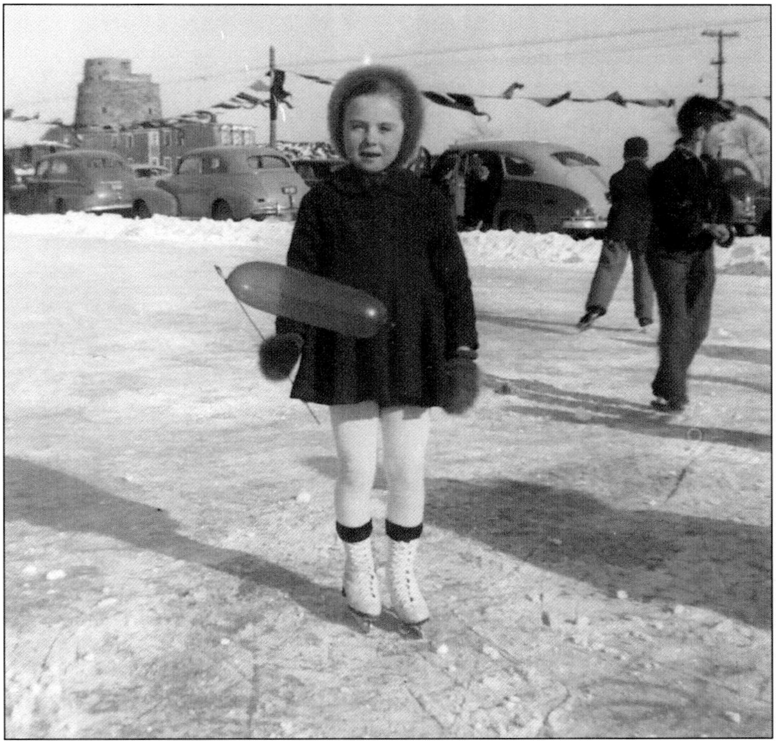

WINTER CARNIVAL, c. 1951. The area across from Beaconsfield School was flooded and made an ideal outdoor rink for carnival skating. The Beaconsfield Winter Carnival was sponsored by the Beaconsfield Athletic Club. In 1955, the president was Councillor Hartley G. Green. His daughter Judy is holding the balloon, while her sister Carol strikes her best pose! (Green family.)

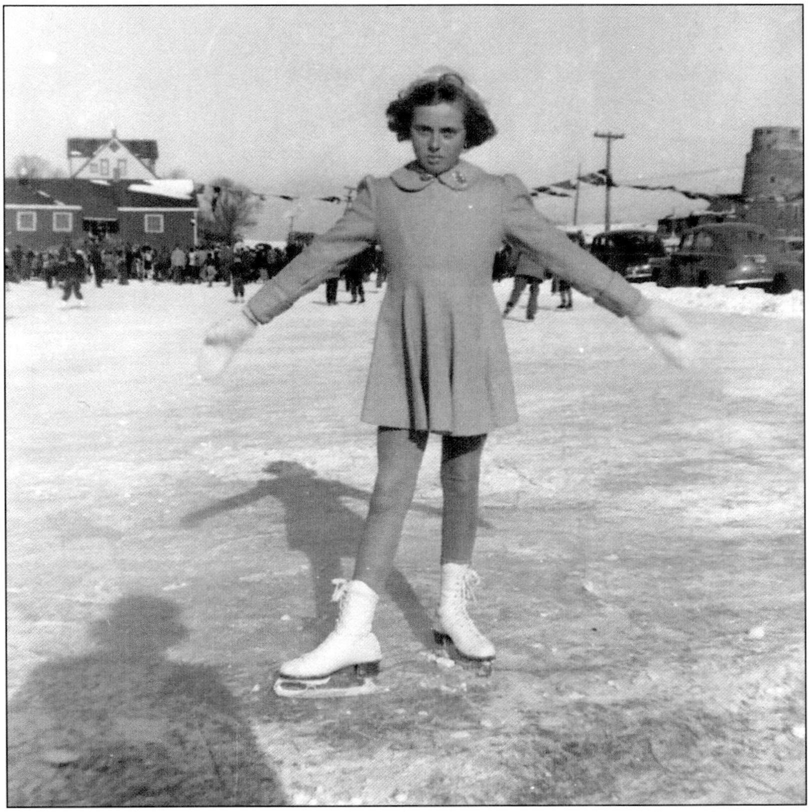

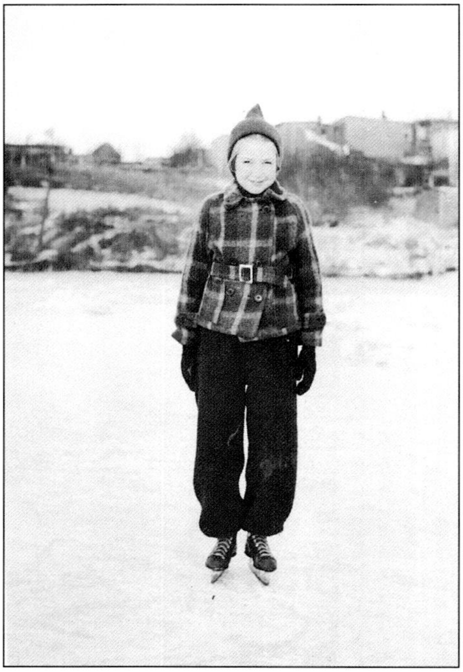

Winter Skating, c. 1940. The old water reservoir on Ready Street made an ideal skating rink for Carol Harris and all the neighbours' kids. (Harris family.)

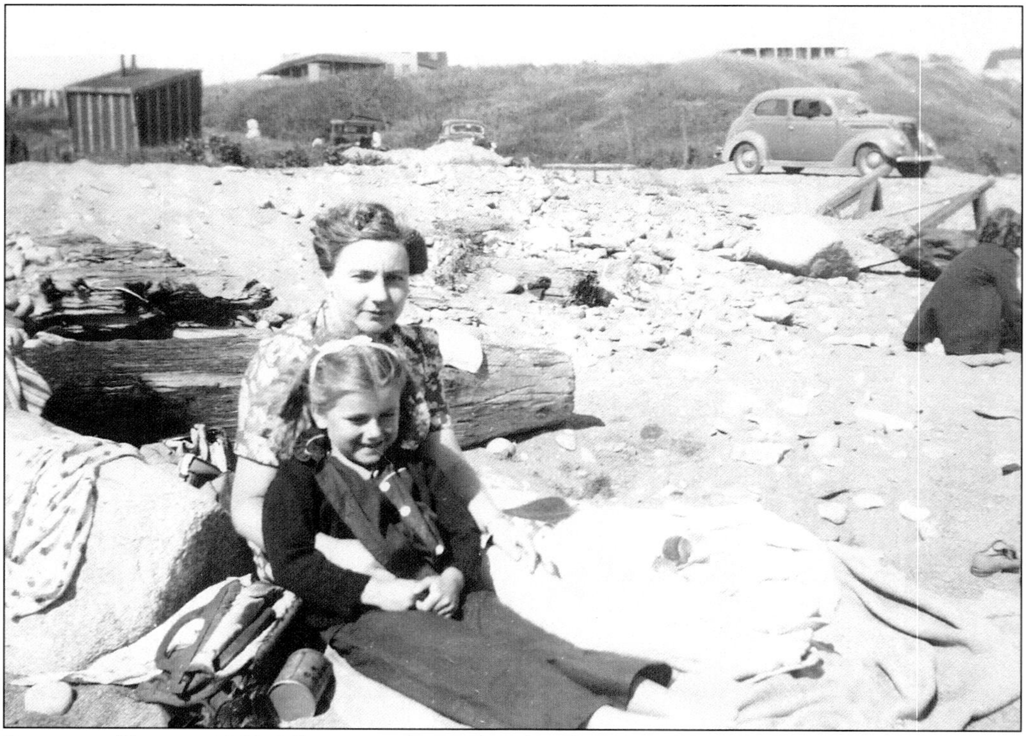

Bayshore Beach, 1950. There were lots of beaches for summertime swimming fun—including MacLarens, Bayshore, and Dominion Park. It was MacLarens, though, that offered changing huts and a canteen. However, over the years both MacLarens and Bayshore were allowed to deteriorate so that today they hold little attraction for swimmers. Enjoying this summer's day is Laura Walton with her daughter Linda. (L. Rolston.)

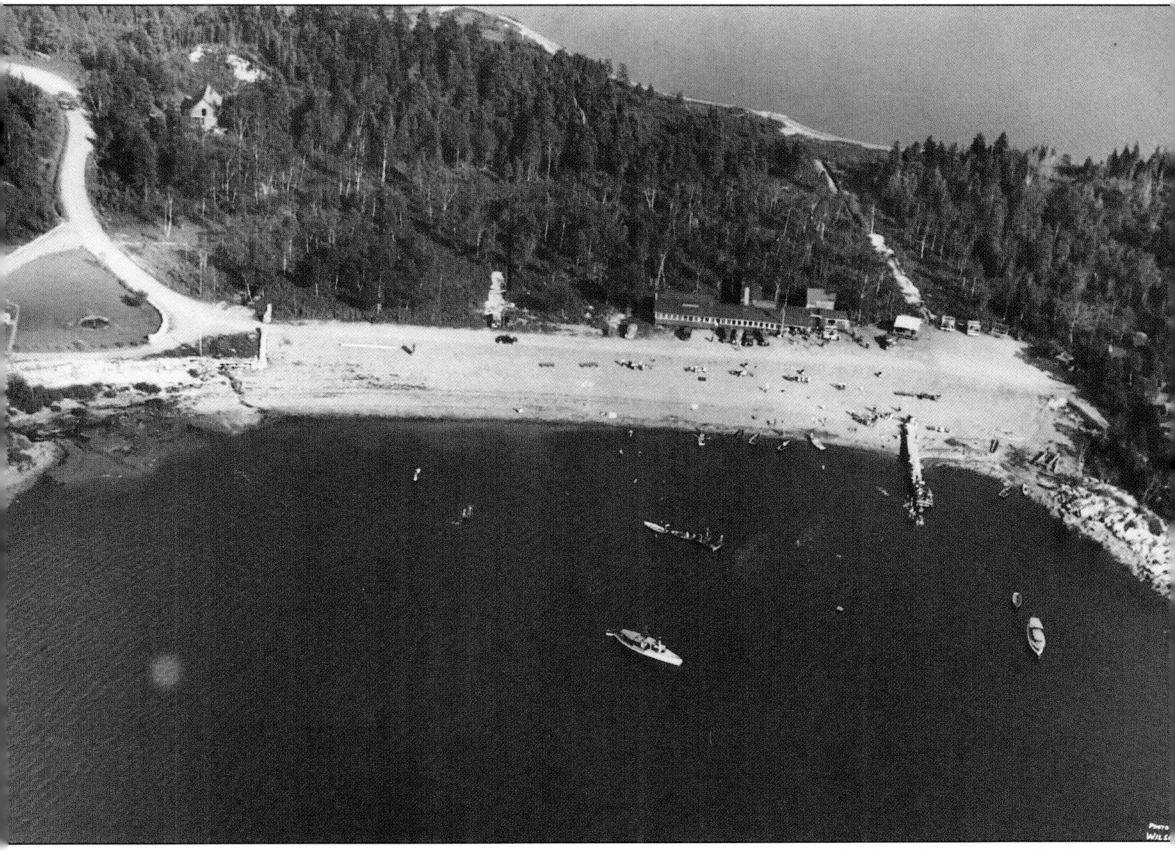

Raynes Beach, c. 1935. Those from Lancaster knew it as Raynes Beach, but by 1946 it had been renamed Dominion Park. The park was operated by the Saint John Municipal Parks Commission. The dancing and restaurant pavilion, shown near the top of the beach, was operated by many over time, including Al Olsen and his mother, Helen; Dan Haggarty; Mert Lester; and Al Goody. (Olsen collection, PIRP #7787.)

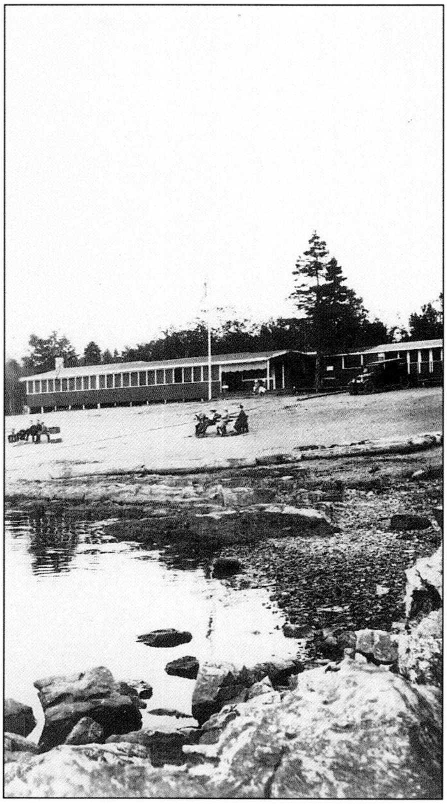

RAYNES BEACH, 1921. "Located on a sheltered cove of the St. John River within a short distance from the centre of the city, the sparkling river water warmed by the summer's sun provides an ideal place for swimming. Started only a few years ago, the facilities of the park are extended annually and on busy days are taxed to capacity. A large area is reserved for parking and buses operate to and from the park on extended schedules". (M. Kingston.)

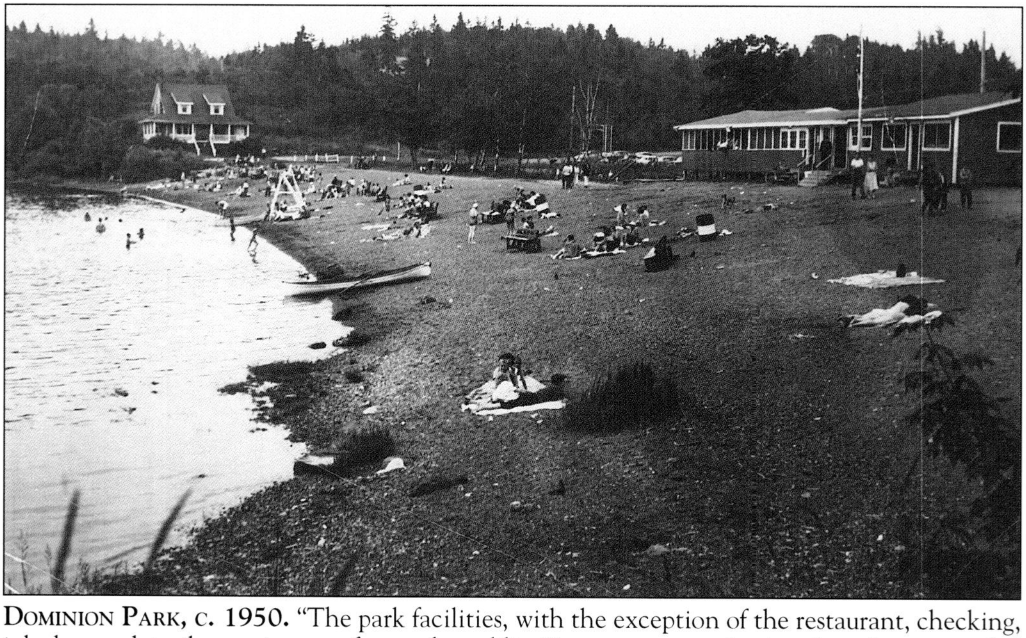

DOMINION PARK, C. 1950. "The park facilities, with the exception of the restaurant, checking, juke box and similar services, are free to the public. Teeter-totters and swings have been provided for the youngsters who like a little variety from swimming, sunning, and making castles in the clean white sand. Pony rides are available, too, but like ice cream and soft drinks, must be paid for". (Olsen collection, PIRP #7921.)

BEACONSFIELD MARTELLOS, C. 1955. Teammates are, from left to right, as follows: (front row) ?, ?, Harry Brittain, goalie, Barry Kane, and George James; (middle row) Fred Whipple, unidentified, Neil McKay, and Stanley Collins; (back row) Hartley Green, Don Whipple, Billy James, and Raymond Trecartin. Co-manager Hartley Green, who couldn't play sports due to a childhood illness, spent thousands of hours over the years supporting hockey. In 1954–55 the Martellos were the Saint John City and District Midget Hockey champions. His hockey associations included being president of the Saint John Minor Hockey Assoc., coach and manager of the Saint John Maroon's Junior Hockey League, president of the Lancaster Centennial Hockey League, and coach and manager of the Beaconsfield Kings Senior Hockey Club. He also organized the Three Star Baseball League and was president of the Beaconsfield Athletic Club. (Green family.)

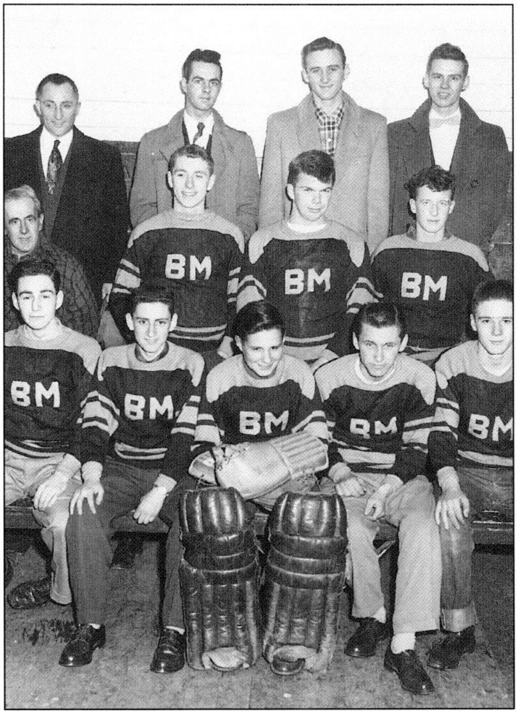

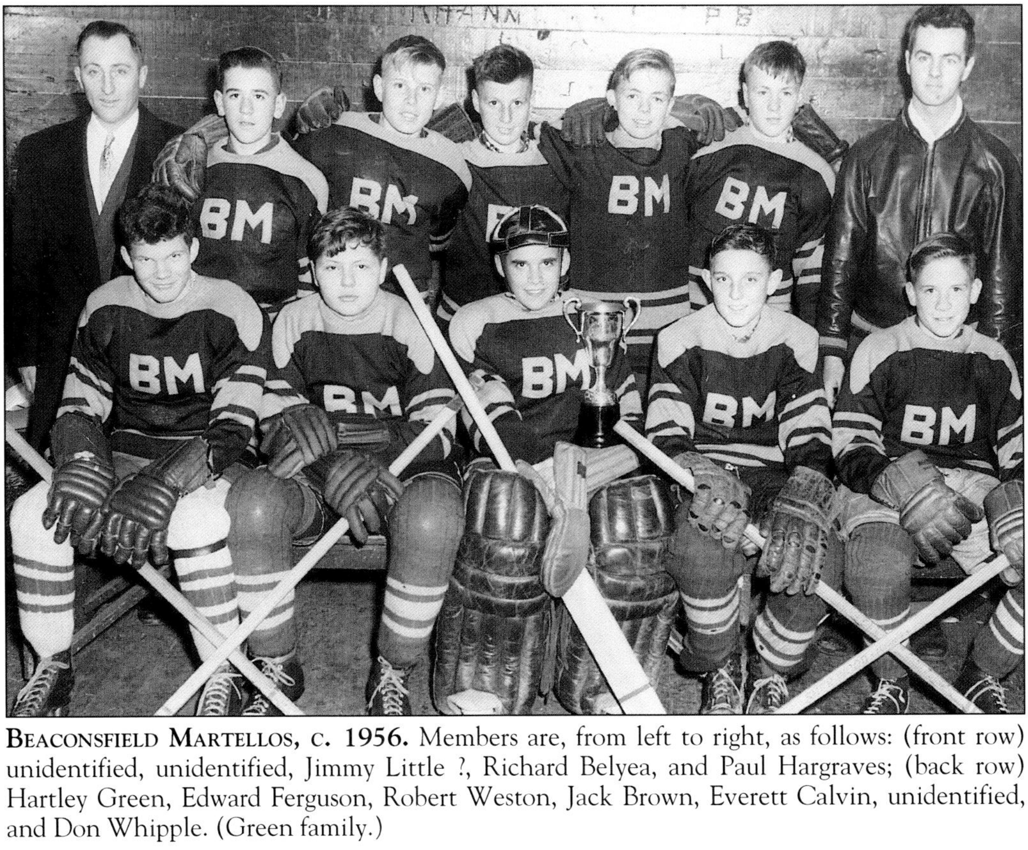

BEACONSFIELD MARTELLOS, C. 1956. Members are, from left to right, as follows: (front row) unidentified, unidentified, Jimmy Little ?, Richard Belyea, and Paul Hargraves; (back row) Hartley Green, Edward Ferguson, Robert Weston, Jack Brown, Everett Calvin, unidentified, and Don Whipple. (Green family.)

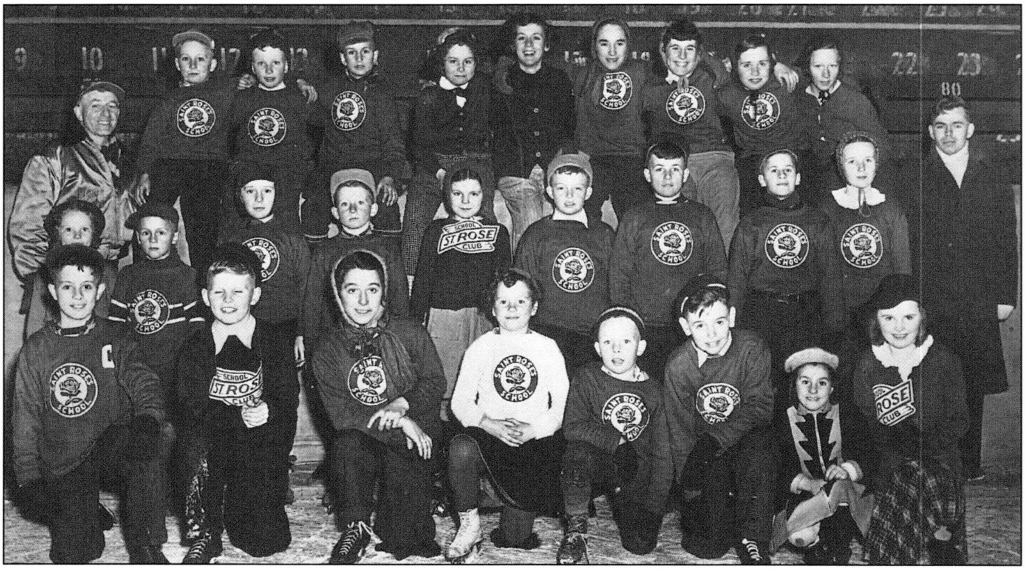

St. Rose School Skating Club, 1953. Skaters are, from left to right, as follows: (front row) Norman Garey, Donny Burchill, Marjorie Sutton, Beth McManus, David Garey, Frank Haggarty, Clair McManus, unidentified, and Germaine Vaut; (middle row) Christine Sherwood, Roger Cyr, Ivan Lacasse, Joe Kane, Sharon McManus, Leonard Sherwood, Ronald Williams, Reno Cyr, Donna Northrup, Fitzjames Kane, and principal; (back row) Jim Fox, coach, Barry McManus, Brian Sherwood, Gerald Cyr, Kathleen Morton, Joan O'Neill, Lola Lacasse, Joan Quigg, Mary Joan Maloney, and Patricia Mallette. (Garey collection, PIRP #9419.)

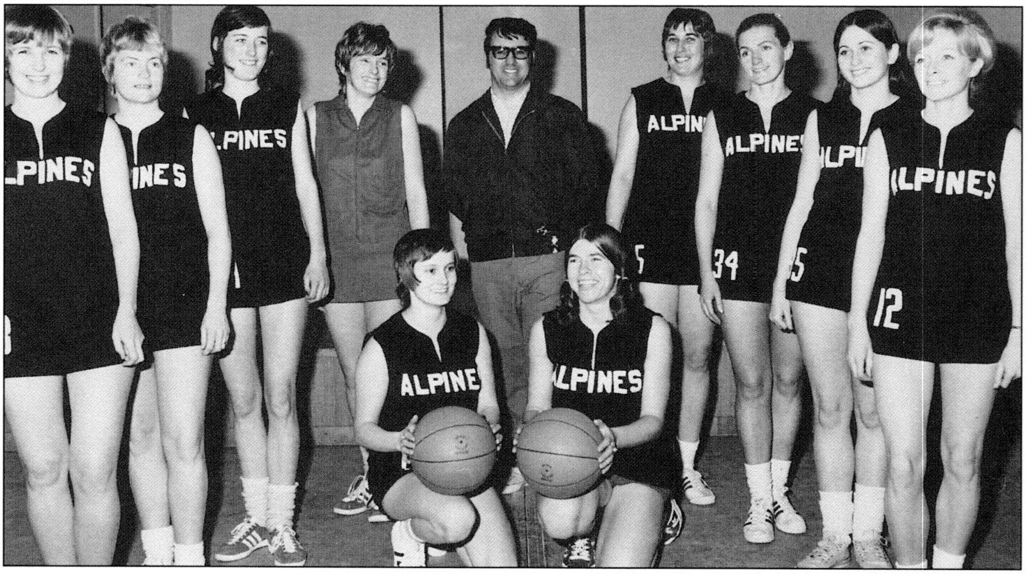

Moosehead Champs, 1972. The Alpines were the New Brunswick and Atlantic basketball champions. For decades Moosehead Breweries has sponsored sports teams in both Lancaster and Saint John. The team members in 1972 were, from left to right, Marlene Vaughan, Rose Donovan, Ellen MacDonald, Jean Hutcheson, Bill Vaughan, Marg McGarrity, Pauline McHugh, Marlene Kenny, and Crystal Jones. Kneeling are Marilyn Dougherty and Bunni Nurmi. (Moosehead Breweries.)

Nine

Politics

Rink Opening, 1967. Mayor Bert Huestis officially opened the Lancaster Centennial Arena. Why the ladies washroom was chosen as the site of the ribbon cutting will probably never be known. The cornerstone ceremony took place on October 2, 1966, with the cornerstone being donated by H.H. Barbour in memory of his wife. In 1958 the Saint John Board of Trade's Civic Affairs Committee had recommended that Lancaster and Simonds Parish amalgamate with Saint John. On January 1, 1967, Lancaster amalgamated with Saint John. Bert served on the Con-Joint Council from January 1 until June 30, 1967, to smooth the way for this amalgamation. He did not re-offer to serve on the new council. Bert recalled "We had a real good city . . . The majority of the population of Lancaster and of its council didn't want that amalgamation." (Huestis collection, PIRP #9446.)

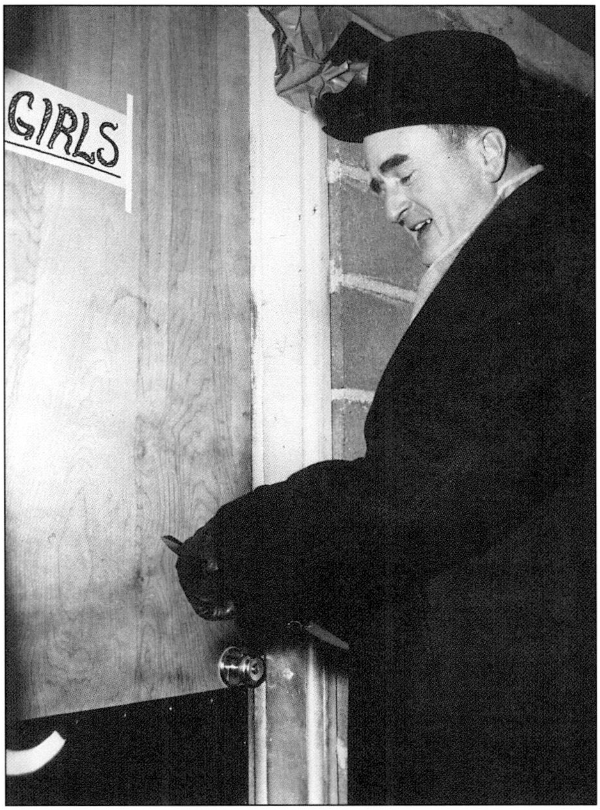

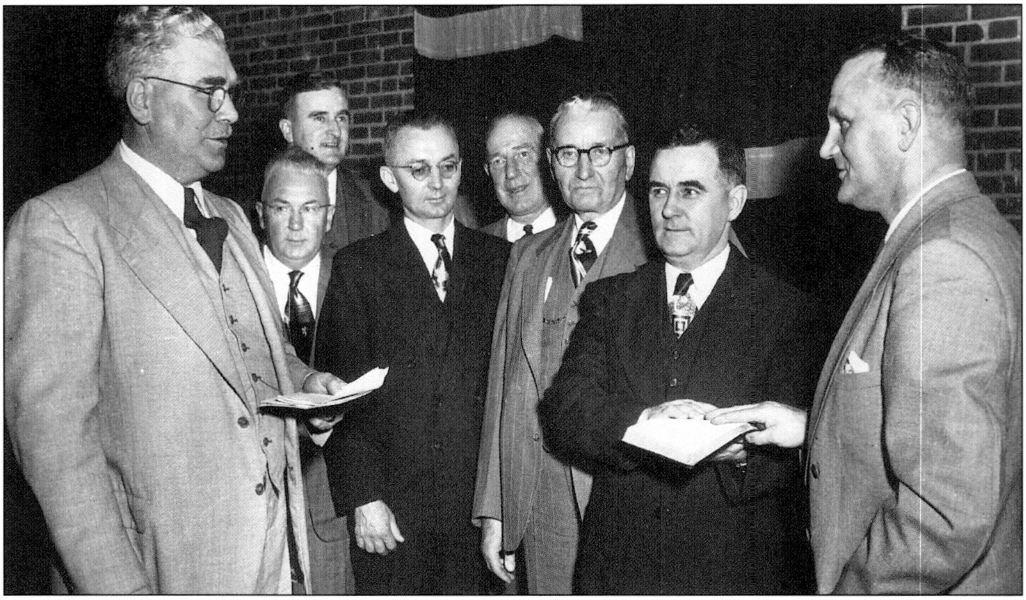

First Council, December 2, 1952. The first Lancaster Council was sworn in at Barnhill school, almost a month before the official incorporation of Lancaster. Judge Reginald Kierstead administered the oath of office to Bill Golding, Bert Huestis, Parker D. Mitchell, Arthur Doherty, Claude Seeley, John Garey, and Mayor Thomas Horsler. During the election campaign Horsler had campaigned with the slogan "H-a hustler O-an organizer R-reliable S-sincere L-leader E-energetic R-responsible." He won the election by 64 votes over Arthur W. Carton, M.L.A. (Huestis collection, PIRP #9438.)

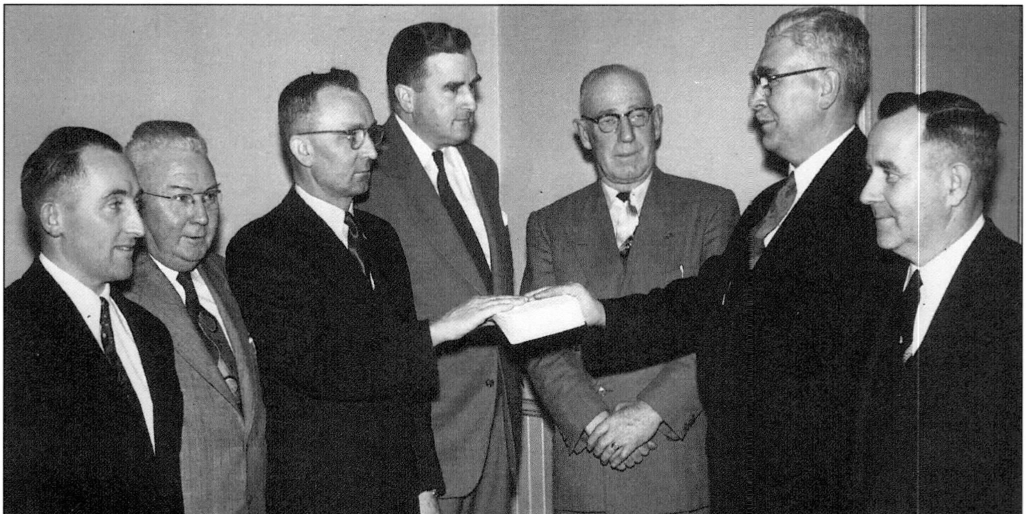

Second Council, December 2, 1954. This was the swearing in ceremony of the new Lancaster Common Council. Shown here, from left to right, are Hartley Green, William M. Golding, Mayor Parker D. Mitchell, Berton W. Huestis, Arthur Doherty, Judge Reginald Keirstead, and John Garey. In the 1958 election, Mayor Mitchell did not re-offer, and Bert Huestis was successful in becoming mayor. His councillors in 1958 were William Golding, Hartley Green, John Garey, Roland Kirkpatrick, and Lloyd Hartt. Huestis led Lancaster into amalgamation with Saint John in 1967. (Huestis collection, PIRP # 9423.)

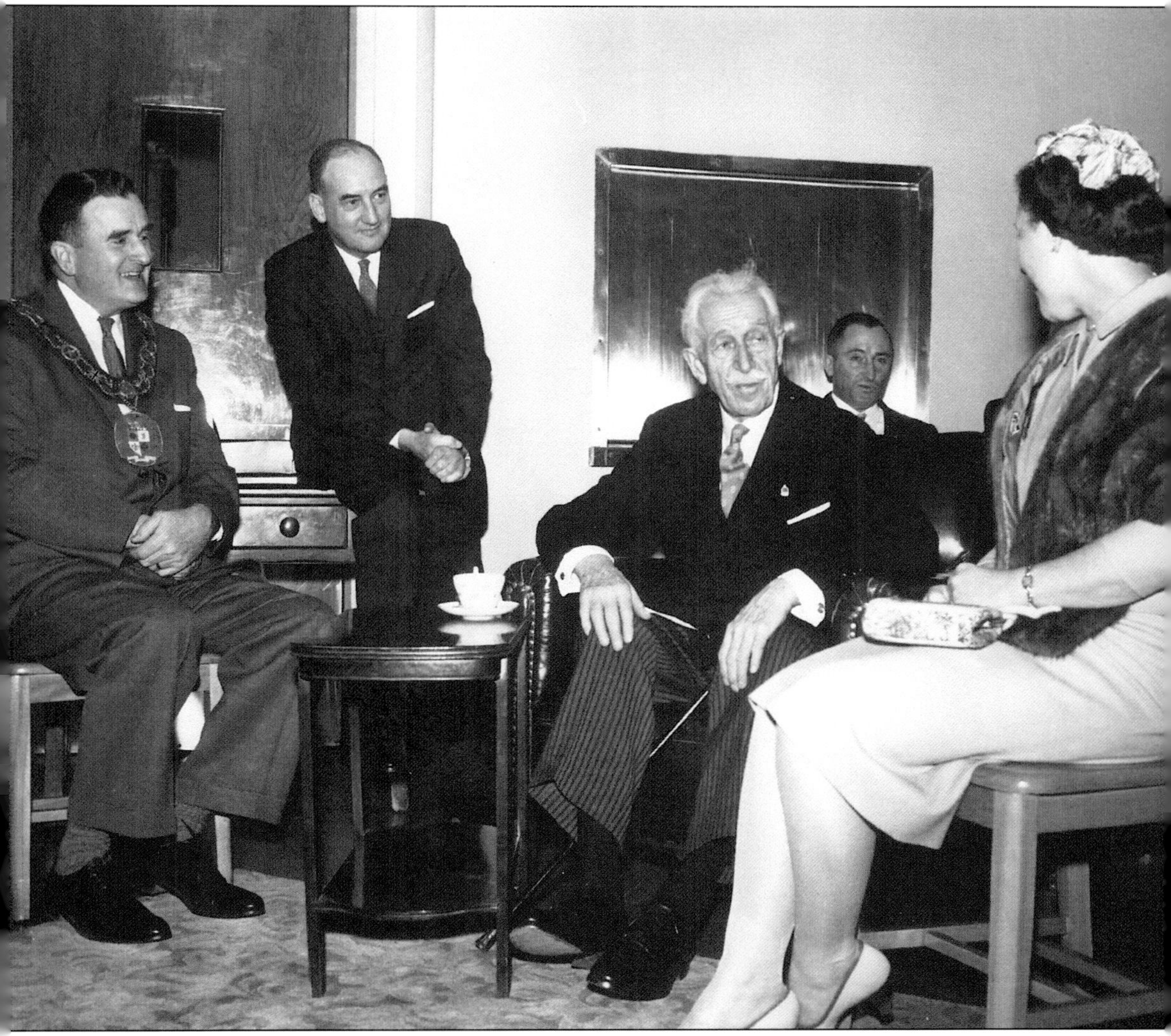

VICE-REGAL VISIT, C. 1963. Mayor Bert and Mrs. Huestis pose for a photograph with Governor General George P. Vanier. Tom McCarthy of the Lancaster Chamber of Commerce is at Mayor Huestis's left. Councillor Hartley Green is behind Governor General Vanier, who was in office from 1959 to 1967. He visited Lancaster and Saint John several times during his tenure as governor general. (Huestis collection, PIRP #9436.)

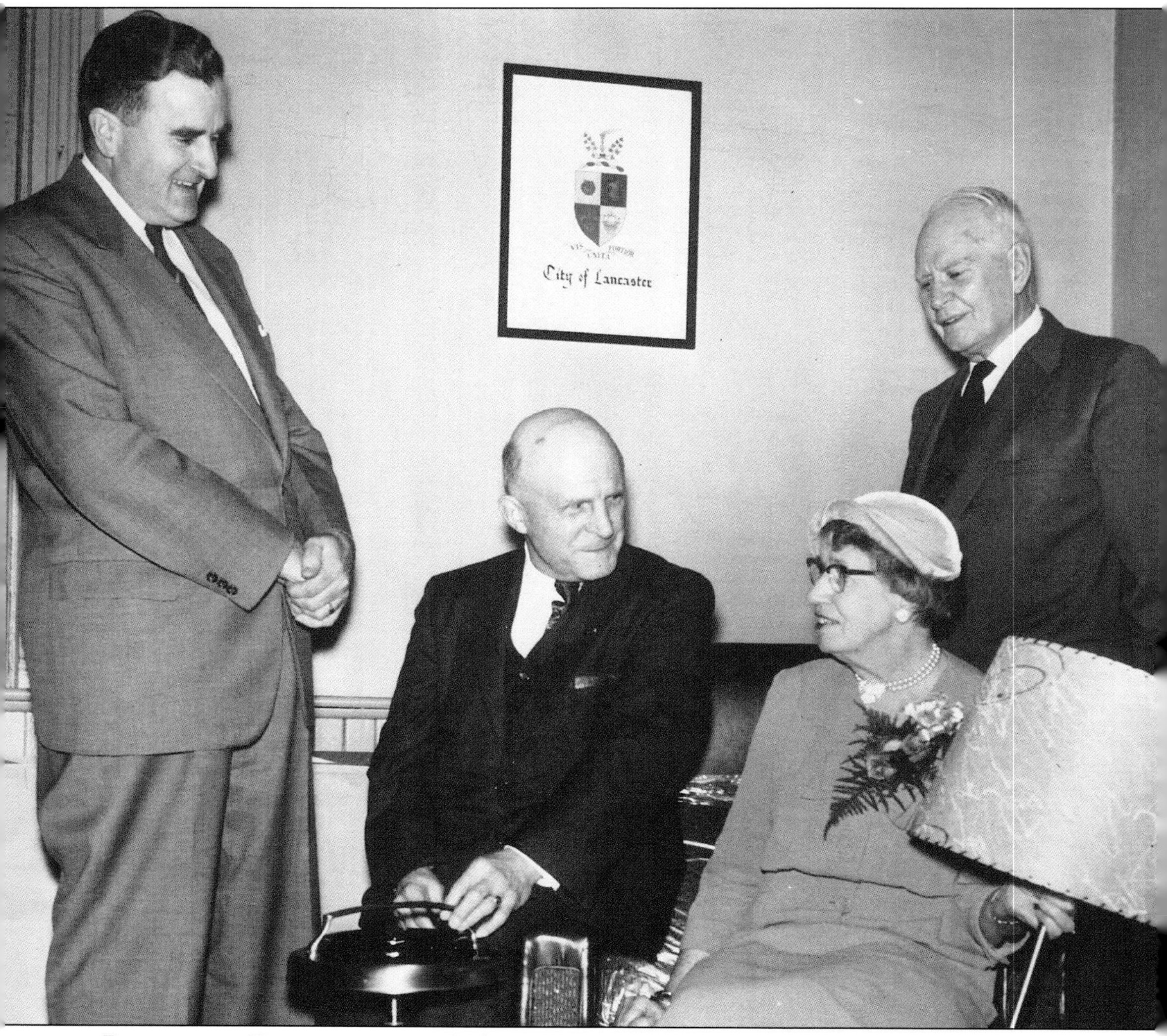

RETIREMENT, DECEMBER 1958. Arthur R. Everett was the longtime treasurer of Lancaster. He attended Saint John High School and the Currie Business College, he then spent 25 years with T. McAvity & Sons, becoming their chief accounting clerk. In July 1933, he joined the Municipal Accounting Department in the county courthouse, becoming treasurer there in November 1937. He joined the City of Lancaster staff in 1953 and died on June 24, 1959. Pictured here, from left to right, are Mayor Bert Huestis, Arthur Everett, his wife, Ethel, and Arthur Carton, M.L.A. Everett was replaced as treasurer by Harold Ellis, who on the eve of amalgamation in 1967 noted that the City had raised $60,000 more than anticipated that year. (Huestis collection, PIRP #9439.)

Ten

BUSINESSES

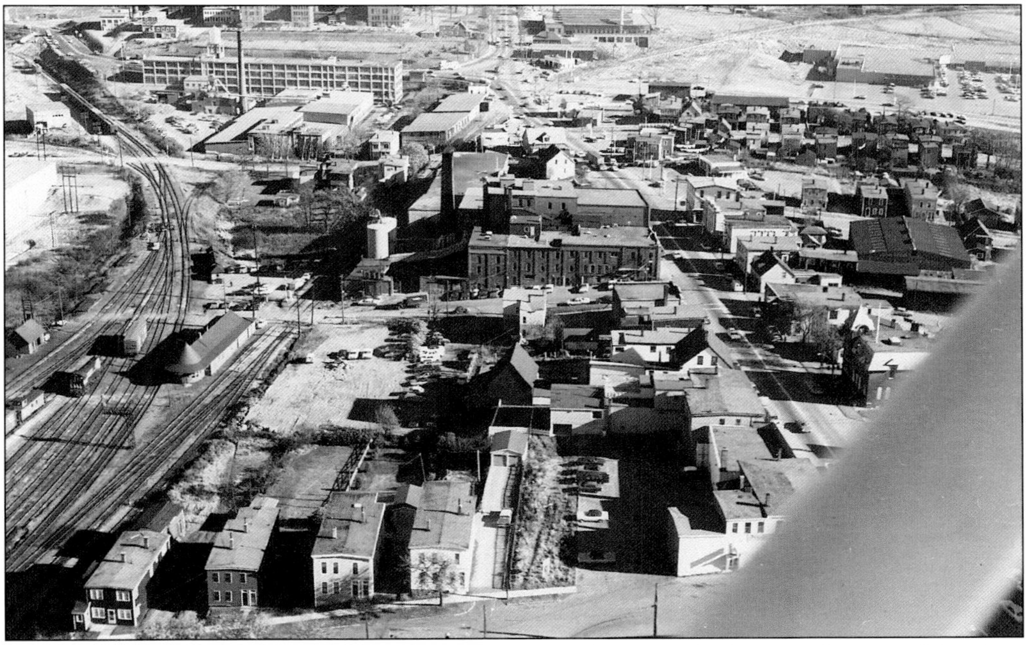

MOOSEHEAD—THE CENTRE OF THE COMMUNITY, 1969. Starting clockwise at the rear of the plant is the Fairville train station, the T.S. Simms Brush Factory, Centracare, the Ford Motor Plant, and the Lancaster Mall. Moosehead traces its roots to the Army & Navy Brewery in Halifax in 1867. The brewing patriarch was Susannah Oland, who in 1877 bought controlling interest in the brewery, renaming it S. Oland Sons & Co. The Oland name has been synonymous with Maritime brewing ever since. Her grandson, George B. Oland came to Saint John after World War I, and he and his father bought interest in the Simeon Jones brewery. George B. eventually took over interest of the Ready Brewery in Fairville. George was followed by his son, Brig. Philip W. Oland, whose generosity to the social and cultural life of Saint John will be felt for decades. After P.W.'s death in 1996, his son Derek became company chairman. Today Moosehead products are available in Canada, the United States, England, and Australia. (Moosehead collection, PIRP #9094.)

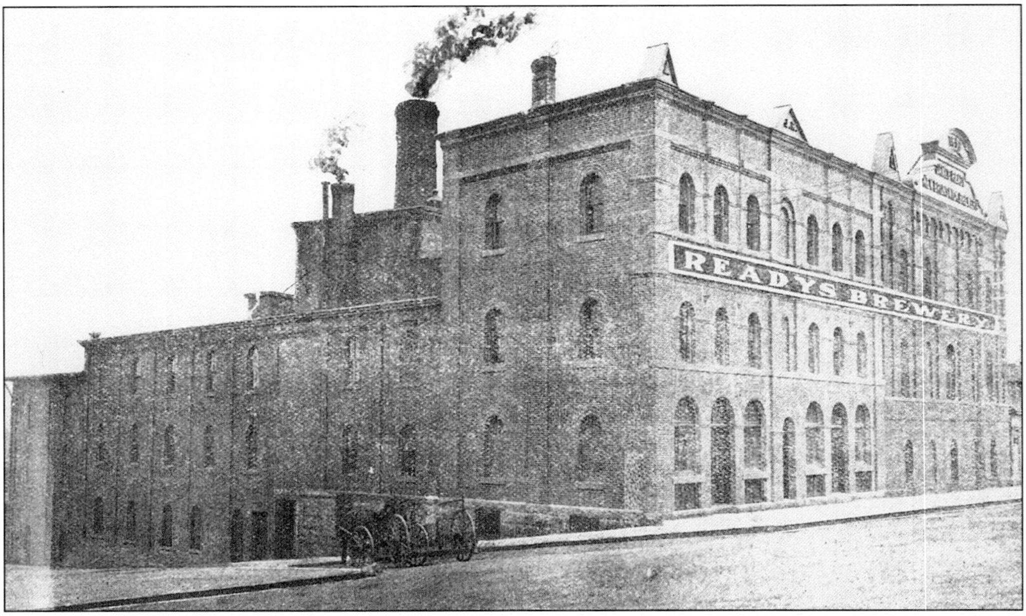

READY'S BREWERY, 1896. James Ready opened his Fairville brewery in 1867 and offered stiff competition to the Simeon Jones brewery on Carmarthen Street over town. By 1916, the brewery was owned by W.B. Tennant, an astute former Baptist minister. From 1916 until 1928, New Brunswick prohibition laws forced the company to make "near-beer" at 2 percent alcohol. In 1928, George B. Oland purchased Readys and renamed it New Brunswick Breweries Ltd. In 1947, the name was changed to Moosehead Breweries Ltd. (HSJ collection, PIRP #830.)

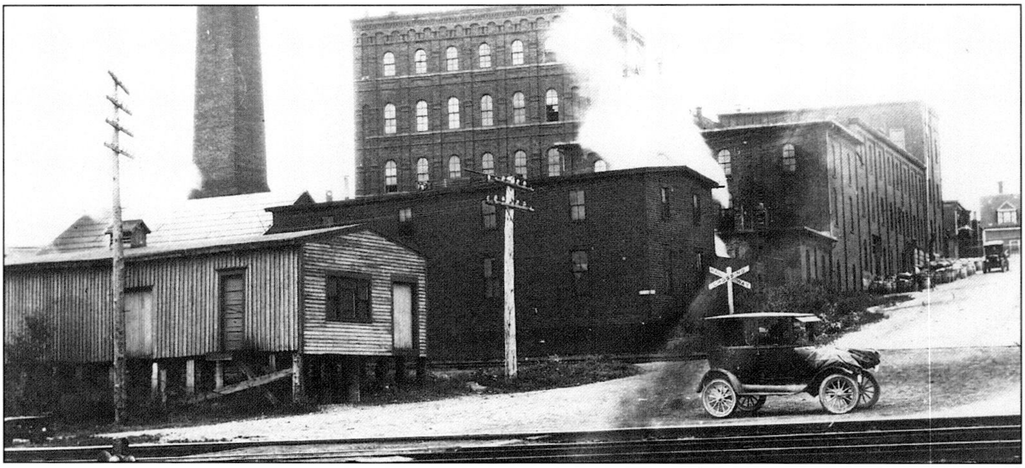

THE REAR OF THE BREWERY, c. 1919. For the brewery to survive, it depended on a range of transportation modes—from hand carts and wagons to delivery trucks and trains. Moosehead sold its product only in New Brunswick, but then expanded to the Maritimes, and now it is available across Canada and the United States. In 1931, Moosehead Pale Ale was added to the Ready's Ale line. George Oland was reminded of the "king of animals" and of the great New Brunswick outdoors with the Moosehead name. In 1934, he introduced Ten Penny Old Stock, named for the best of the old English ales. In 1937, he introduced the company's third famous brand, Alpine. While new products have been added over the years, these three beers have continued to serve the company well. Ten penny brand is no longer sold. (Byers collection, PIRP #4618.)

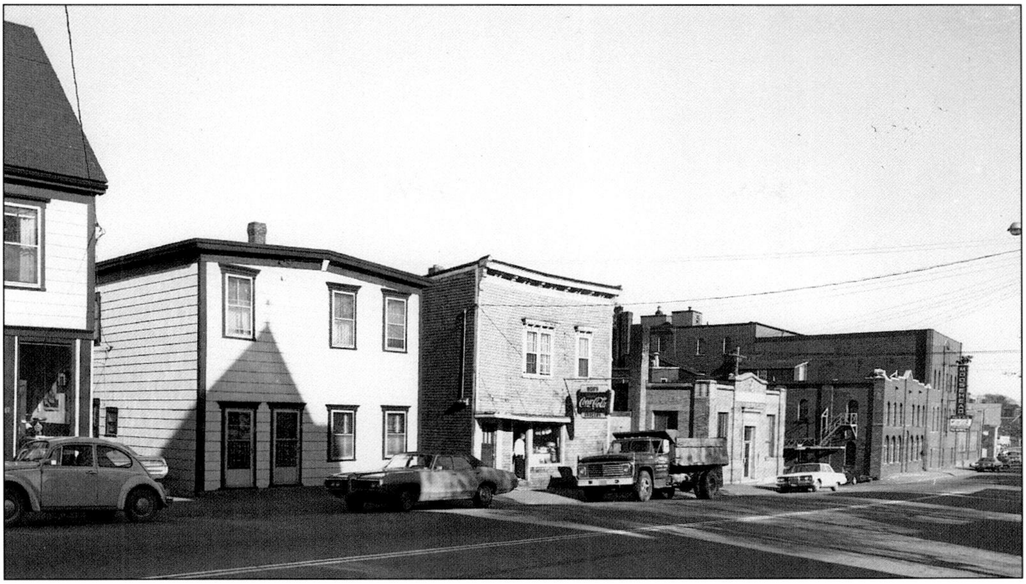

MAIN STREET, 1969. As opportunities arose, Moosehead expanded and eventually acquired all of the businesses shown here for plant expansion. At the left is the former Collin's meat store, Bob's Grocery, and the old Bank of Nova Scotia at the corner of North Street. In 1978, Moosehead entered the American market, quickly gaining prominence as the fourth largest selling import beer. In 1985, Moosehead began selling its product in England. (Moosehead collection, PIRP #9089.)

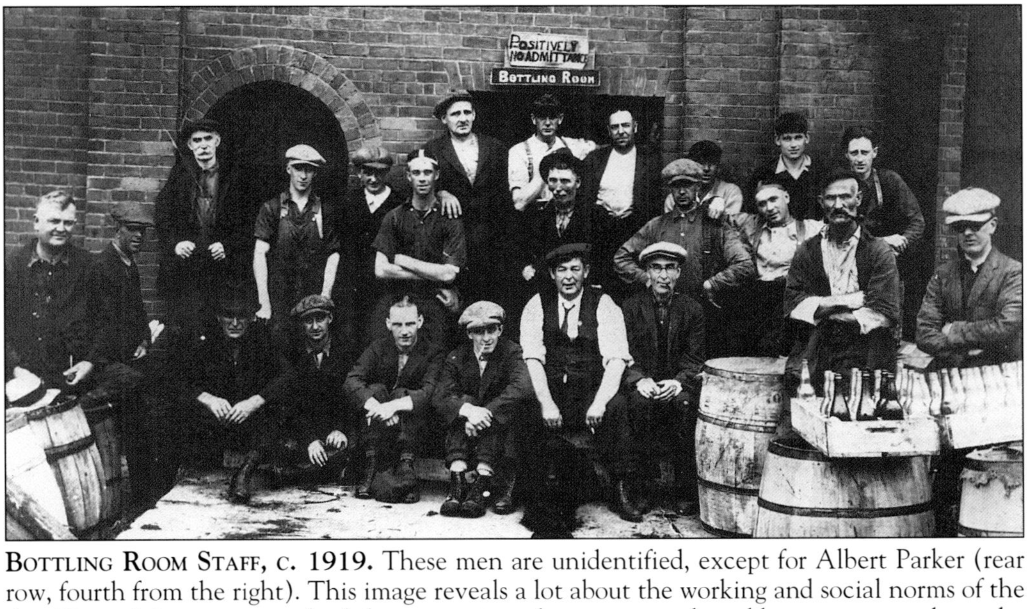

BOTTLING ROOM STAFF, C. 1919. These men are unidentified, except for Albert Parker (rear row, fourth from the right). This image reveals a lot about the working and social norms of the day. Two of the men near the left are wearing what appear to be rubber aprons—to keep the beer from staining their clothes. Most of the men wear hats, whereas today they would wear safety helmets. Six of the men are smoking, and three of them have pipes. Note the obvious range in ages. Many started working at the brewery as young men, and remained their entire working lives. While there were few, if any, social and retirement packages at the time, the company did have a reputation for taking care of its own. (Byers collection, PIRP #4619.)

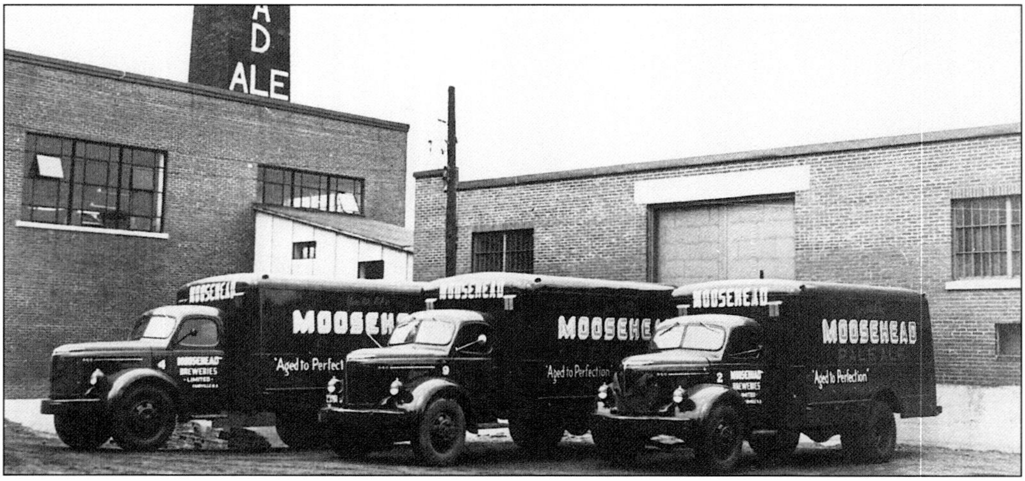

THE DELIVERY FLEET, C. 1948. Moosehead's fleet has expanded a multiple of times from these three trucks. Not only do transport trucks travel the North American highways delivering the product, but container ships take Moosehead to overseas markets. The local fleet of trucks can be seen throughout the day delivering draft kegs and cartons of Moosehead or Alpine to local clubs and pubs. (Moosehead collection, PIRP #9090.)

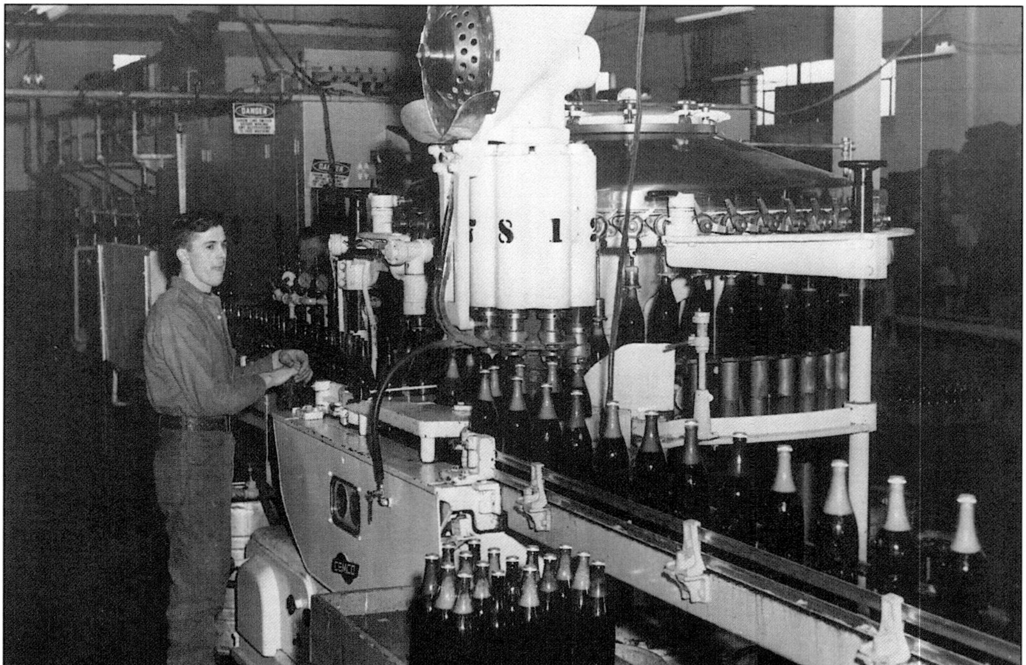

THE BOTTLING ROOM, 1947. After the malt solution is extracted from the barley malt and corn, it goes through a fermentation process, and is then aged before it is packaged into bottles, cans, or kegs. Jerry McGraw began working for Moosehead in 1946 and stayed there until his retirement in 1987. Being a family-owned business, Moosehead places great emphasis on family values. Jerry's father-in-law, Micky Logan, worked there for over 40 years, retiring as a foreman. His brother-in-law, Paul Logan, still works there driving a local delivery truck. Jerry's son Tony also works there, as did Jerry's two brothers Vanance and Alvida. (Moosehead collection, PIRP #9445.)

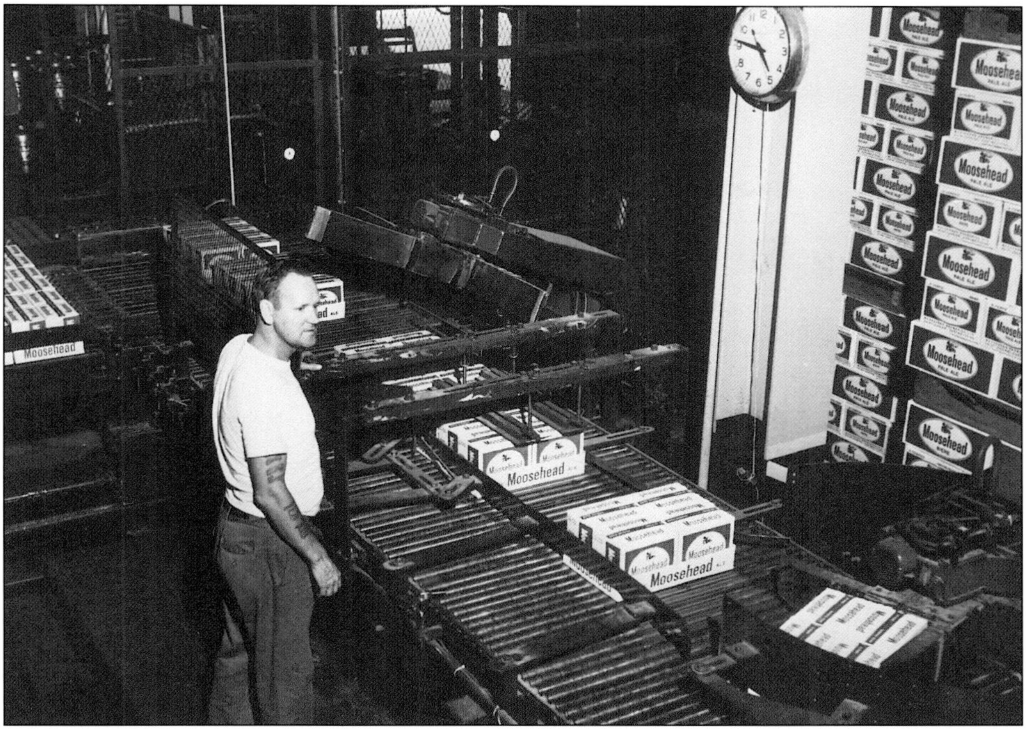

Packing Room, August 1971. Charles Perkins oversees boxes of Moosehead ale traveling along the conveyor heading to be palletized for shipping. (Moosehead collection, PIRP #9444.)

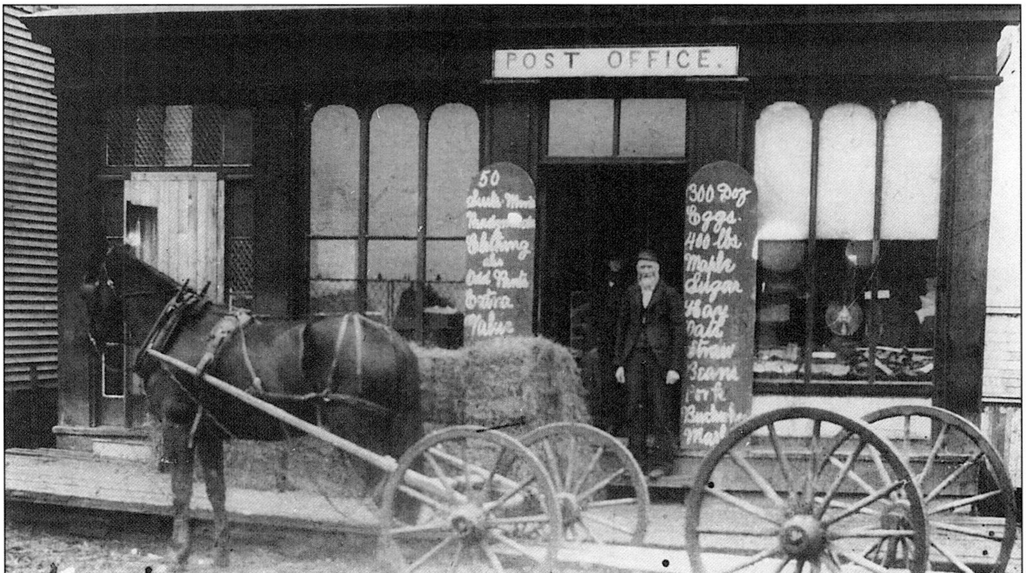

Fairville Post Office, c. 1890. This is Michael Collins. Johnny carried on with the butcher shop from the 1950s to the 1970s. Goods for sale included 300 dozen eggs, 400 pounds of maple sugar, hay, oats, straw, beans, pork, buckwheat, mash, clothing, and "odd pants". (HSJ collection, #4398.)

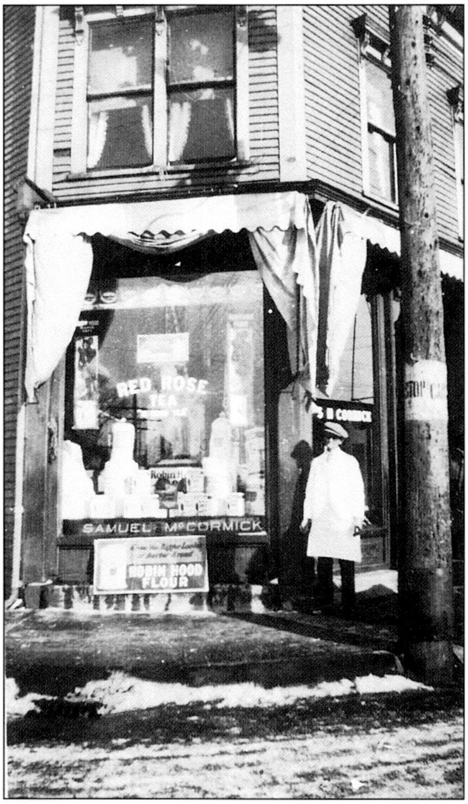

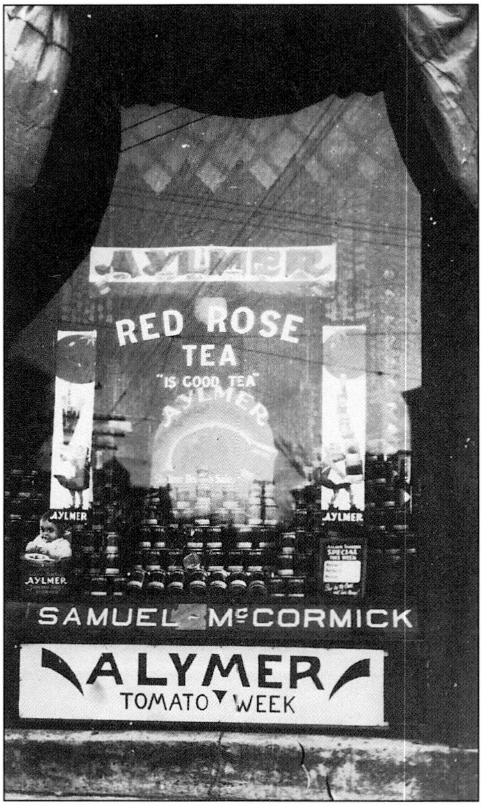

Corner Grocer, c. 1935. Samuel McCormick, in the doorway, became a clerk in James E. Bryant's corner store at 10 Main Street around 1904. Before working at the store, he was a postal clerk. He took over the business and ran it until 1944. In 1945, he became manager of Minchin Barker's grocery at 117 Main Street. He retired a few years later. In the left photo his window display is for Robin Hood flour, and right, it is for Alymer's Tomato Week. (E. Boyd.)

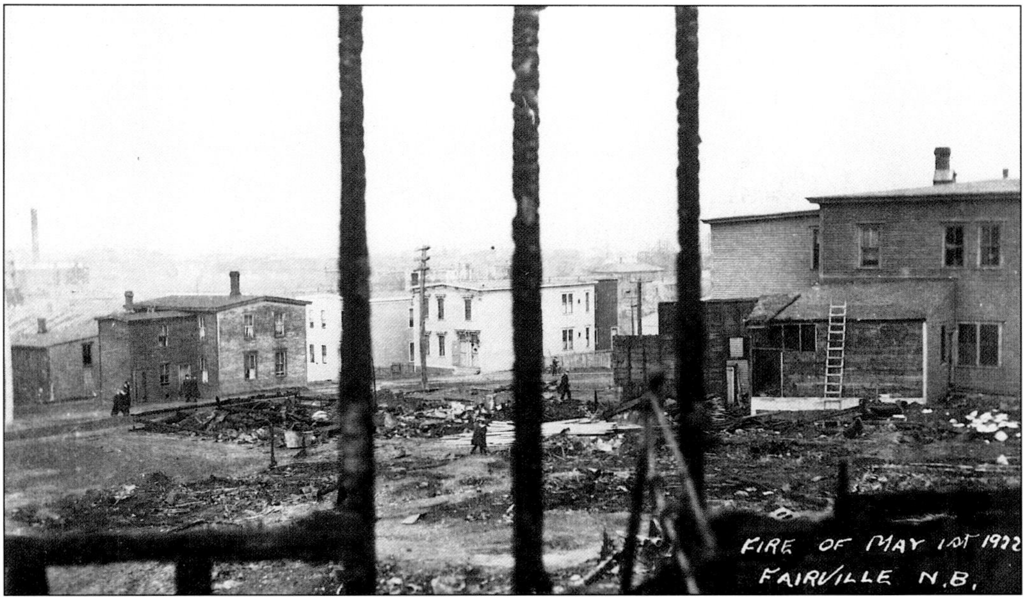

Main Street Fire, 1922. "The fire demon created terrific havoc in the heart of the Fairville business district yesterday . . . A little baby was rescued by its mother, Mrs. Perley Durdan, just in time to save its life the bed, in which it was lying at the time, was blazing freely". The fire started in the rear of the Durdan home and destroyed or damaged the Fairville Drug Store, Fred A. Chittick's Shoe Repair Shop, Jeremiah J. Hennessy's Dry Goods Store, Jeremiah Stout's House Furnishings Store, Wetmore's Cash and Carry Store, W. Gould's Billiard Parlor, the Windsor Confectionary Store, and Boyle Brother's Tinsmiths. "While J. Driscoll's general novelty store, on the opposite side of Main Street from the fire, had all its plate glass windows cracked by the flame. They fell out when some water came in contact with them". "A particular amusing site was witnessed when several freezers of ice cream were carried out of one of the burning shops. The kids made good use of their opportunity and grabbed the ice cream by the handful and crammed it into their mouths". (E. Boyd.)

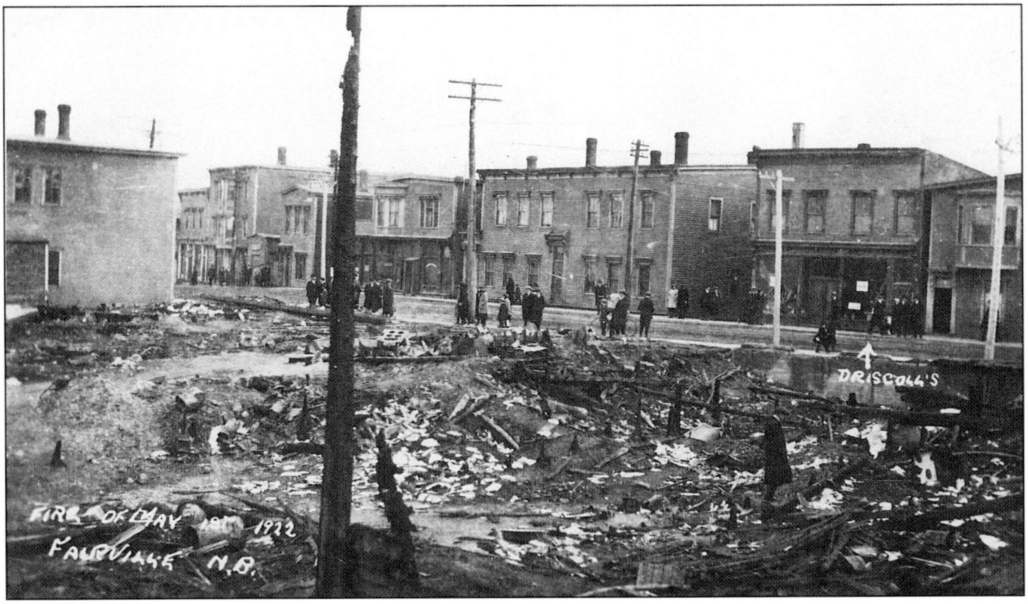

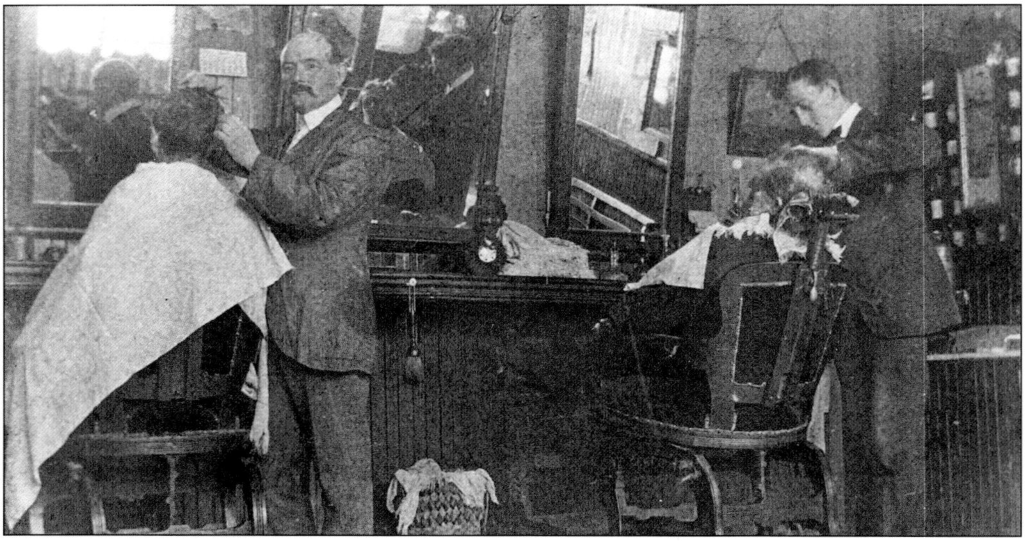

Best Tonsorial Artist in the (lower.) West. Jasper R. Cameron Sr. and his son Jasper (Jap) Jr. operated their barber shop for almost a century until it closed in 1979. "Just imagine the number of haircuts given over all those years . . . and all the yarns and stories swapped by the clientele . . . and all the friendships made, and all the goodwill shared, not to mention all the sticks of gum given out to little boys for their good behavior, while Mr. 'C' sheared their first baby curls". They began business at 9 Rodney Street (site of these photographs.), then moved to 121 Union Street, and eventually to 159 Market Place. Jasper Sr. is at the left in both photographs. One of the barber chairs in the top photo, c. 1900, still exists. Cameron's first hydraulic chairs were installed in 1903 as shown in the bottom photograph. The mirror and shelve unit in the 1903 photograph is now on exhibit in the New Brunswick Museum. (Cameron collection, PIRP #7925, #7657.)

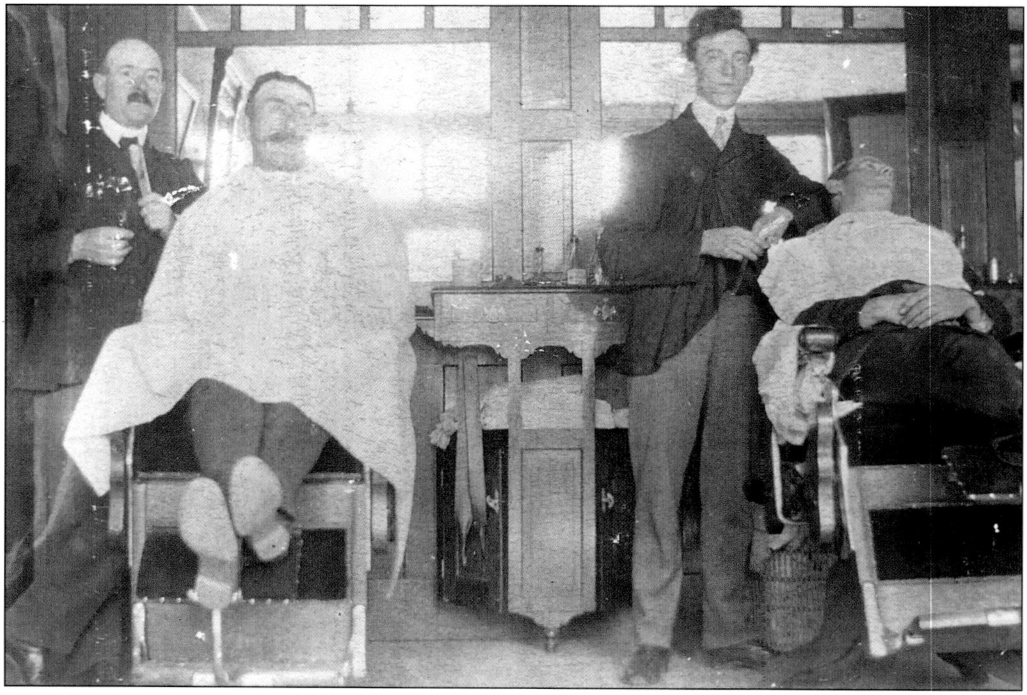

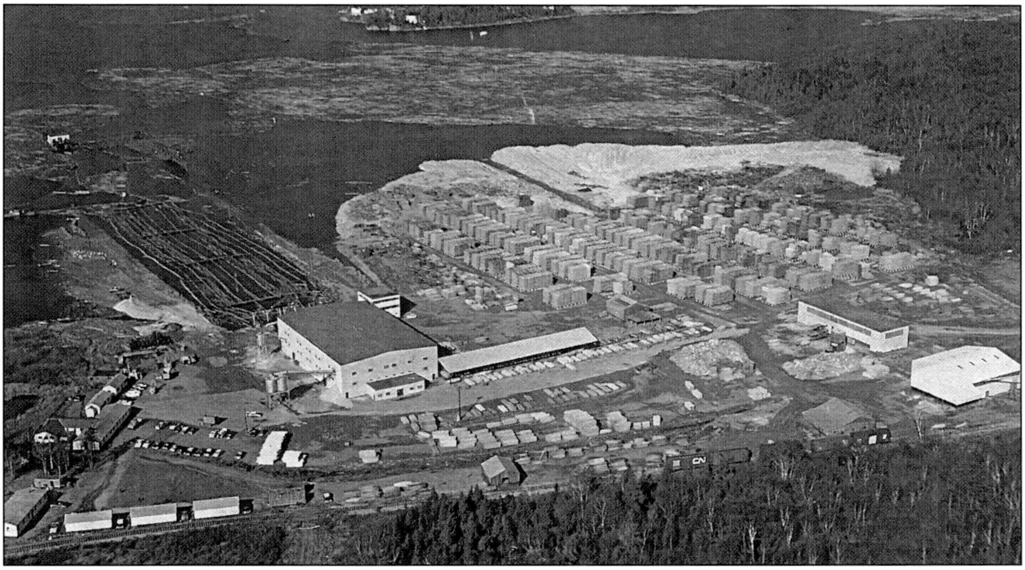

J.D. Irving Long Lumber Mill, South Bay, c. 1960. After K.C. Irving bought the pulp mill in 1946 he needed "a large new sawmill . . . capable of turning out 30 million board feet a year". The two-storey mill building opened in 1957. Three sets of Swedish gang saws were used. "Most of the logs for the sawmill came from the State of Maine". Andre Cushing, who built the sawmill at Union Point, probably set up shop in Saint John under a unique American law that allowed logs cut in Maine to be manufactured in Saint John and then shipped duty free back into the U.S. The mill had to be owned and operated by an American citizen. Cushing fit the bill! This law was repealed in 1911. In 1964, the Irving Sawmill employed about 475 men, excluding the river and boom crews. The last log drive down the St. John River finished with the construction of the Mactaquac dam in the late 1960s. This ended the life of the South Bay Mill. Custom Fabricators & Machinists now operate from the plant. In the background is Dominion Park and Greenhead. (H.E. Wright.)

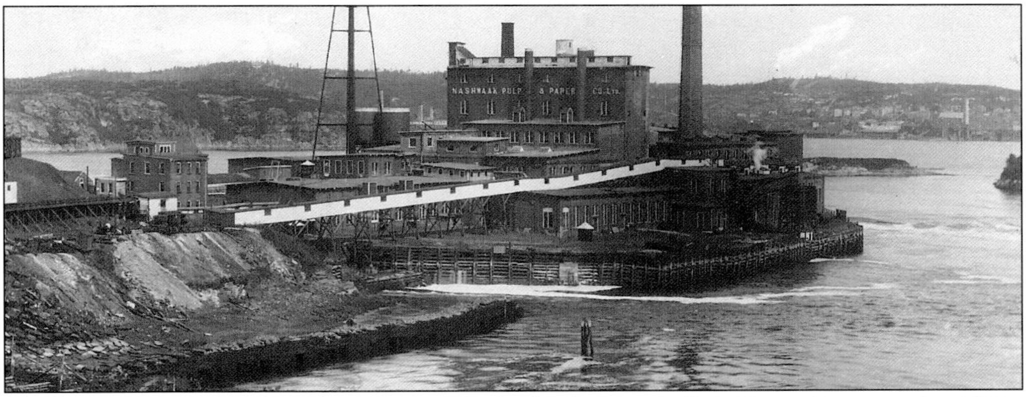

Pulp Mill. Andre Cushing, from Maine, built the first sawmill at Union Point in the 1850s. Next to his mill was the Goddard Sawmill. In the 1830s, a canal had been cut across the point to allow navigation around the rapids. The sawmill was replaced by a sulfite mill in 1899. It was known as the Nashwaawk Pulp & Paper Co. until 1932, when it was purchased and renamed the Port Royal Pulp & Paper Co. Irving bought the mill in 1946 and renamed it the Saint John Sulfite Ltd. In 1951 it was renamed the Irving Pulp & Paper Ltd. and underwent a $20 million expansion. Since Irving took over the mill, the employees have had steady employment. (M. Bernard.)

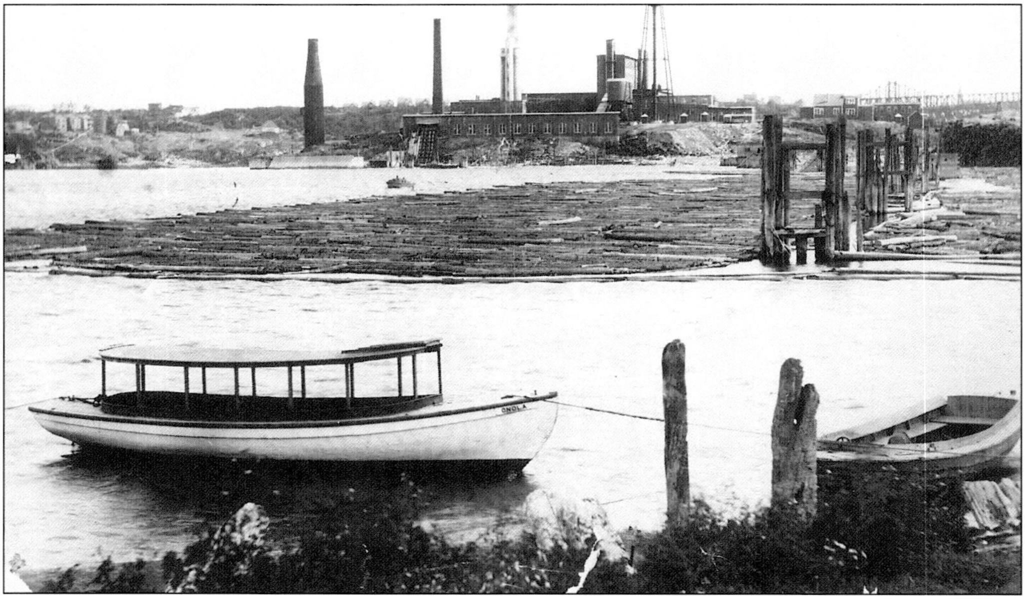

Pulp Mill Log Pond. The top photograph shows the log pond from Milford, and the bottom photograph looks to Milford. Along the Milford shoreline in the 1870s was James deWolf Spurr's NB Distillery and B. Hopkin's brick yard. Today a portion of the pond is filled with wood chips but the mill still uses it as a log pond. For almost a century, the mill poured contaminants into the air and the river, and the rotten egg smell was an on-going joke about living and breathing (choking!) in Saint John. Over the past several decades, Irving has spent hundreds of millions of dollars on expansions that sought to reduce or eliminate these pollutants. (M. Bernard.)

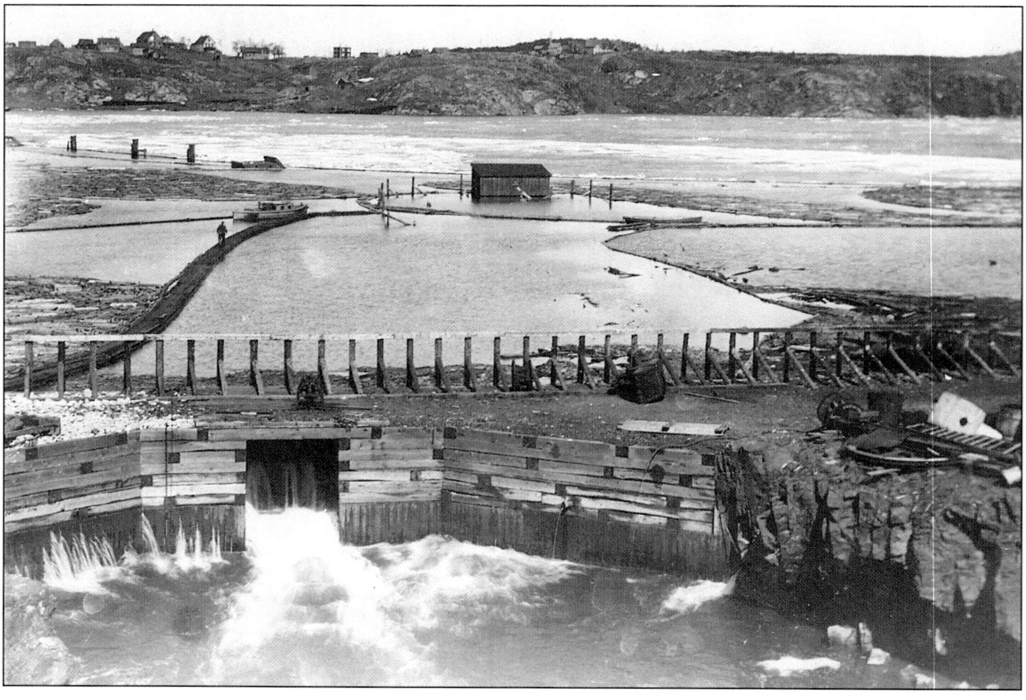

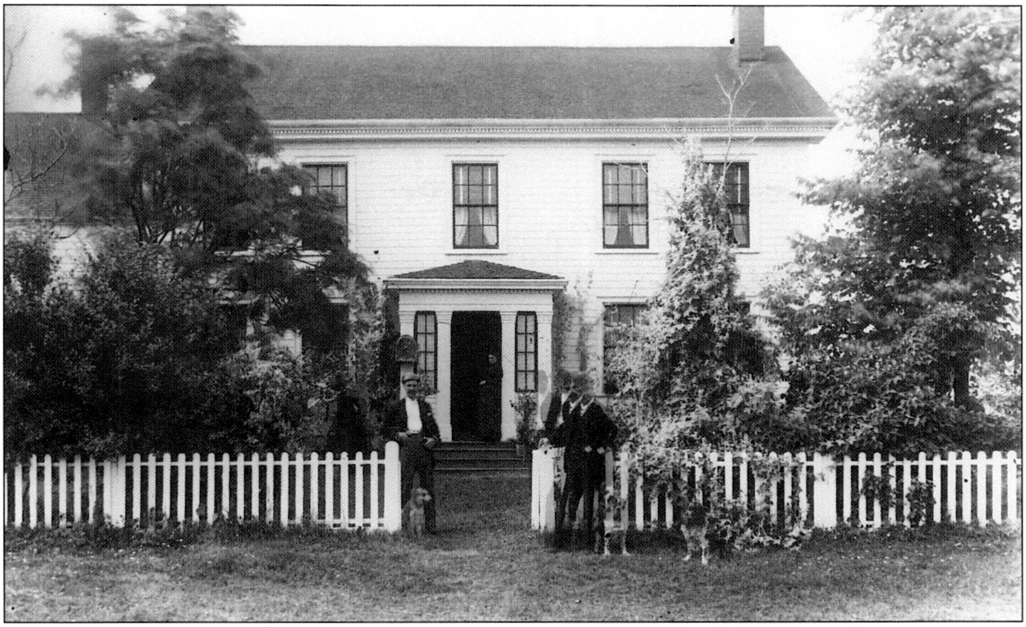

QUINTON FARM, C. 1870. Jesse Quinton, son of pre-loyalist settler Hugh Quinton of Conway (the original name for Lancaster), built this Georgian farmhouse between 1815 and 1830. The farm was subsequently owned by William A. Quinton, a member of the Common Council and the New Brunswick Legislature, and superintendent of the Provincial Lunatic Asylum. From Quinton, it went to grandnephew James Q. Hall, whose family kept the property until selling it in 1990. The house was saved from demolition with designation as a municipal heritage site in 1990. (Hall collection, PIRP #3267.)

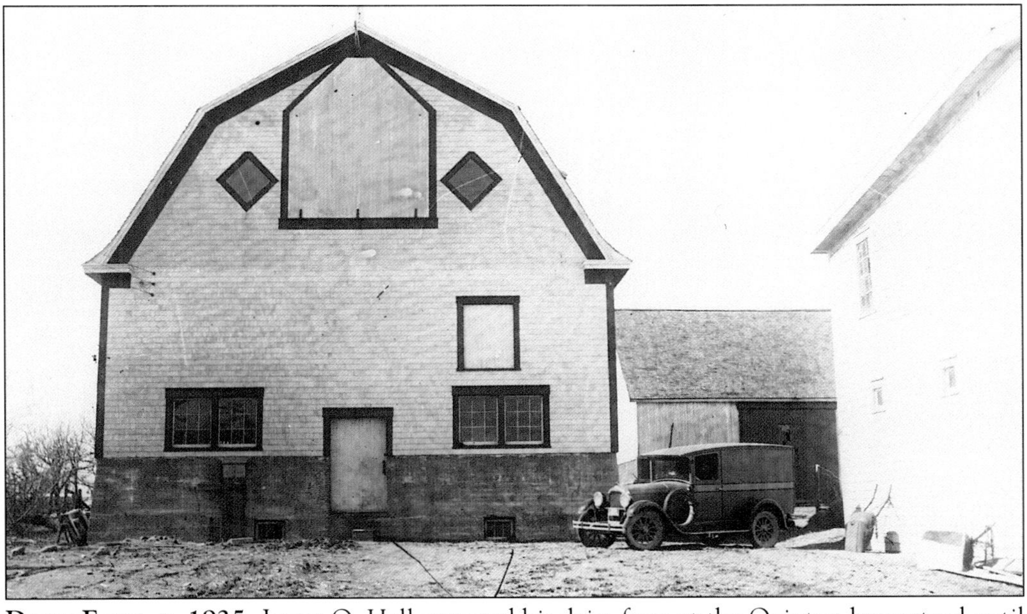

DAIRY FARM, C. 1935. James Q. Hall operated his dairy farm at the Quinton homestead until his death in 1959. The Hall dairy wagon took milk and cheese to merchants in Fairville. One farmhand, Charlie Chamberlain, later gained fame on Don Messer's Jubilee. The barn still stands, converted into an apartment building. (Hall collection, PIRP #2675.)

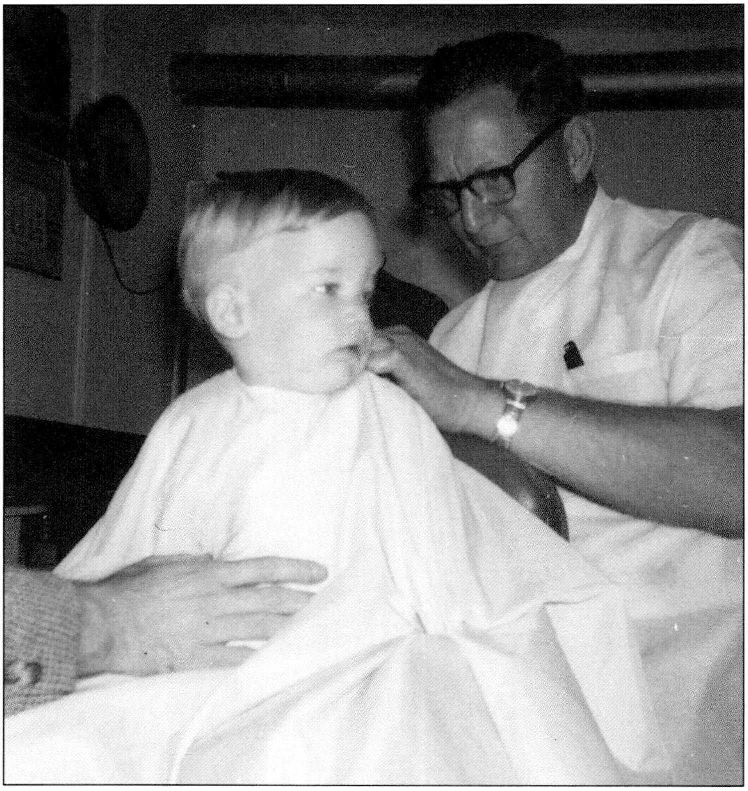

First Haircut. One-year-old David Rolston was taken to Frank Moore's shop at 44 Main Street in August 1964 to get his thick blond hair cut. David is now a marine biologist in Terrace, B.C. Lancaster has been home to numerous barbers on Main Street—Frank's, Louis Poirier's, Ken Steen's, Willard's, and the Lancaster Barber. There have also been numerous beauty salons in Lancaster, both on Main Street and in the Lancaster Mall. (L. Rolston.)

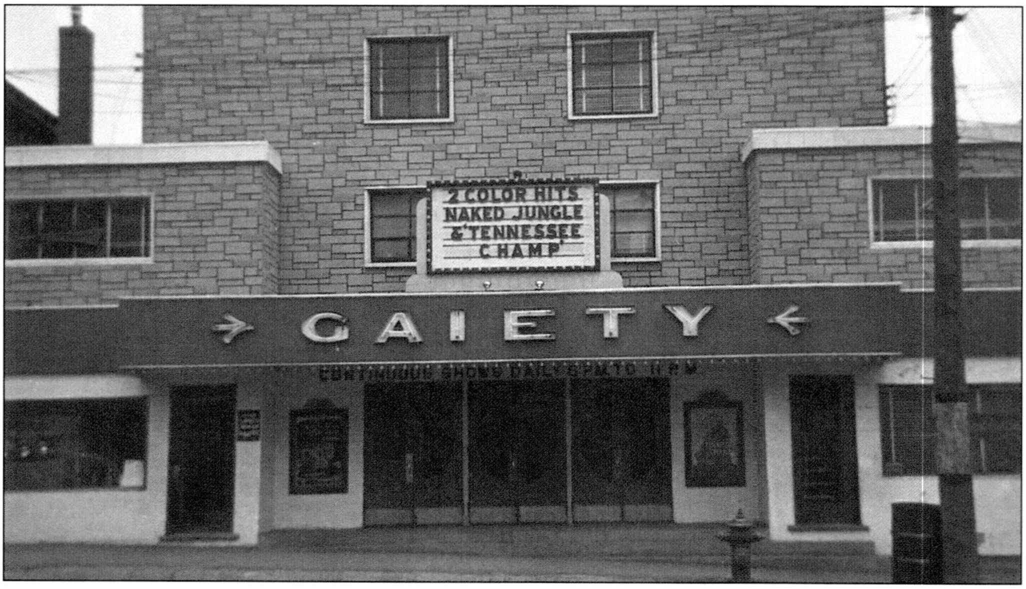

The Gaiety, c. 1957. Thomas J. O'Rourke opened the Gaiety's doors on Main Street in 1920. In 1936, Les Sprague became his partner. In 1947, they, with partner Gilmour Armstrong, formed a new company, Lancaster Theatres Ltd., and bought and modernized the Gaiety. Within the darkened auditorium Lancasterites watched shows such as Duffy's Tavern, The Naked Jungle, and its last show, The Bridge on the River Kwai. In October 1958, Tom Horsler bought the building and closed the cinema. (K. Steen.)

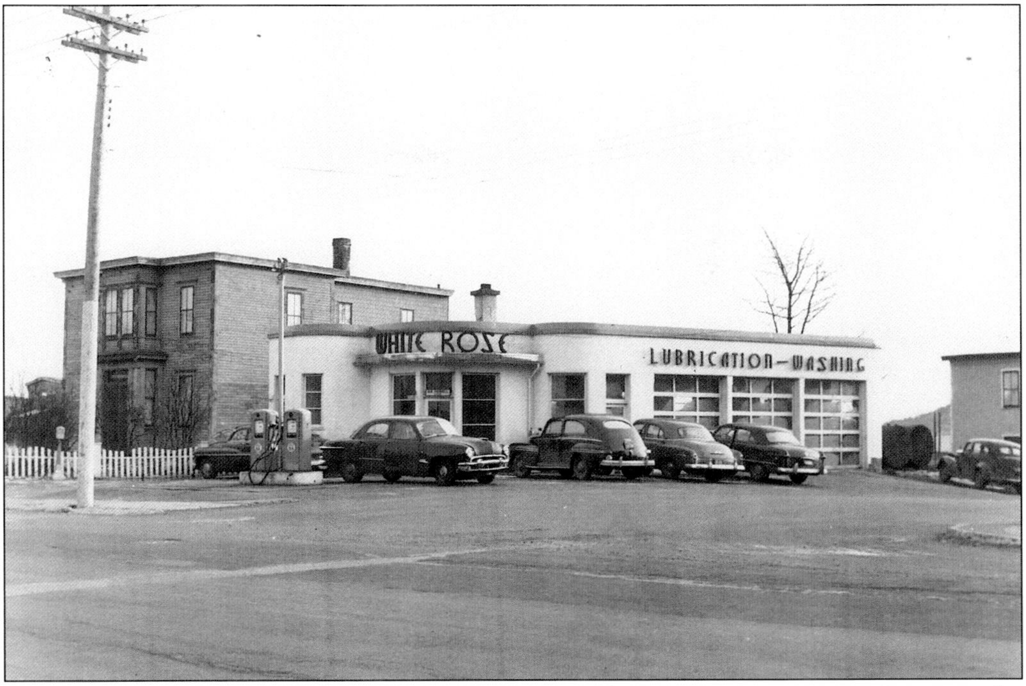

WHITE ROSE, C. 1958. Art Morrell was the lessee at this station at 112 Main Street, at the corner of Harding Street. The station is still at the corner, although it is now a Shell. Note the air pump to the left of the telephone pole. (HSJ collection, PIRP #9015.)

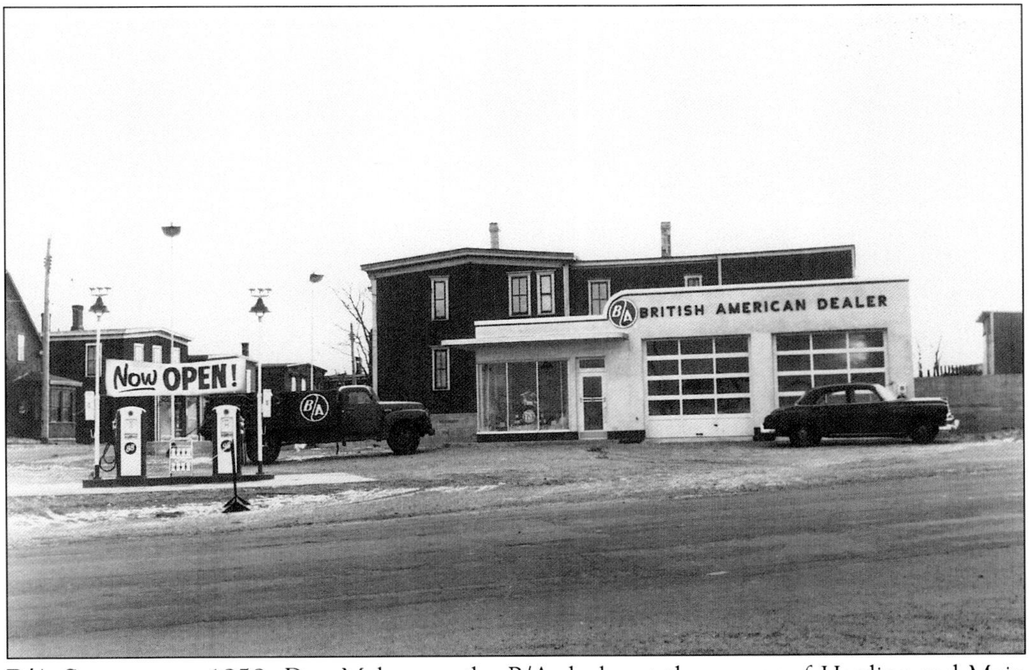

B/A STATION, C. 1958. Don Myles was the B/A dealer at the corner of Harding and Main Streets. By 1963, he was delivering oil for Irving Oil Ltd. The B/A Oil distributor was Bill Chahley on Lawrence Street. His motto was "Sunshine Comfort with our Dependable Service and Fuel Oil". The building was demolished in 1994. (HSJ collection, PIRP #9020.)

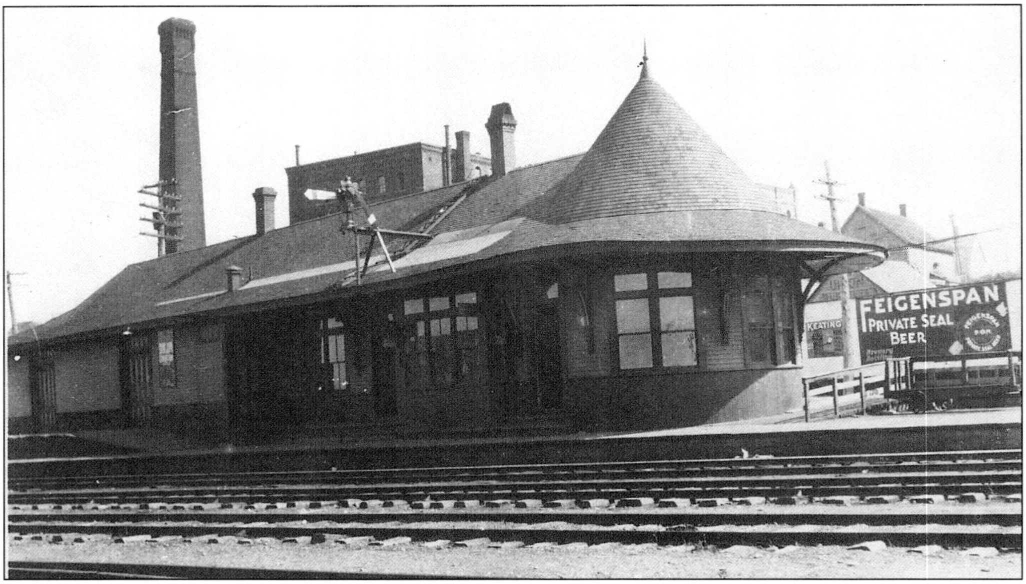

Fairville Station. The CPR built the station in 1893. Through the station, Lancaster merchants transported the fruits of their labour. Locals took the train into Saint John, or hopped aboard to go to summer camps in Belmont or Epworth Park. The "Loire Valley" tower and circular bay was added in 1910 for use as a ladies waiting room. The station was demolished in 1992. (McKinnon family.)

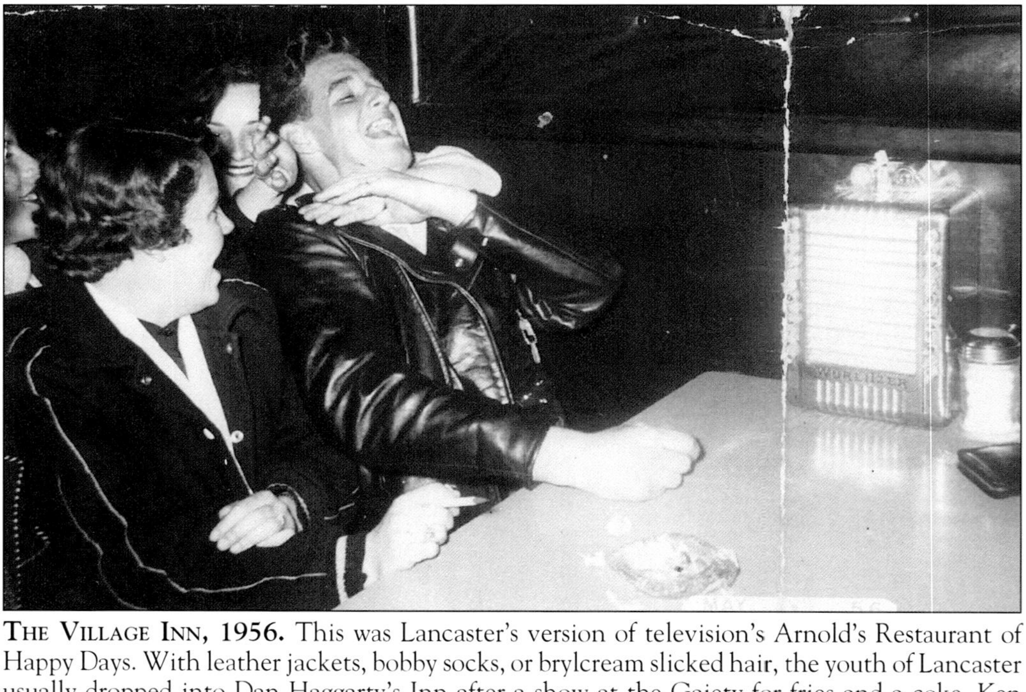

The Village Inn, 1956. This was Lancaster's version of television's Arnold's Restaurant of Happy Days. With leather jackets, bobby socks, or brylcream slicked hair, the youth of Lancaster usually dropped into Dan Haggarty's Inn after a show at the Gaiety for fries and a coke. Ken ? has probably dropped a dime into the table juke box to play Presley's latest hit for Beverly Williams, Joan Rumson, and the unidentified lady behind him. (L. Rolston.)

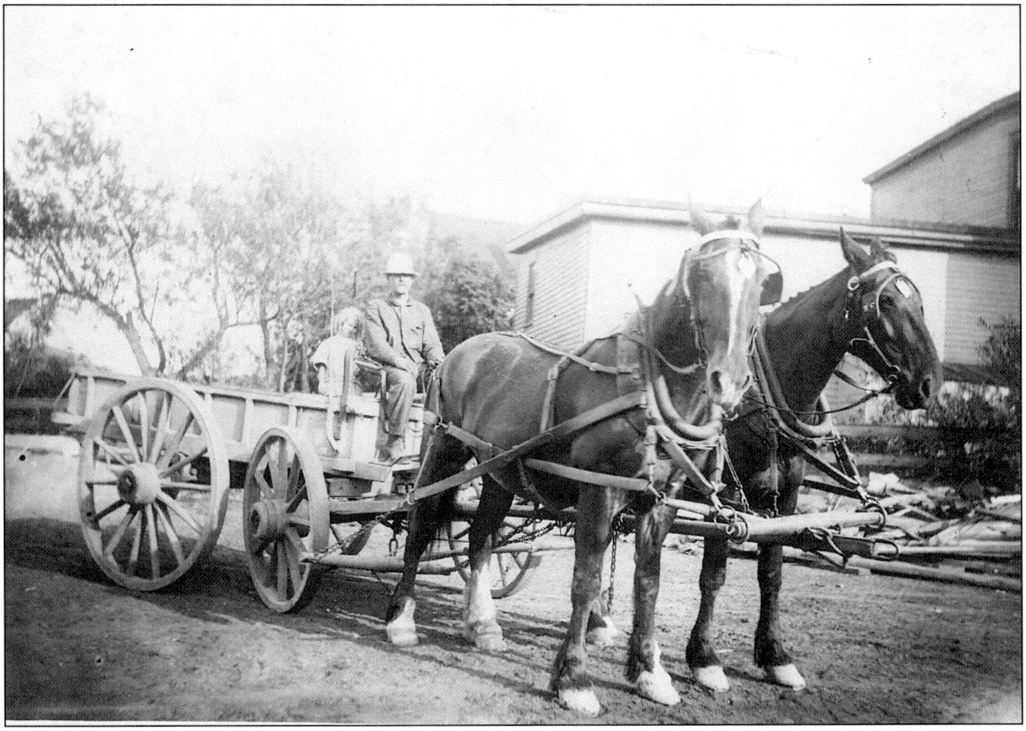

YANKEE McCORMICK. Fred was born in New Hampshire and thus his nickname. While his brother Sam operated a grocery store, Fred was a teamster (trucker.) all his life. His daughter Bessie, who later worked as a hairdresser in MRAs, is beside him near their home on Church Avenue. (E. Boyd.)

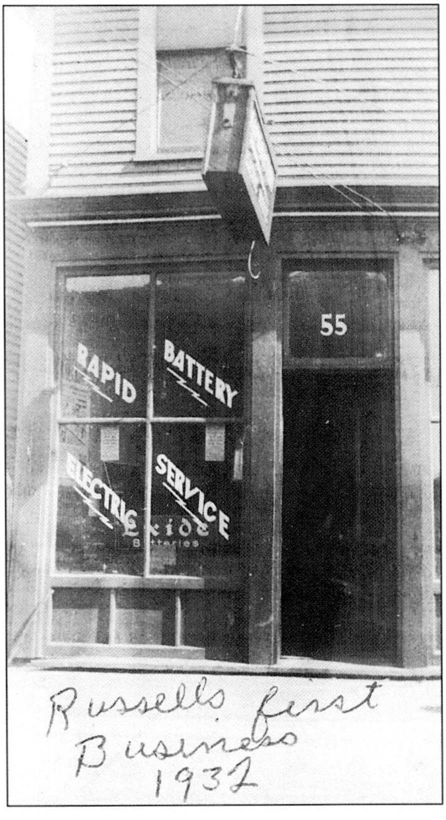

FIRST BUSINESS. In 1932, Russell Webb opened Rapid Battery Electric Service at 55 Main Street as part of Masson's garage. Two years later he borrowed $300 from his aunt and bought out Tibbitt's Esso lease at Barnhill corner. (Webb family.)

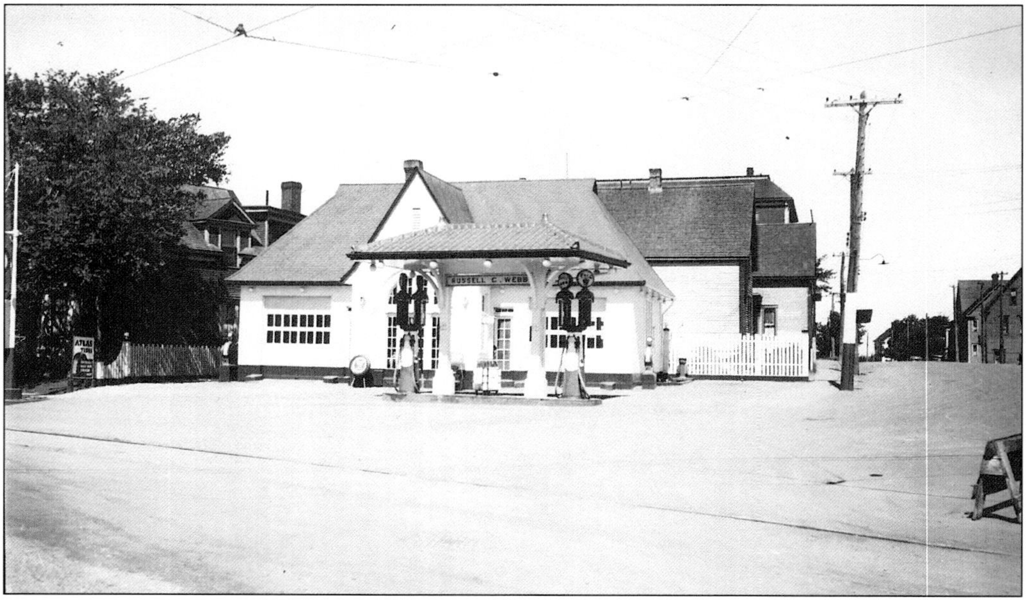

WEBB'S ESSO. In 1934, Russell bought this Esso franchise from George Tibbett. He stayed in business until 1969. Russell passed away in August 1969. Dr. Baxter's house is at the left of the station. The two buildings at the right were moved by Russell, and he built his first garage here in 1948. (Webb family.)

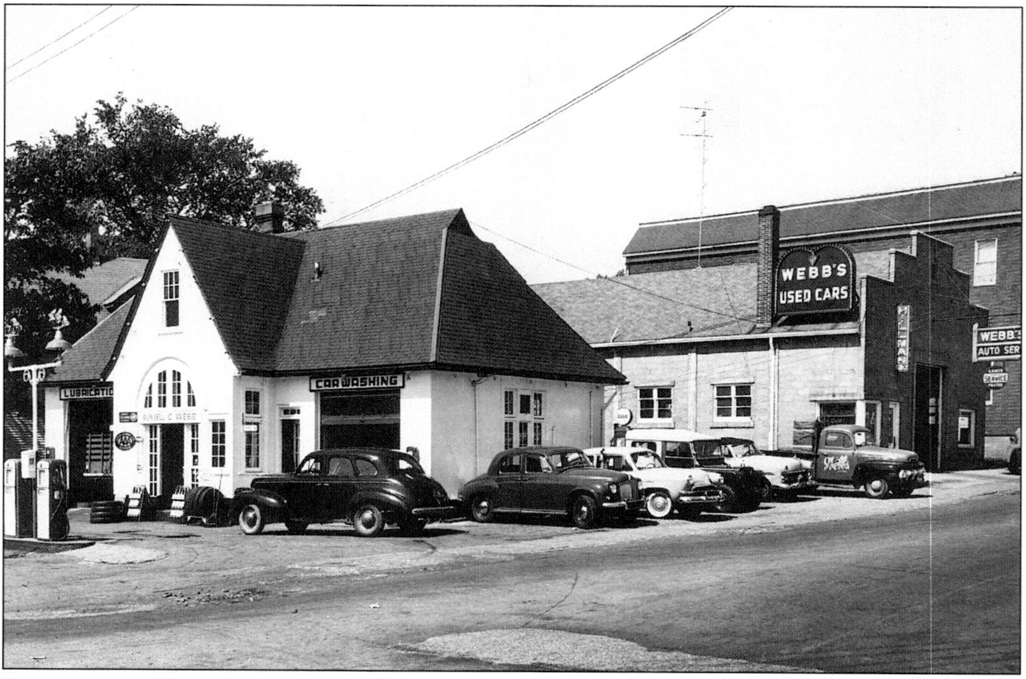

SERVICE AND CARS. In 1948, Russell built this garage behind his service station. In addition to being a Hillman dealer, in later years he also sold and serviced Volvos and Land Rovers. To the right of the garage is Willis #70 Orange Lodge. A new station and car wash are at this site today. (Webb family.)

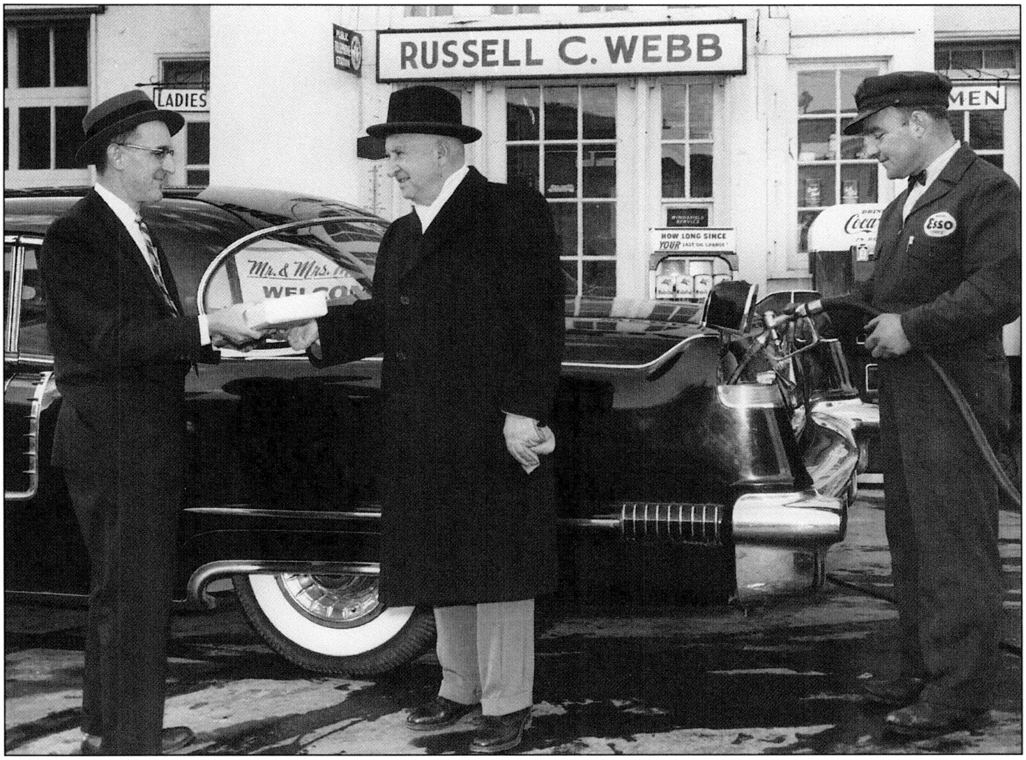

Twenty-fifth Anniversary. In 1959, Russell received a 25th-anniversary gift from Councillor Harry Tippett. A few years later Russell built a new car showroom on the Golden Mile, specializing in Sunbeam cars. (Webb family.)

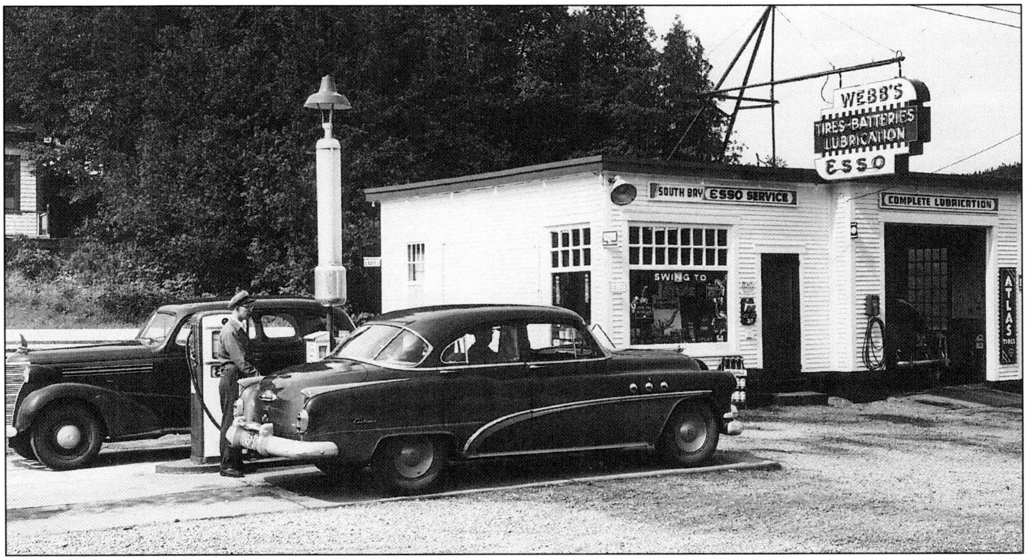

South Bay Service. Around 1950, Russell opened his second service station in South Bay. The station attendant is wearing a uniform—recalling a time when gas stations gave service—and looked the part. The station only lasted a few years. (Webb family.)

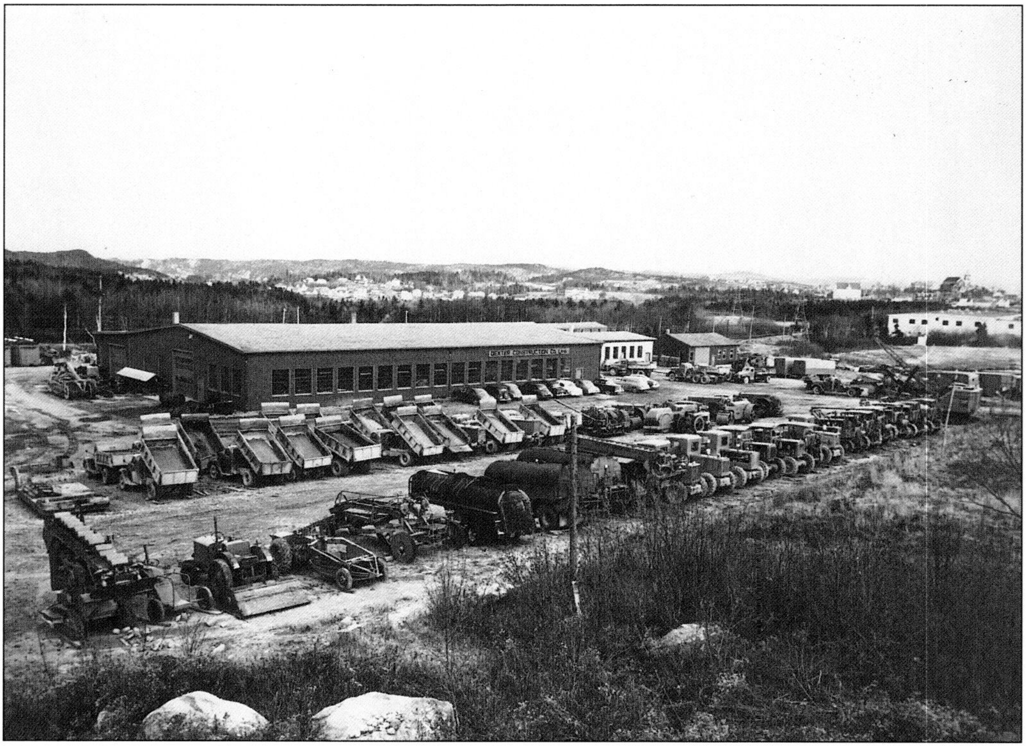

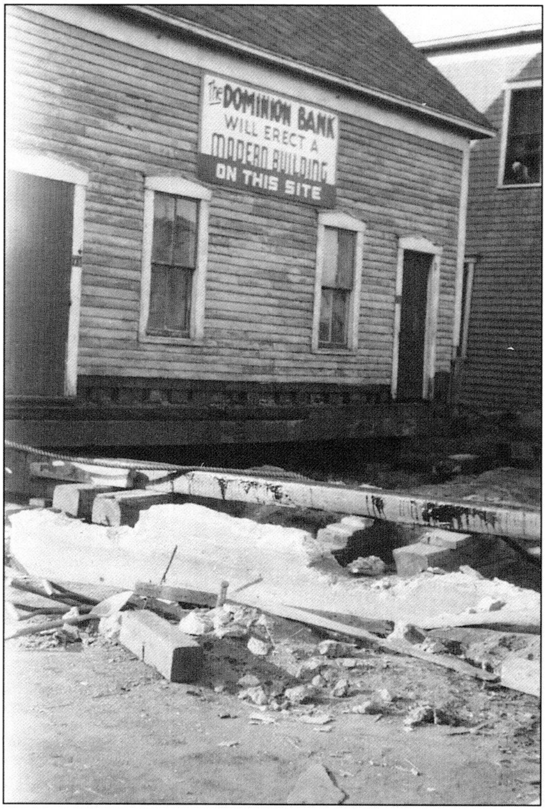

DEXTER CONSTRUCTION, C. 1946. Cecil Dexter started his construction company during World War I. The company specialized in road construction, with most of their work stemming from outside Saint John. His brother Russell joined the company in 1932, followed by Russell's son Val in 1947. Their office was at 800 Dever Road. The company was sold in 1975. (V. Dexter.)

DOMINION BANK, 1952. The "Dominion Bank has purchased a lot directly opposite the present Bank of Nova Scotia building on Main St. and . . . the building that now occupies the site will be removed . . . The establishment of this institution appears to be another mark of confidence in the future of Lancaster". George Chittick moved the building. (Chittick family.)

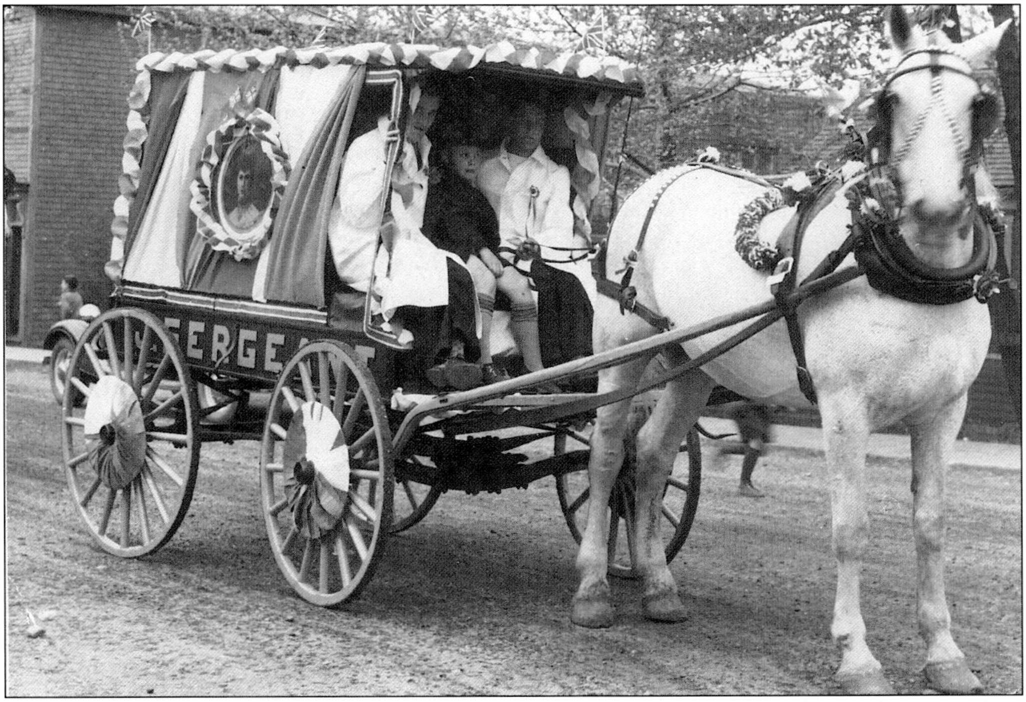

Home Delivery. John Sergeant's grocery at 43 Main Street did not always decorate their delivery wagon in this manner. This is believed to be the 1935 Jubilee Celebration of King Edward and Queen Mary. (E. Boyd.)

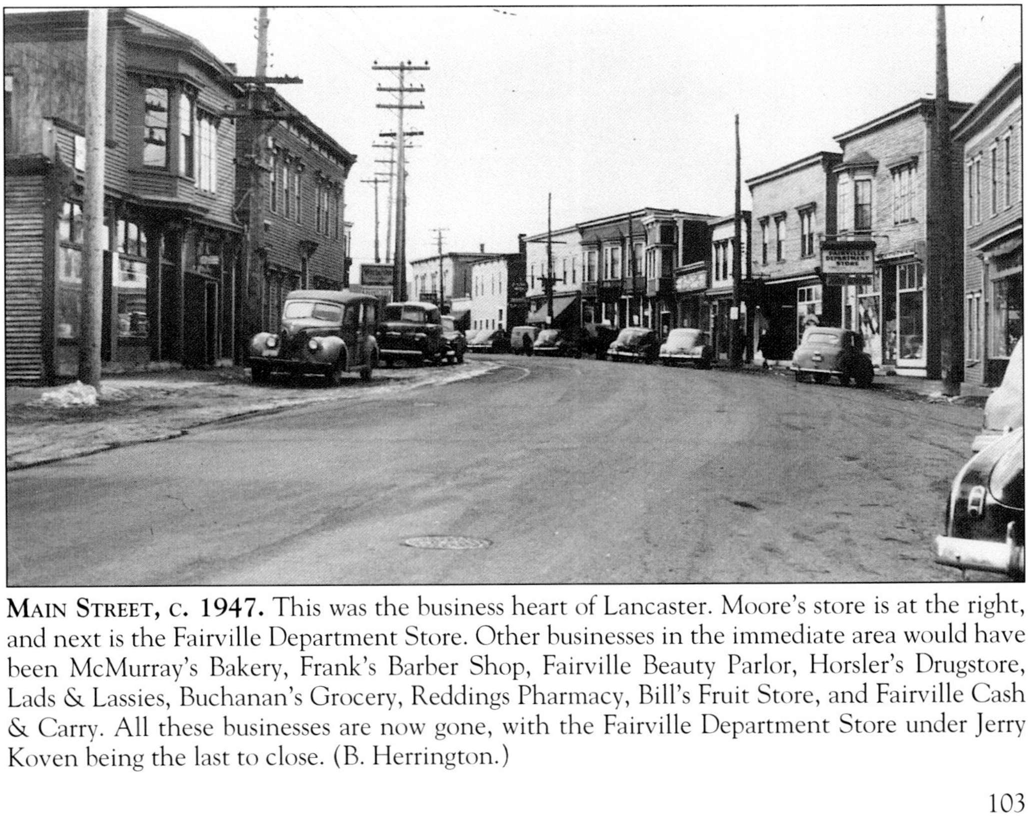

Main Street, c. 1947. This was the business heart of Lancaster. Moore's store is at the right, and next is the Fairville Department Store. Other businesses in the immediate area would have been McMurray's Bakery, Frank's Barber Shop, Fairville Beauty Parlor, Horsler's Drugstore, Lads & Lassies, Buchanan's Grocery, Reddings Pharmacy, Bill's Fruit Store, and Fairville Cash & Carry. All these businesses are now gone, with the Fairville Department Store under Jerry Koven being the last to close. (B. Herrington.)

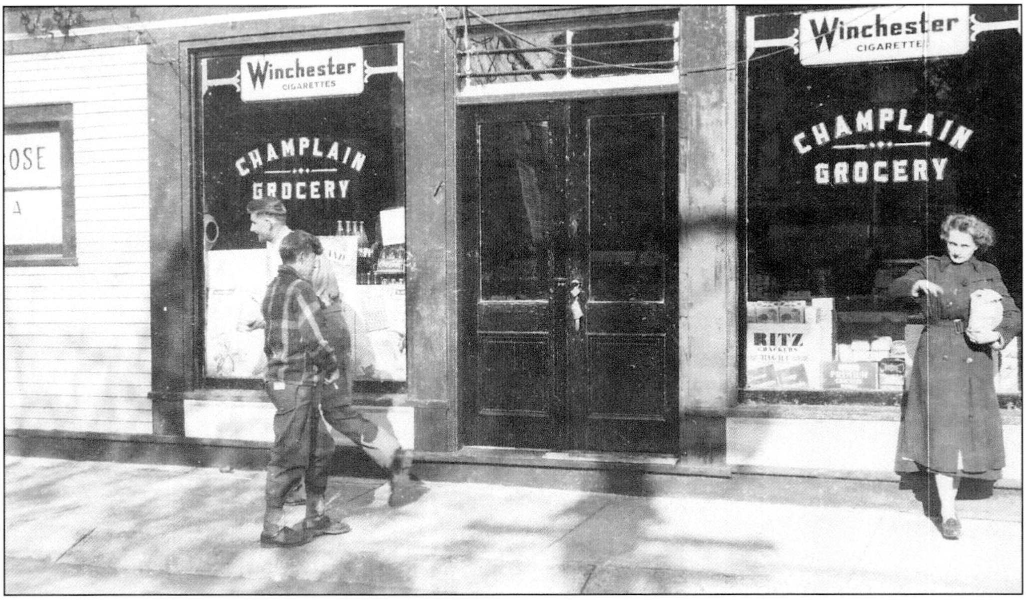

Champlain Grocery, 1958. Buzz Devenne and his wife, Alma, operated this store on Champlain Street for over a decade. Alma's family had also owned a grocery store on Waterloo Street in the 1930s and '40s. After Buzz's wartime service in Saint John, this was a logical option for them. Buzz is standing next to his Tea for Canada Week (April 14–19.) display of Red Rose, King Cole, Lipton, and Salada teas. (Devenne family.)

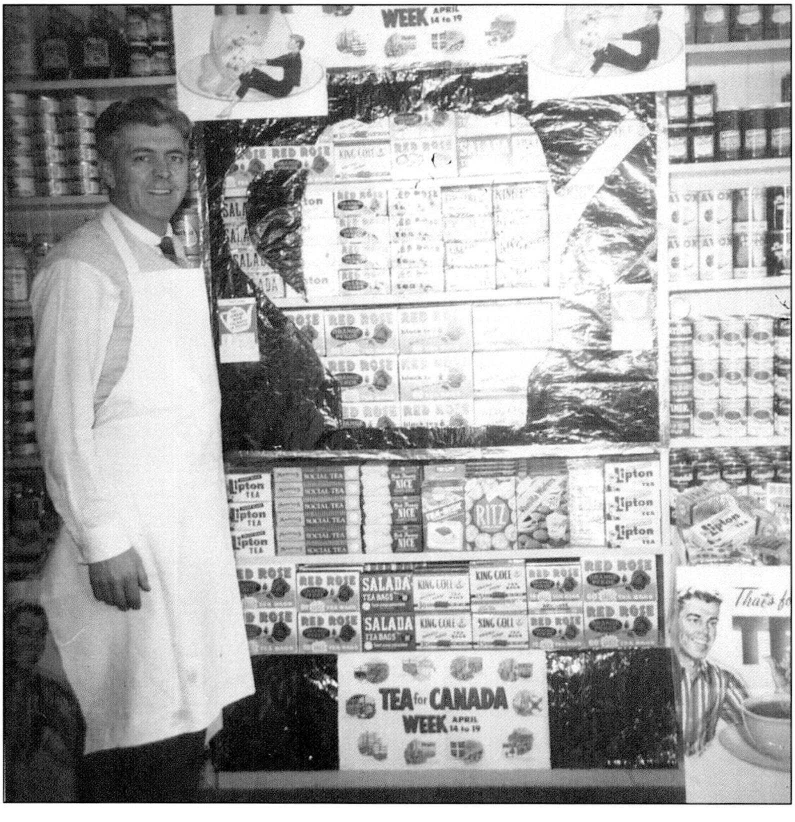

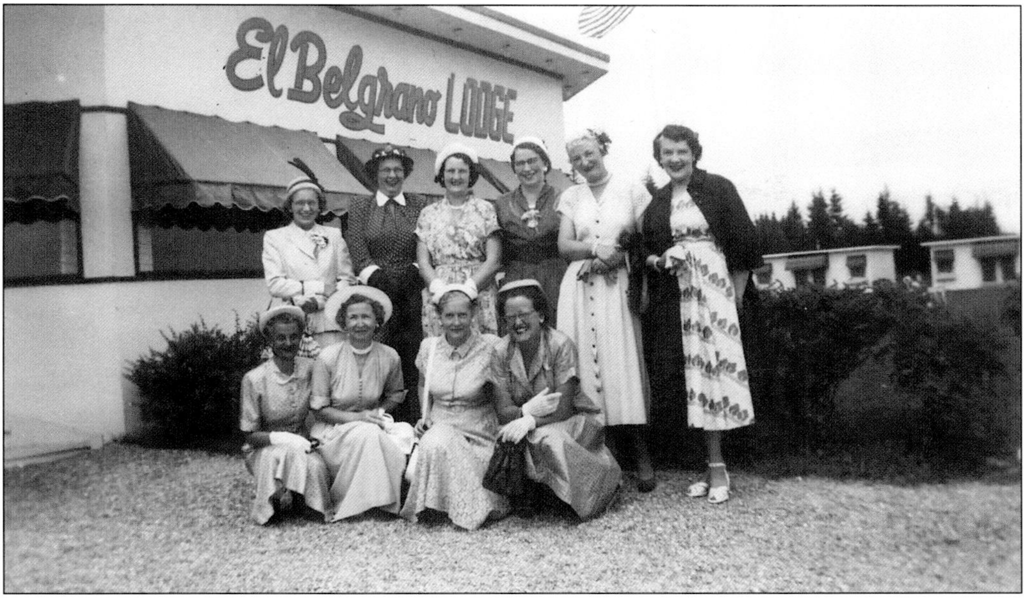

Fine Dining. The El Belgrano opened in 1946 as the "modern dine and dance place" in Lancaster. The owners were J.J. Joyce and his wife, Marjorie. It closed in 1980 after his death. Its most recent use was a location for the movie *Children of a Lesser God*. This was a neighbour's tea party about 1950. The guests, from left to right, are (front row.) Marjorie Brown, Mildred Black?, Bessie Cushing, and Marge Haley; (back row.) Barb Tippett, Nan Scott, Rhona Carter, Fern Lawson, Trixie Plourde, and Ella Horsler. (Marlene Ross.)

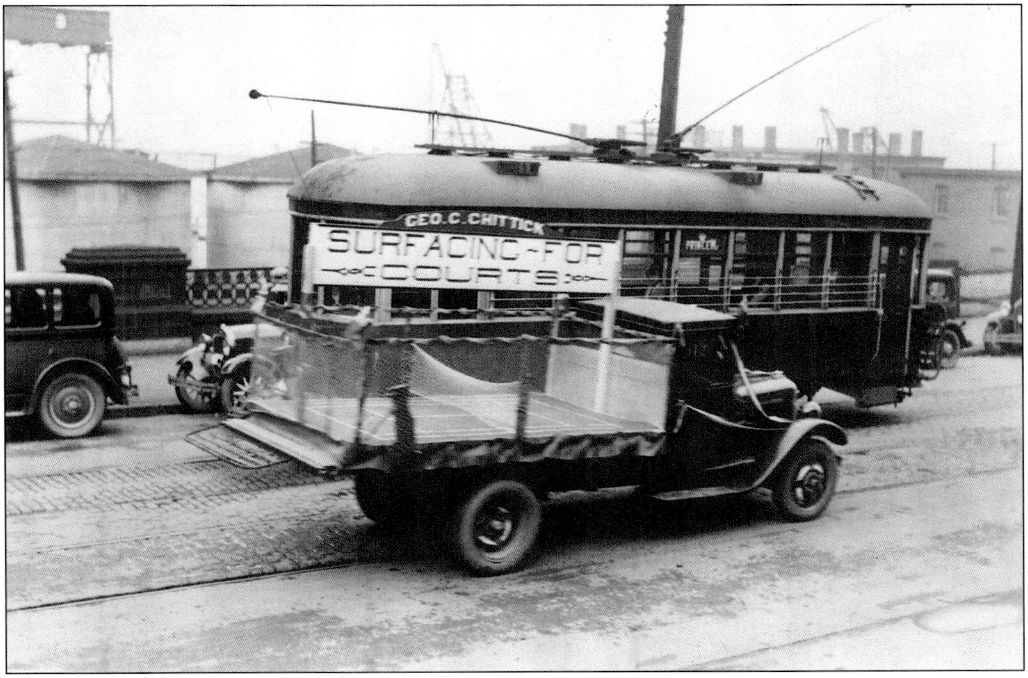

Parade Float, 1935. For the jubilee Transportation Day parade, the Chitticks entered this tennis court float. The streetcar is the Prince Street west car. (Chittick collection, PIRP #9240.)

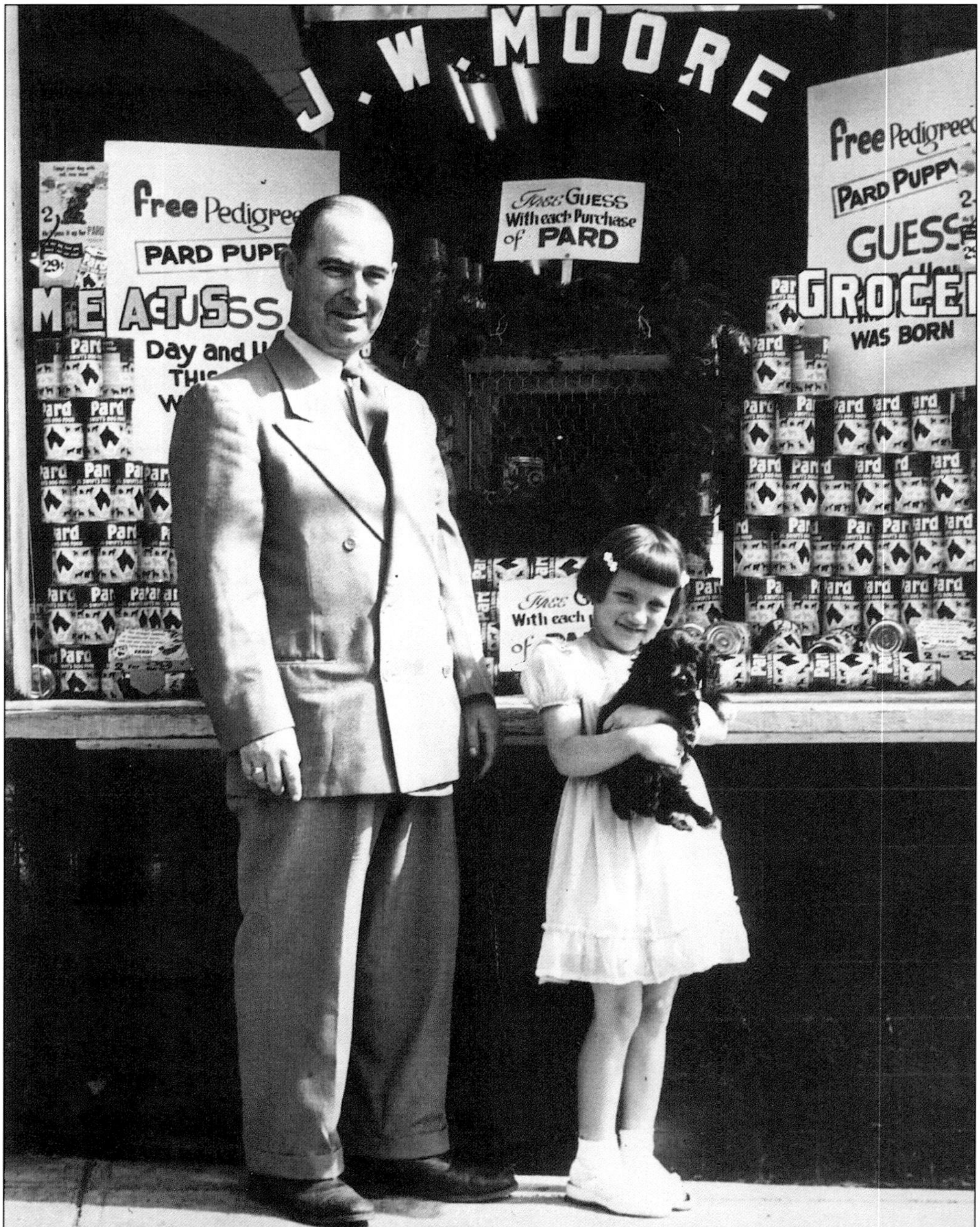

Puppy Love. In the 1950s, Swift's held a contest to guess when this puppy was born. Every time you bought their Pard dog food you received one free vote. Willard Moore, whose motto was "No cheap service, just service cheap", presented his puppy to this young girl. Willard remained at this Main Street location at the corner of Walnut Street until 1965, when he sold his property to the Bank of Nova Scotia, which now stands on the site. (Willard Moore.)

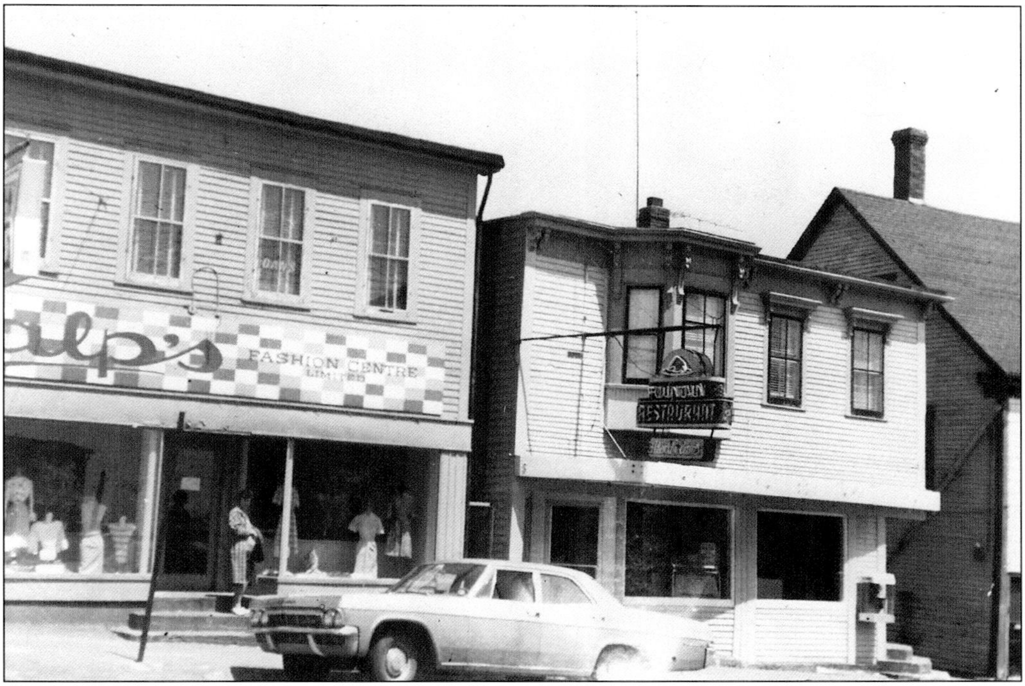

CALP'S AND FOUNTAIN. While Calp's was a landmark on Charlotte Street uptown, its stay at 57 Main Street was rather short-lived—about 1964 to 1966. Next door was the Fountain, operated by Al Olsen for many years. Long-gone businesses include The Palms Restaurant run by the McManus brothers, John Hooley's Poolroom, Joe Boyle's Hardware, Chittick's Shoe Repair, Koven's Fairville Department Store, Reid's Diner, and Eddie Snodgrass's Ice Cream Parlour. (Olsen collection, PIRP #7923.)

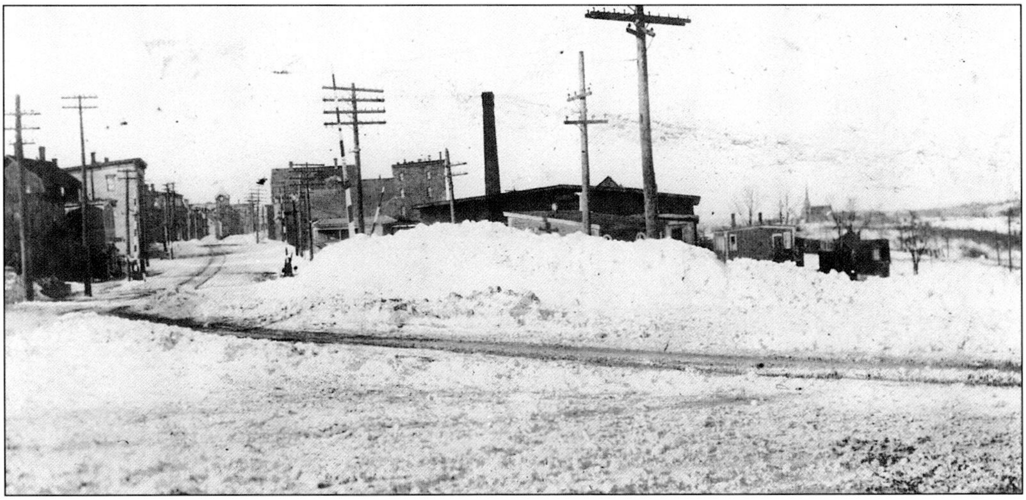

SIMMS CORNER. Willard Moore remembers: "It was the streetcars. There was no snow removal then, and whenever it snowed they'd put them out with those big revolving brushes on the front. They cleared the tracks and threw the snow away up over the doors of buildings. I remember we wanted the parish councillors to clear our entrances for deliveries, but they said if they did that on Main Street, the people on Manawagonish Road would want it too." (Jones collection, PIRP #5911.)

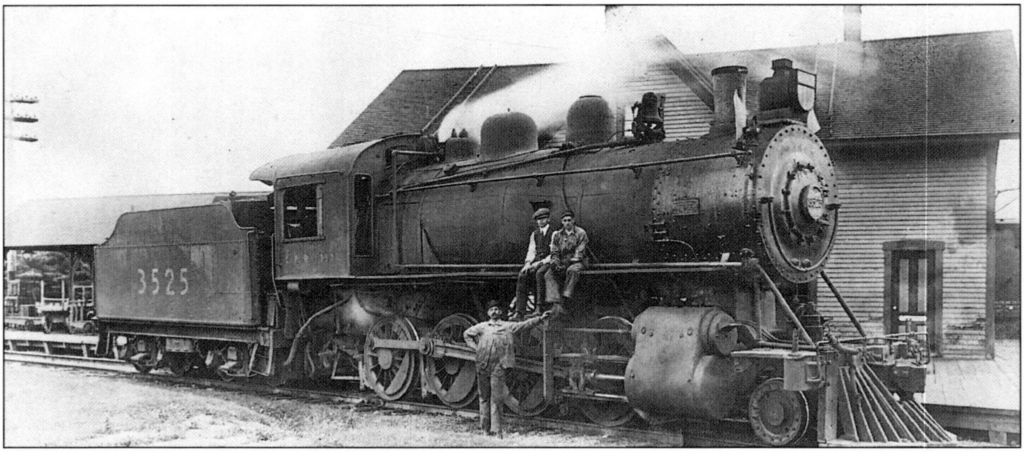

THE RAILWAY. In 1889 the Canadian Pacific Railway came to Saint John and headquartered on the west side. While it primarily served the port, the train was the lifeblood for many Lancaster businesses. The second Fairville station was located behind Moosehead Breweries. Engineer George Cheeseman is standing in front of locomotive 3525. (Campbell collection, PIRP #7881.)

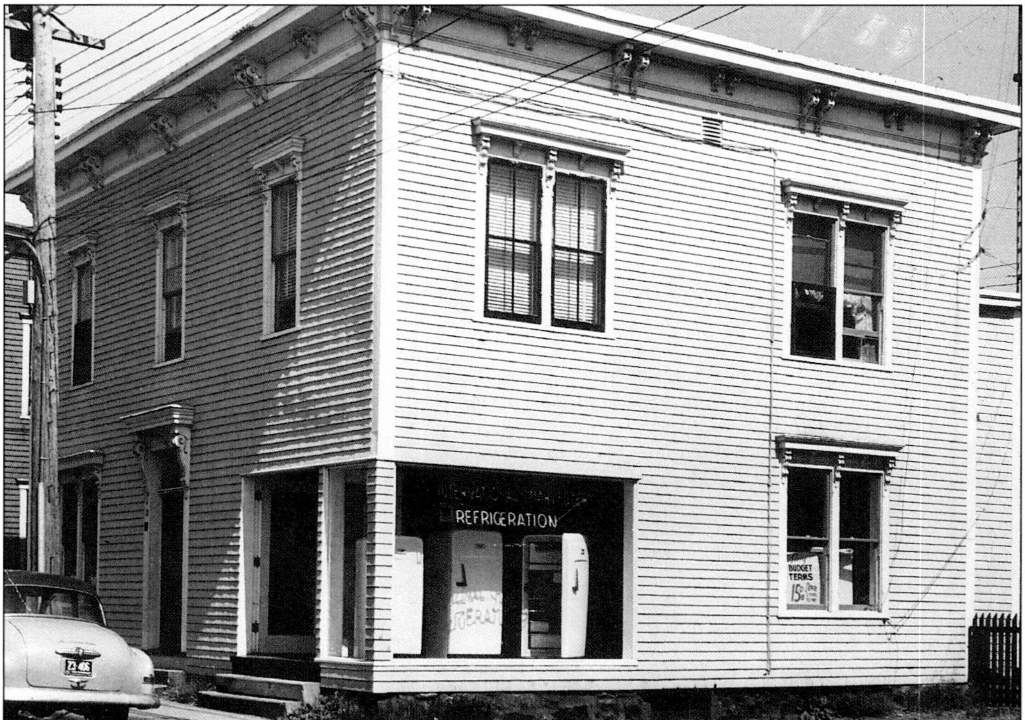

WEBB'S TELEVISION & REFRIGERATION, 1952. "The 102 foot tower (behind the building.) erected . . . is attracting the attention of many of Lancaster's residents . . . Webb expects to puck [*sic*] up occasional television broadcasts from the United States, and more successfully it is hoped, when a television station has been established at Bangor, Maine . . . If successful, we predict that Mr. Webb's store featuring electrical appliances will become a popular spot". Saint John's first television station, CHSJ, did not go on the air until 1954. On May 25, 1953, this television tower toppled during a storm. (Webb family.)

WELL-KNOWN MEAT CUTTER, c. 1950. Tommy Butler was both well known and respected in Lancaster. He worked at Johnny Collin's Meat Store (related by marriage.) and was a member of the Lancaster Fire Department. (G. Butler.)

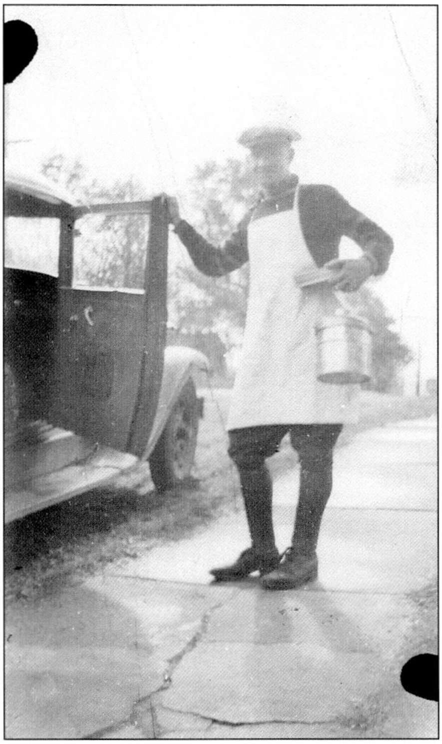

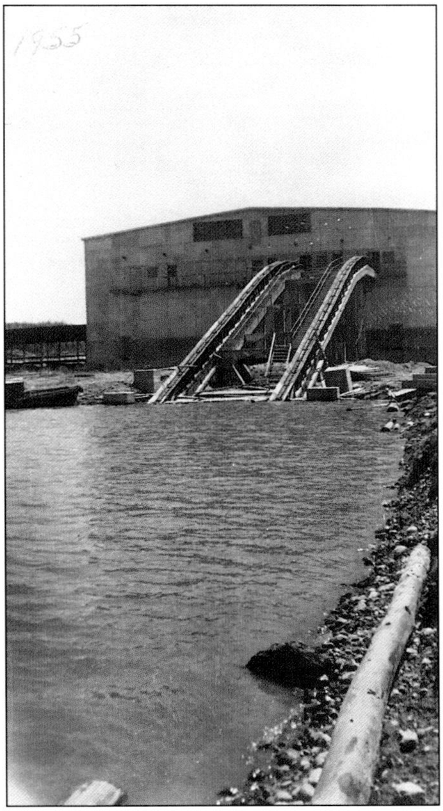

SOUTH BAY MILL, 1955. The logs were carried up the conveyor into the mill. Today the bottom of South Bay is littered with hundreds of sunken logs from various mills previously located in the bay. (B. Herrington collection, PIRP #9105.)

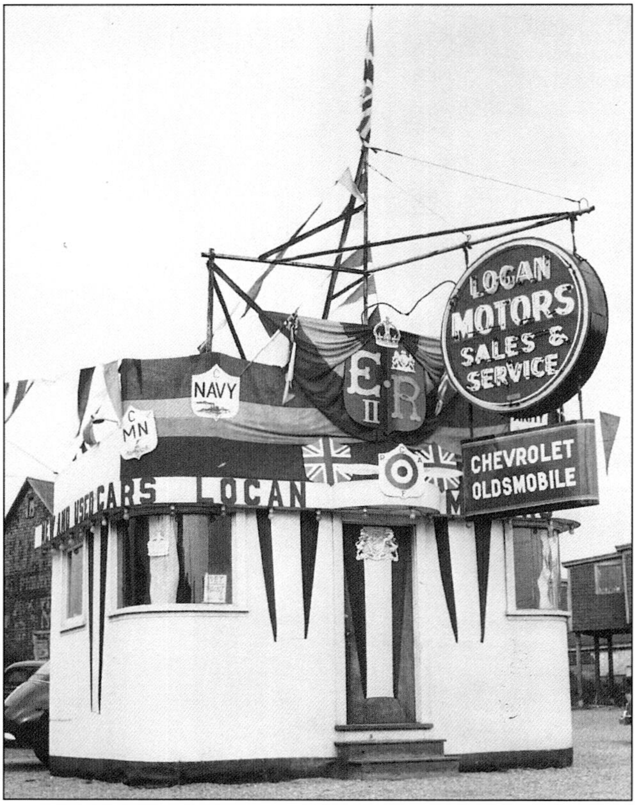

LOGAN MOTORS, 1953. Located at Simms Corner, where Wendy's restaurant is now, Logan's sold both new and used cars. Eventually they expanded into a marine division and relocated to South Bay. The decorations are for the Queen's coronation celebration. (Perry collection, PIRP #9467.)

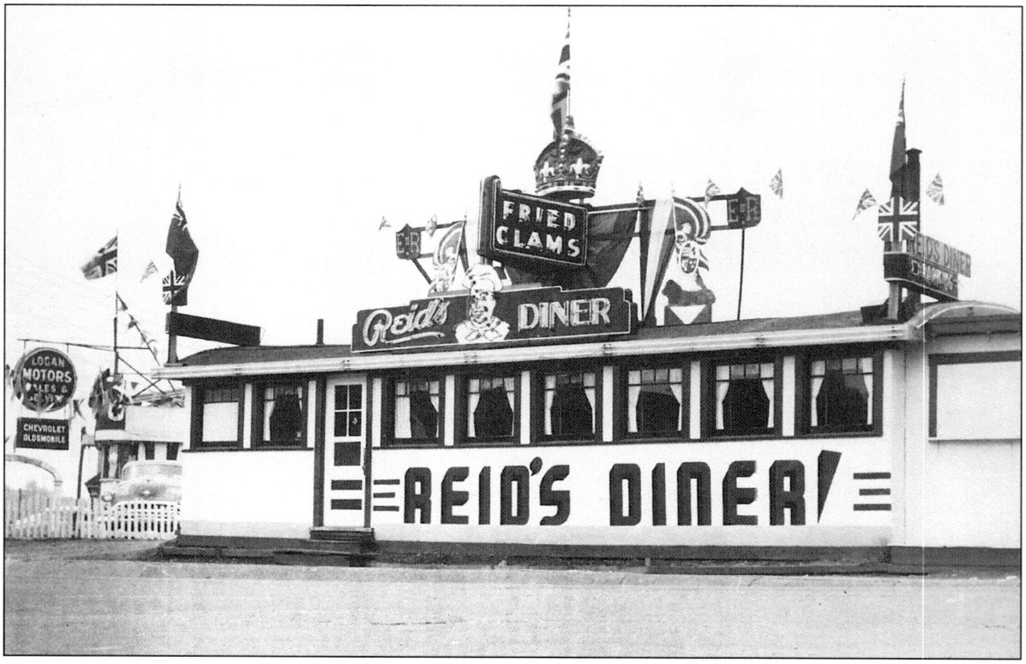

REID'S DINER, 1953. This diner, next to Logan Motors, survived for over 40 years. Charles and Mildred Reid eventually left this structure for much larger facilities nearby where their banquet rooms were the envy of much larger restaurants. (Perry collection, PIRP #9466.)

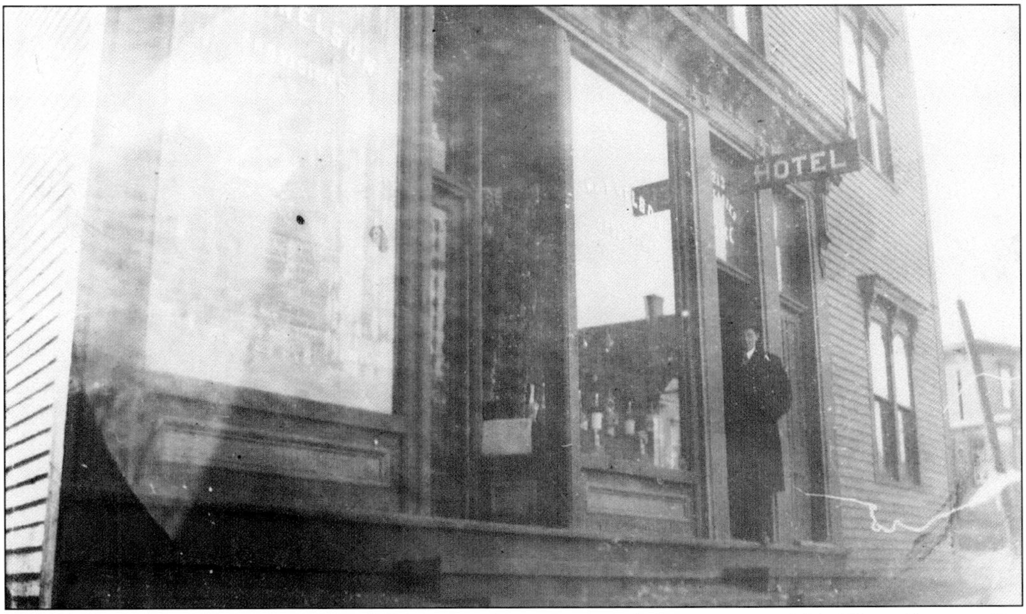

PROVISIONS STORE, C. 1920. William T. Nelson operated this store at 210 Olive Street. His brother was C.R. Nelson. (Chittick family.)

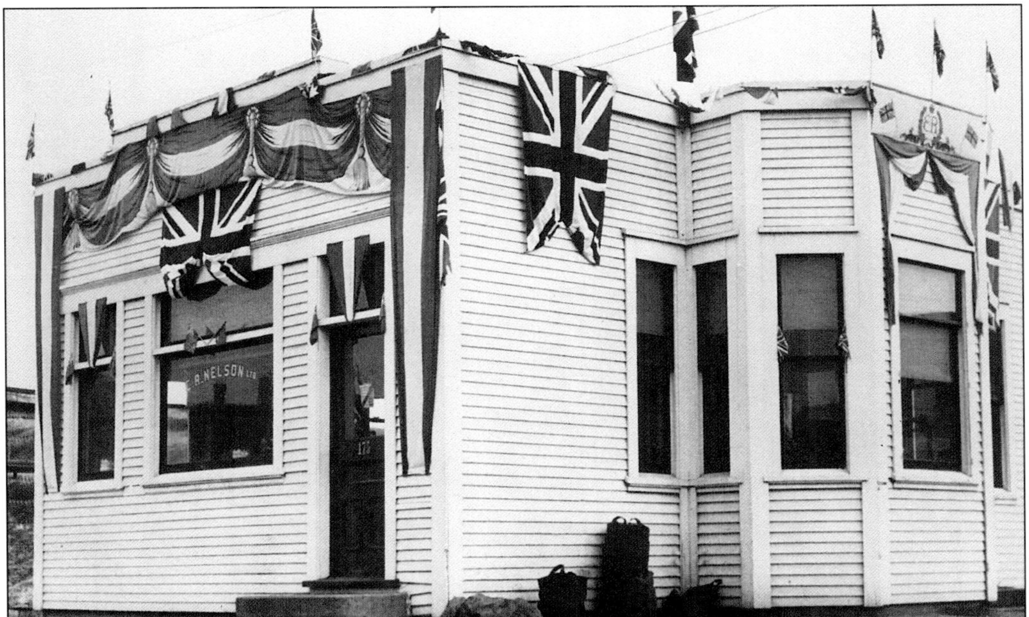

NELSON COAL, 1953. C.R. Nelson was one of the major coal suppliers in Lancaster, and for that matter, in all of Saint John. This office was at Simms Corner, next to Simms. (Perry collection, PIRP #9462.)

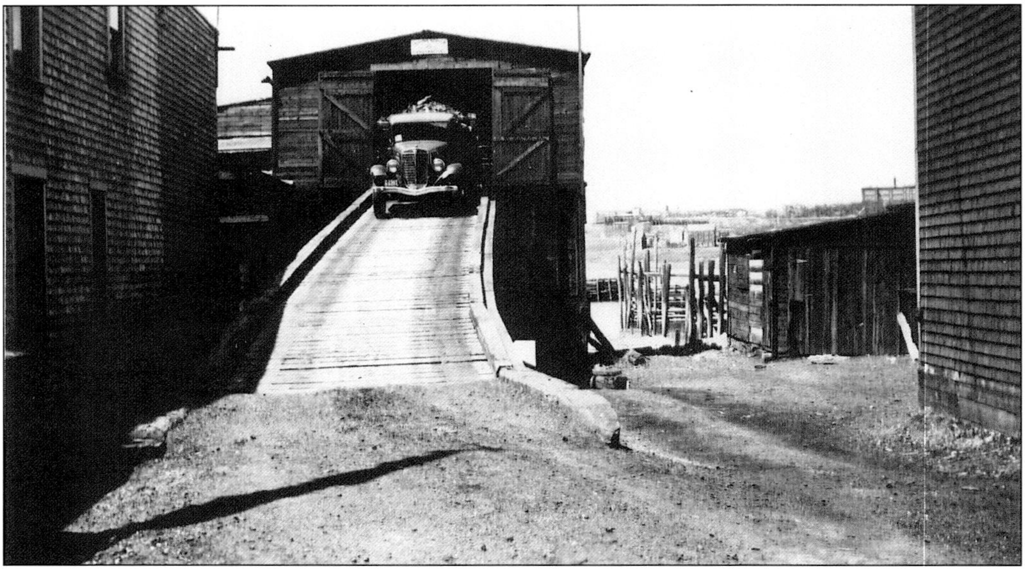

HAMM COAL, C. 1930. Frank Hamm, a veteran of World War I, was another major coal supplier in Carleton and parts of Lancaster. (Hamm collection, PIRP #9490, #9440.)

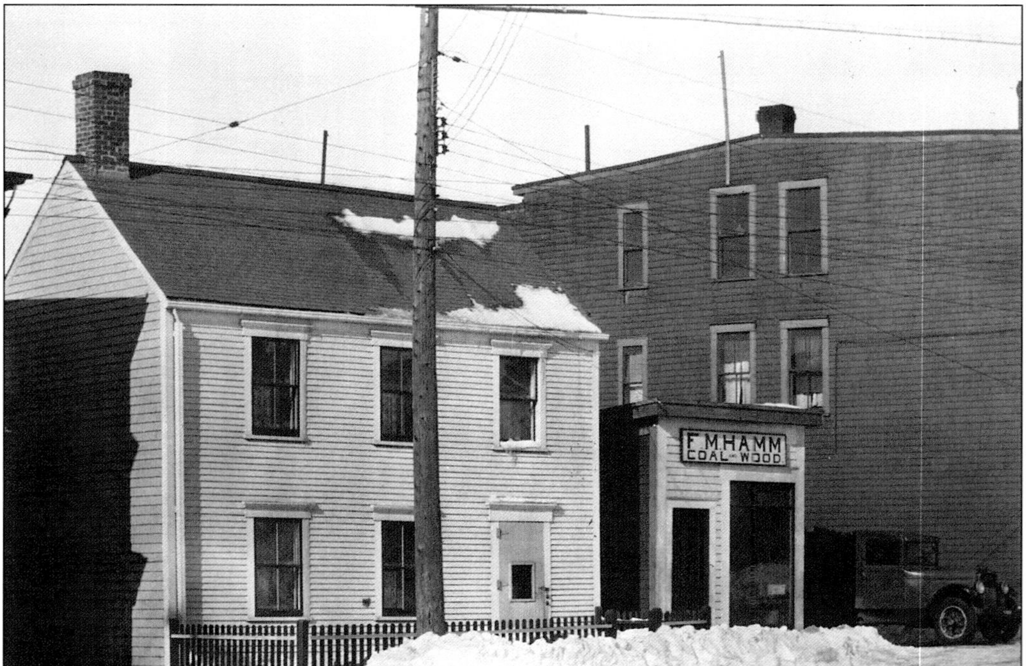

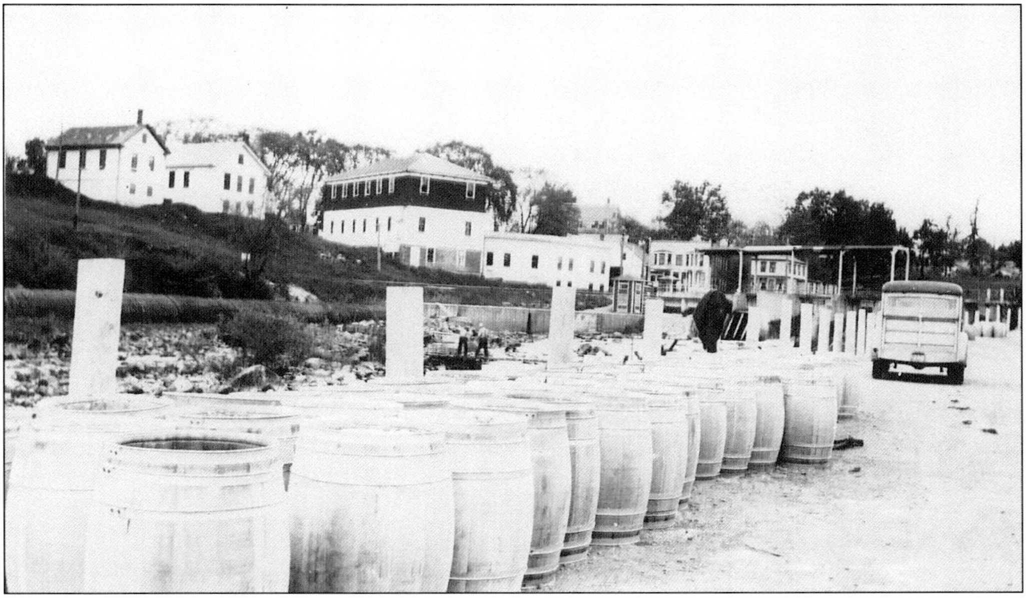

Fishing, c. 1940. Many in Carleton and Lancaster relied on a few jobs or occupations to get them through lean or slow times. In addition to his coal business, Frank Hamm did his best to keep his fish barrels full for sale. (Hamm collection, PIRP #9491.)

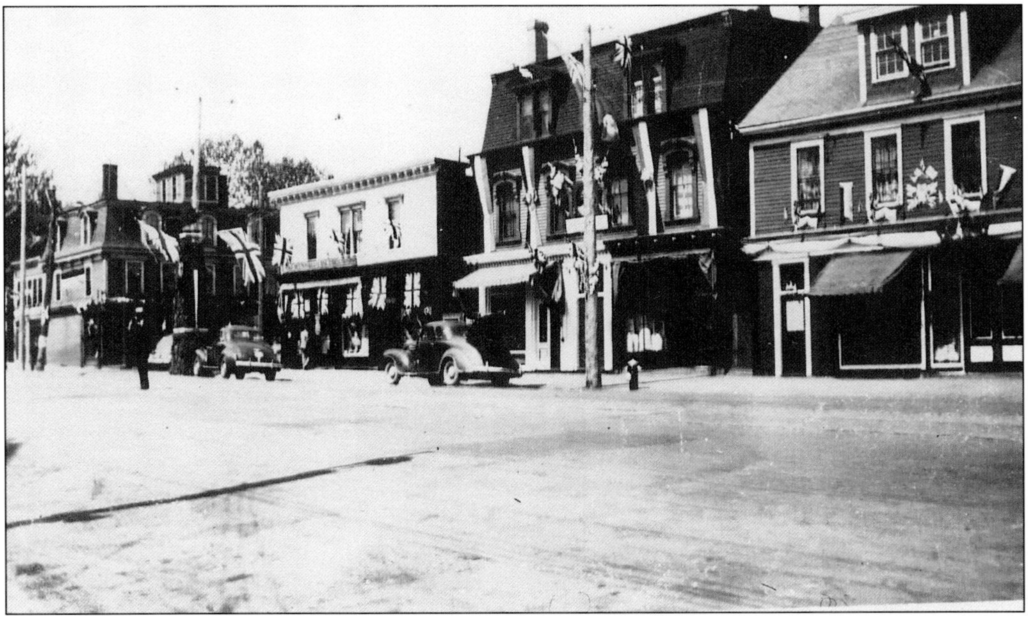

King Street, Royal Visit 1939. Carleton decorated for the visit of the King and Queen. This is now the site of a Tim Horton's shop. (Hamm collection, PIRP #9492.)

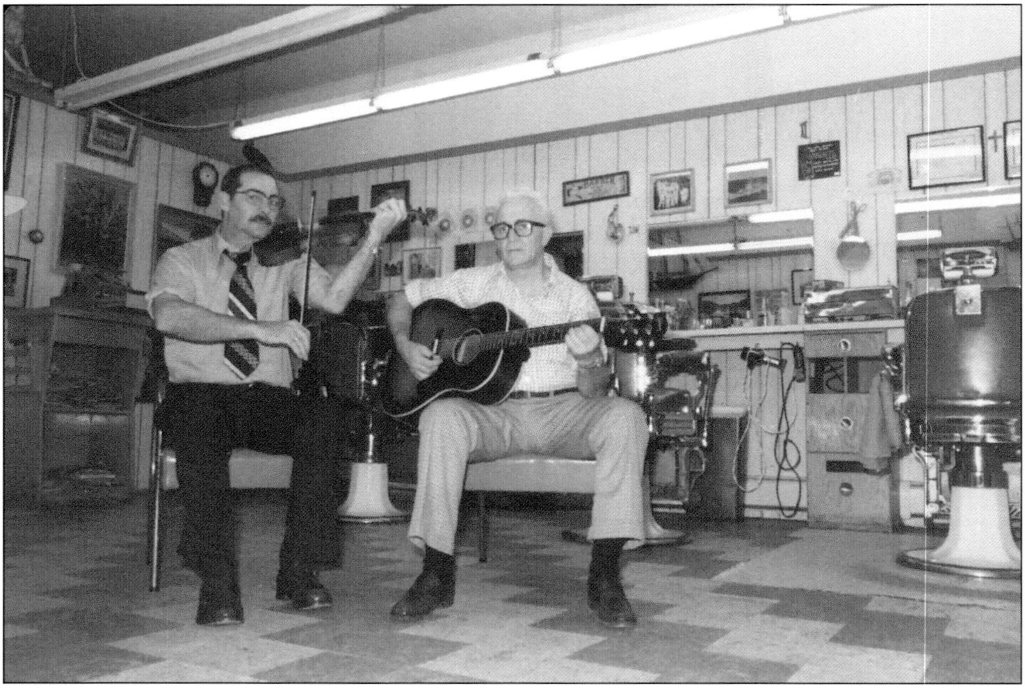

Song or Haircut? Louis Poirier was one of many Main Street barbers, but he was probably the only one who serenaded his customers. With Louis is Chick Philpitt. (Poirier family.)

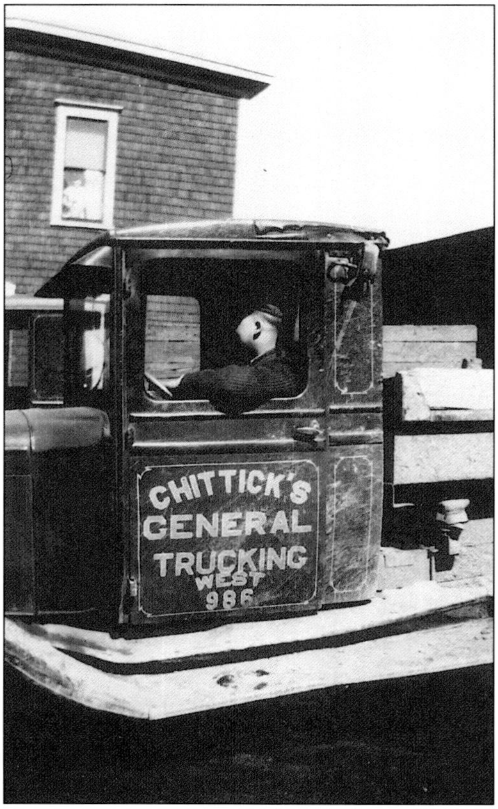

Chittick's, 1956. There were few businessmen in Lancaster and Saint John as well known or respected as George Chittick. He turned his small general trucking business into one of the largest construction companies in New Brunswick. (Chittick family.)

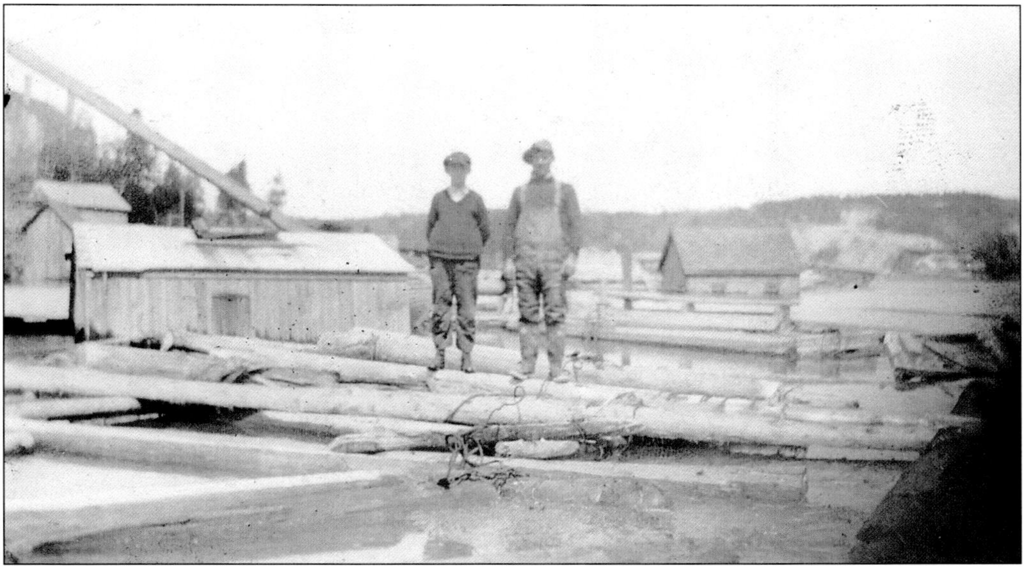

THE R&B MILL, C. 1920. The Randolph & Baker mill was the lifeblood of Randolph for decades. Several generations worked in the mill and lived in the company houses. Many of Saint John's early Acadian families worked here. (Top-M. Bernard; bottom-Perry family.)

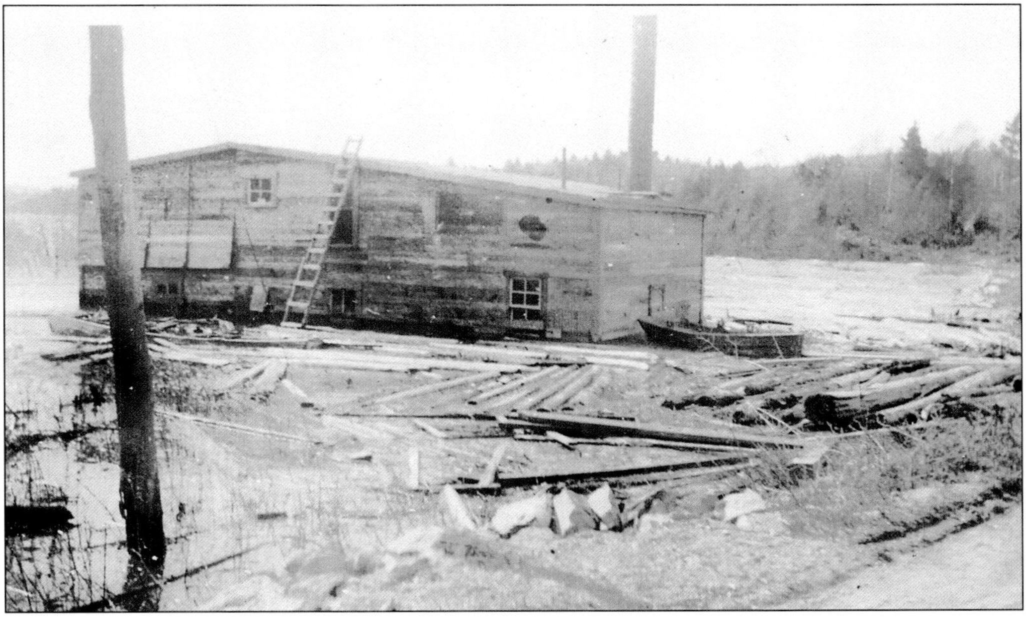

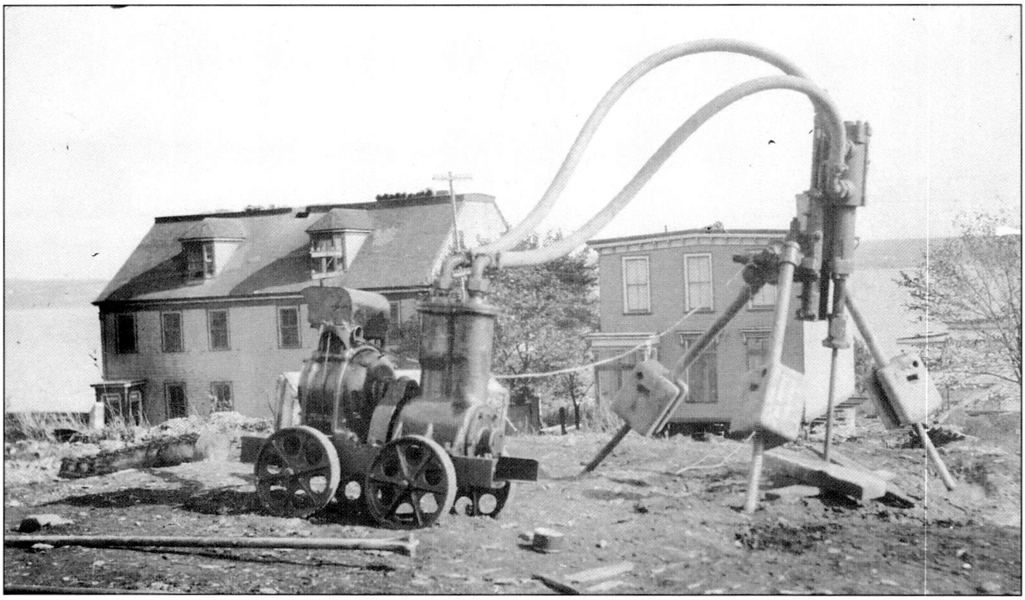

Pneumatic Drill. The R&B Mill used this drill to aid in the construction of more company homes. In all, the company owned at least 18 homes. Can you identify the location by the two buildings in the rear? (M. Melanson.)

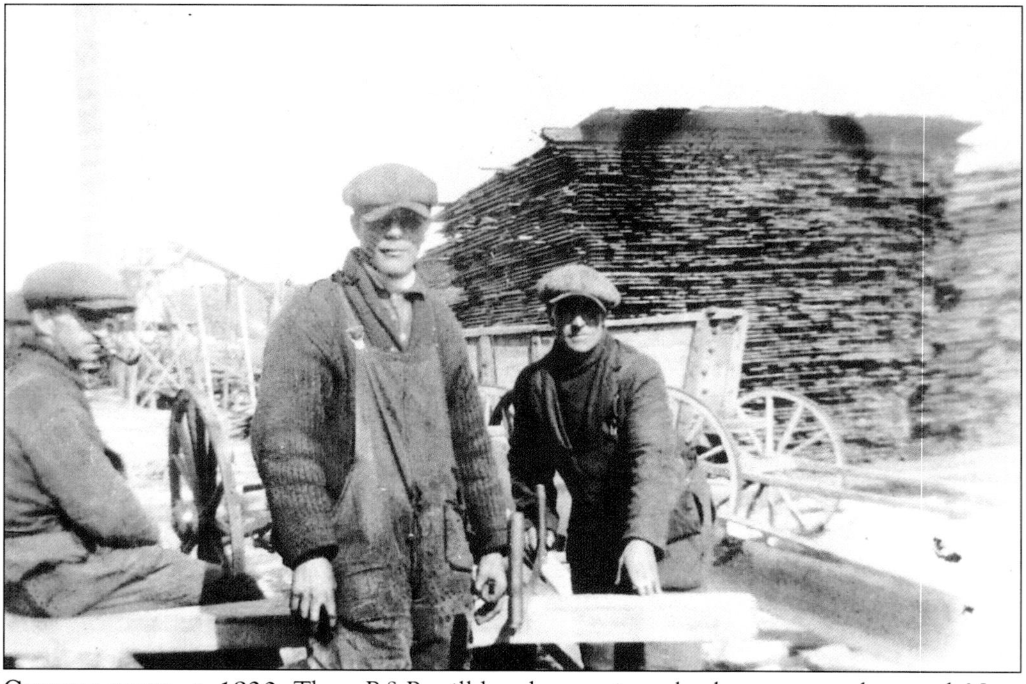

Cutting wood, c. 1930. These R&B mill hands are using a buck saw to cut the wood. Note the wagons, the large stack of sawn timber, and the mill smoke stack. The mill was destroyed by fire sometime in the 1930s but was rebuilt on a smaller scale. (M. Melanson.)

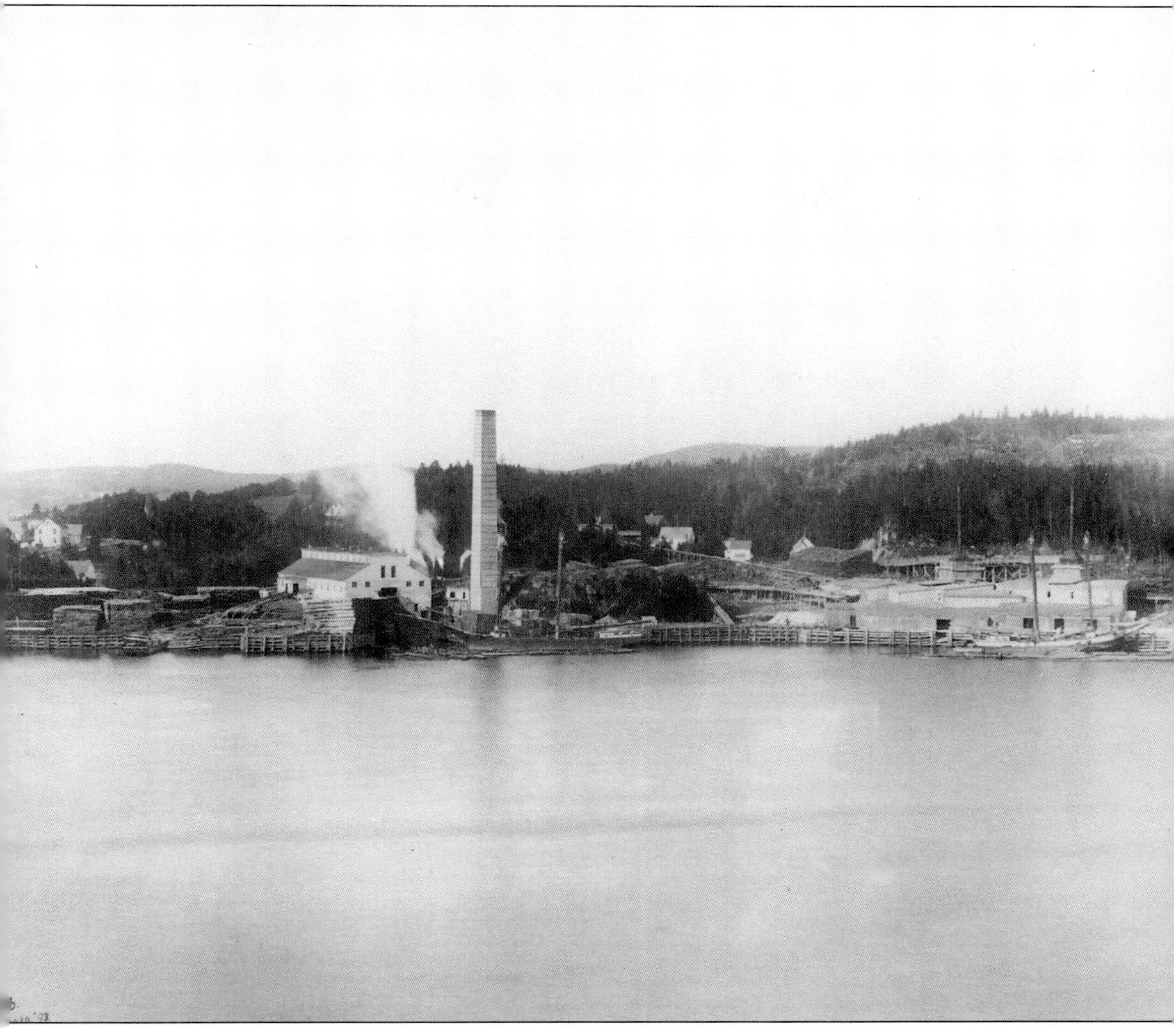

The R&M Mill, 1893. Archibald Randolph and Charles P. Baker's original partnership was in a lime burning business in Randolph. By 1897, the lumber mill's output was over 21 million feet. The mill had "two gangs", three lathe machines, a "stave machine", and a "heading machine". The company owned two tugboats, the *Randolph* and the *Kingsville*, used to bring the logs downriver in booms. Behind the lumber mill was the lime quarry. In 1894, the lime kilns produced 65,000 barrels of lime. (M. Melanson.)

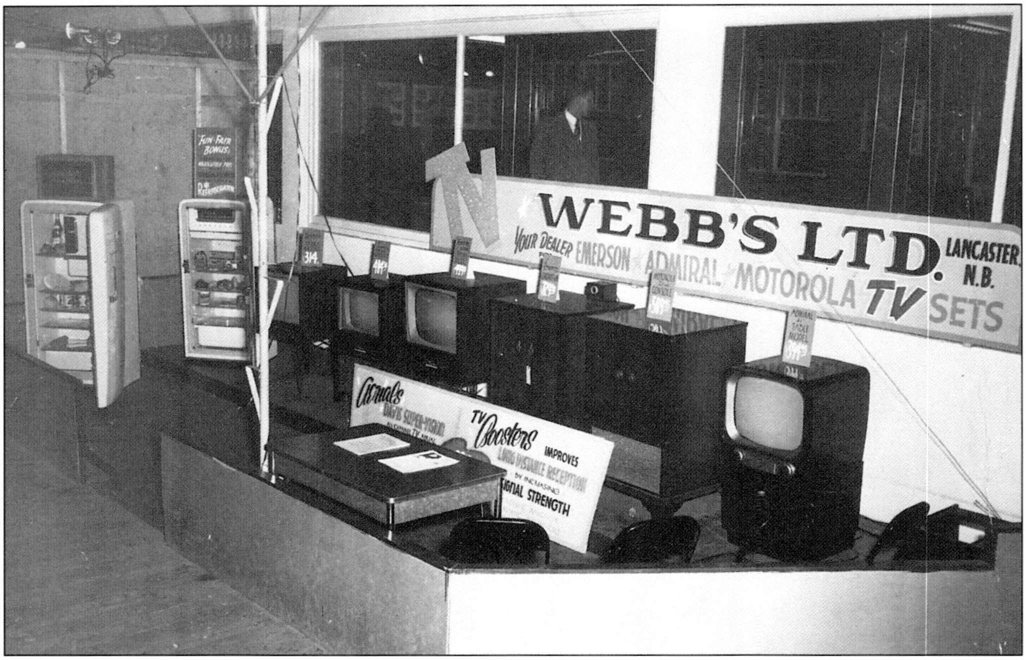

WEBB'S APPLIANCES, C. 1955. Russell Webb offered a free Sunbeam Mix Master if you bought a refrigerator. He also carried Emerson, Admiral, and Motorola televisions, including aerials and "TV Boosters" to improve long distance reception by increasing signal strength. At his Service Centre across the street he carried a wide assortment of automotive and sporting goods, and toys. Intermixed with ice scrappers and cans of Atlas ice remover, there are baseball gloves, footballs, board games of chess, Gobs of Fun, Yogi Bear, Lil Beaver trucks, a tow truck, a tricycle, and hunting rifles, next to the hockey sticks. (Webb collection, PIRP #9475, #9466.)

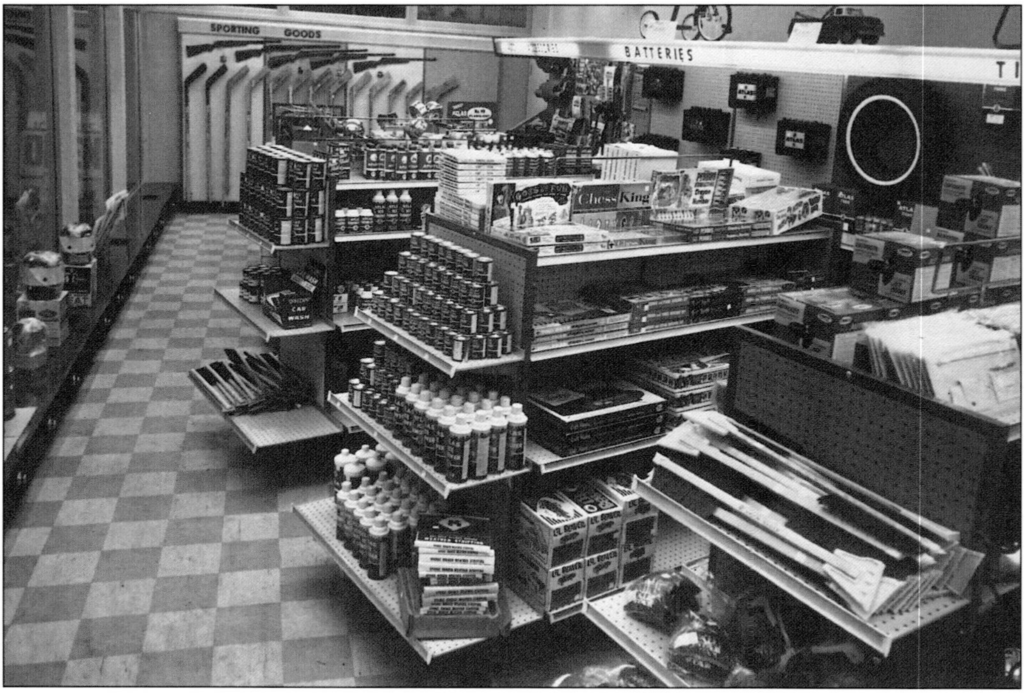

Eleven

More of Lancaster and Her People!

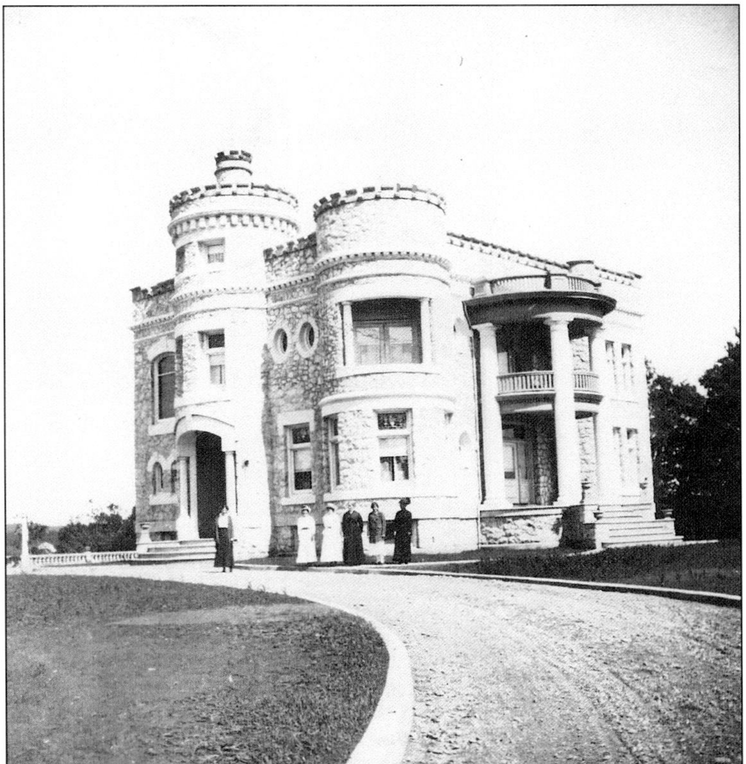

The Castle, July 1915. Commonly referred to as Baker's Castle, this Baronial Gothic home at South Bay was built by Parker Baker between 1912 and 1915. In July, there was an "open house" so neighbours could visit the magnificent home. The house was sold from the family in 1924. The house was also used as a prestigious river inn. It was later owned by Sen. Clarence V. Emerson and also served as a nursing home before again reverting to a single-family residence. (M. Kingston.)

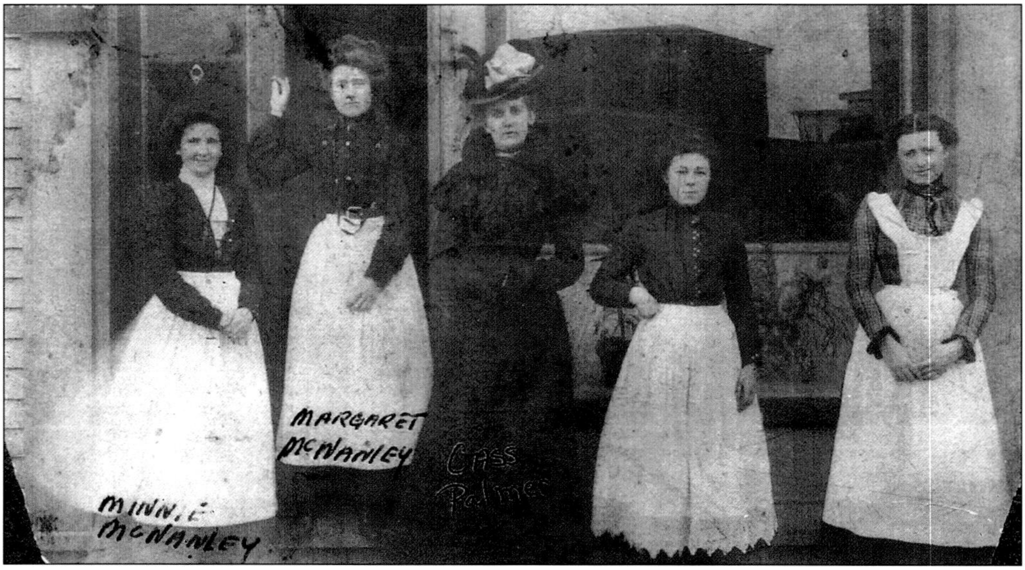

Dress and Mantle Making, c. 1900. Minnie McNanley owned this shop at 17 Main Street. Next to her is her sister Margaret and friend, Cass Palmer. By 1901, she had moved her shop to 5 Spar Cove Road across the river to Indiantown. Between 1893 and 1901 John McNanley, a millman, was listed as living on Prospect Street and at 17 Main Street. (A. Donovan.)

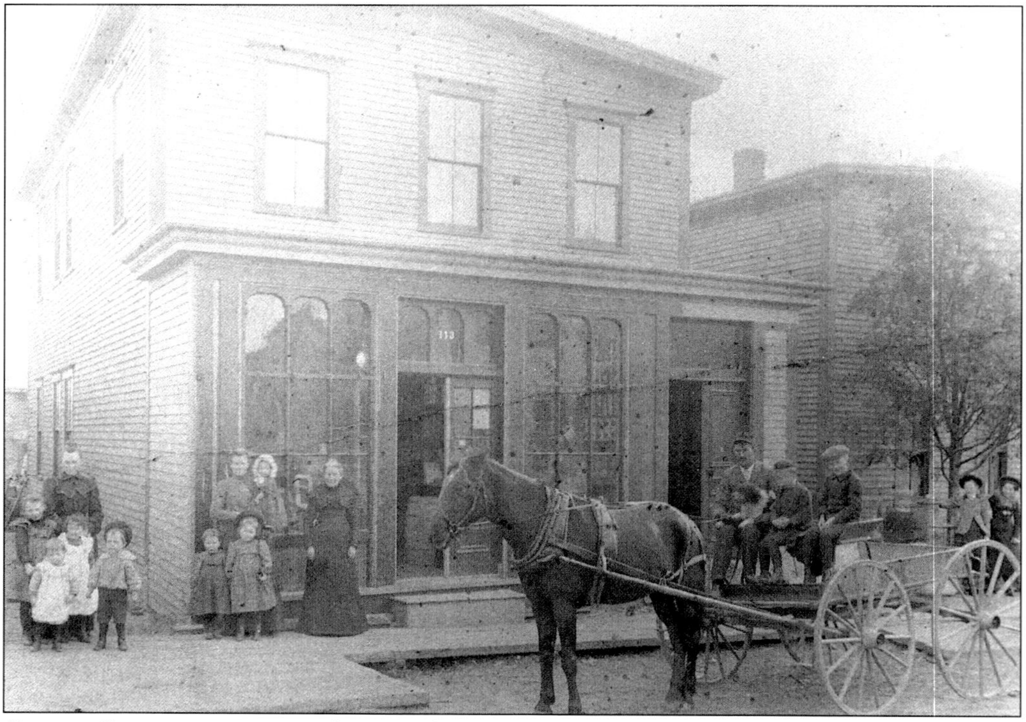

Corner Store, c. 1901. William Andrew McColgan, the wagon driver, operated this store at 113 Harding Street with his wife, Laura, for over 43 years. Seated next to him are his sons Walter, with the dog, and Stan. Standing to the left of the door is Laura, holding Ethel, born in 1900; in front of her are Vivian, born in 1898, and Blanche, born in 1896. Walter was born in 1865 and died in 1948. Laura was born in 1875 and died in 1952. (E. Small.)

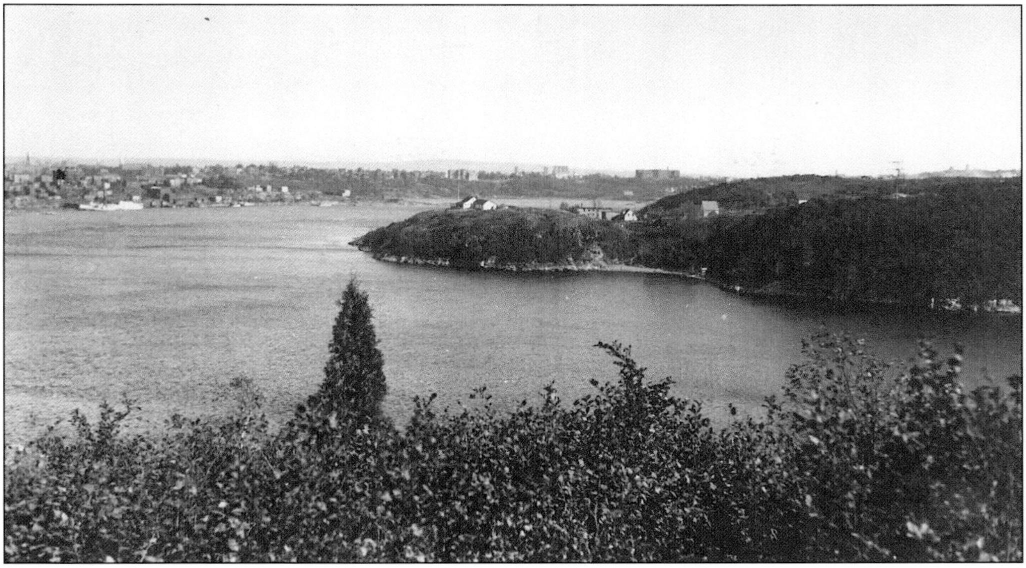

PROSPECT POINT, 1945. In 1920 the Byng Boys purchased a clubhouse in Milford and held their monthly meetings there for 58 years until fire destroyed the clubhouse in November 1978. Formed in 1919, the Byng Boys, named after Lord Julian Byng of Vimy, is a unique club in which members originally had to be brought off the battle field in a stretcher. Now meeting at the Union Club, the membership is open to veterans who saw combat. (Spinney collection, PIRP #5919.)

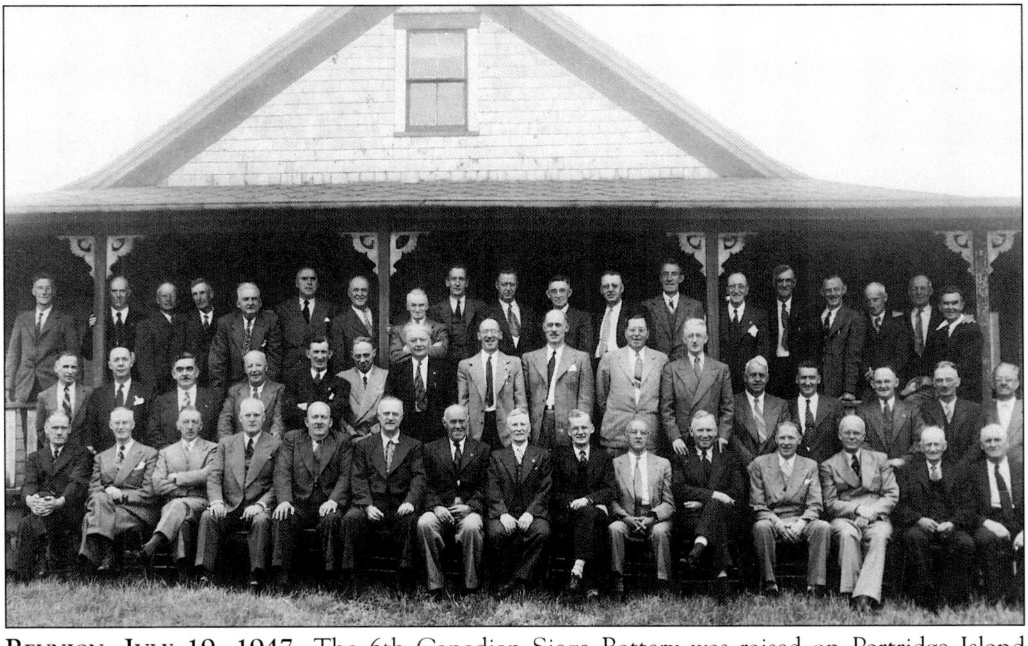

REUNION, JULY 19, 1947. The 6th Canadian Siege Battery was raised on Partridge Island during World War I. After distinguished service during the war, former members of the battery organized an association and held annual meetings until the 1970s. Some of the gunners at this reunion included former Battery Commander Maj. Larry Allen, Lloyd Yeomans, Col. Gil Hart, Fortress Commander of Saint John during World War II, Leroy Armstrong, Murray Dixon, and Harold Fowler. (J.L. Armstrong collection, PIRP #4880.)

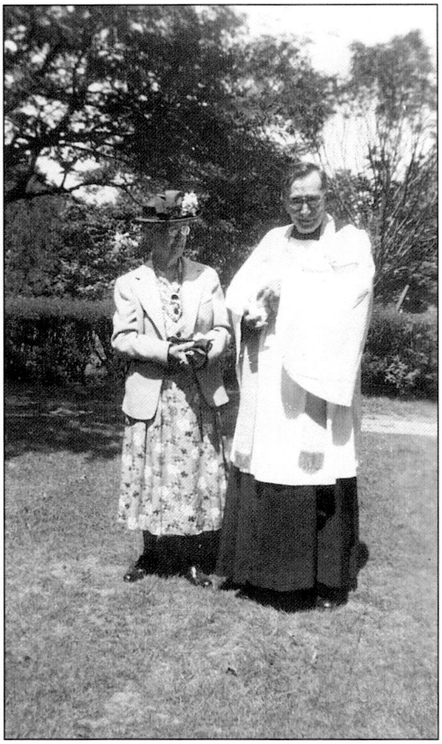

Baptism, July 16, 1950. Rev. Canon Fernand LeRoy holds Carol Ann Henderson behind the Church of the Good Shepherd shortly after her baptism. With Canon LeRoy is his wife, Mabel. On January 15, 1950, Canon LeRoy celebrated his 25th anniversary on his induction as rector of the Parish of Lancaster. He wrote "May I ask you in all earnestness to come to the Anniversary Services as soldiers ready to follow your Leader into a fresh campaign and to pledge unto Him your whole-hearted loyalty and devotion". (C. Craig.)

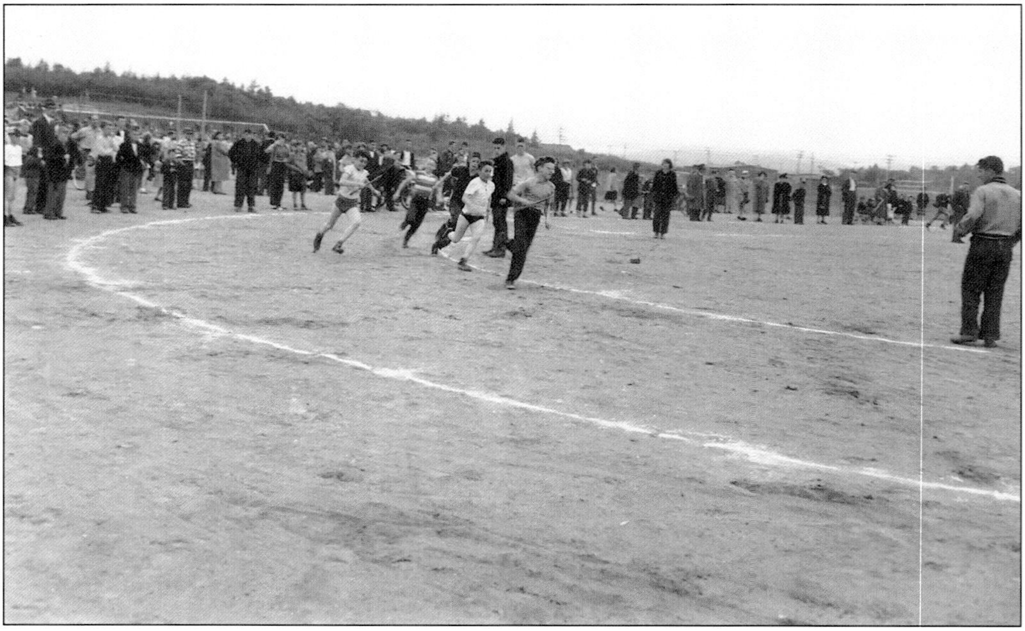

Track and Field, 1954. As part of the first anniversary celebrations of Lancaster, a track and field event and a doll carriage parade were held at the Lancaster War Memorial Recreation Field. This field, which opened on July 14, 1953, was to be developed over several years. A grandstand and baseball park, a soccer field, a running track, and an arched gateway to the field from Dever Road were eventually built. Today the name has changed slightly to the Lancaster Memorial Field. (HSJ collection, PIRP #7811.)

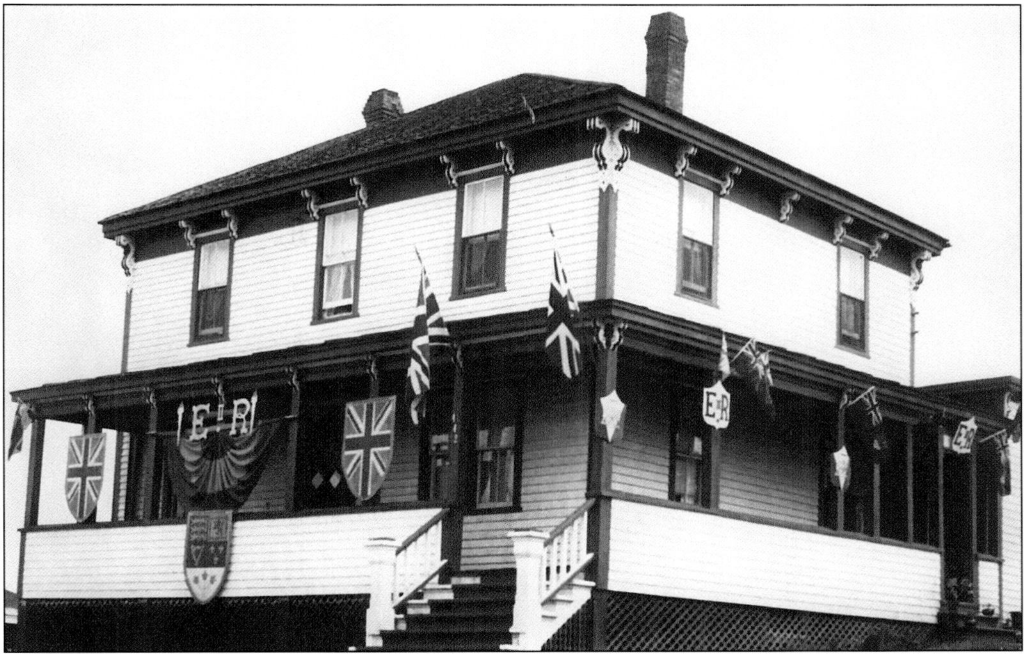

Albert Perry's House at 442 Greenhead Road, 1953. Albert Perry—firefighter, policeman, sportsman, and decorator extraordinaire—decorated his Colonial Revival house for the coronation celebrations of Queen Elizabeth II. His wife and son still live in the house today. (Perry collection, PIRP #9464.)

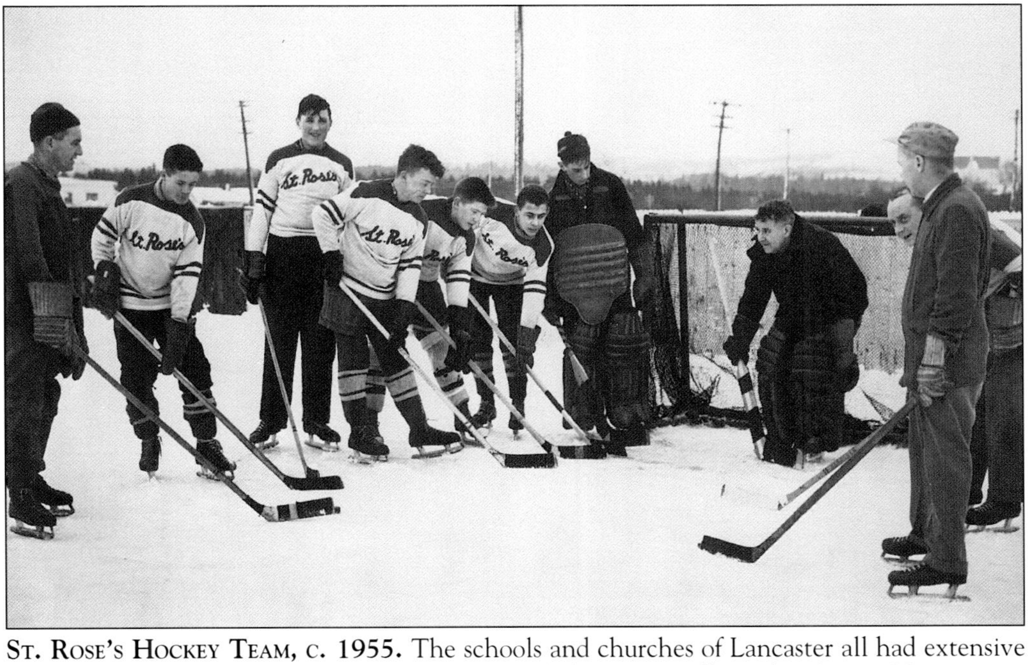

St. Rose's Hockey Team, c. 1955. The schools and churches of Lancaster all had extensive sports programs. Everybody got into the act, including Councillor John Garey. He may not have been a Gump Worsley in goal, but his enthusiasm, and that of his fellow adults, certainly made them good role models for the boys eager to get one past goalie Garey! His son Norm is second from the left, and Joe Flynn is at his left. All others are unidentified. (N. Garey.)

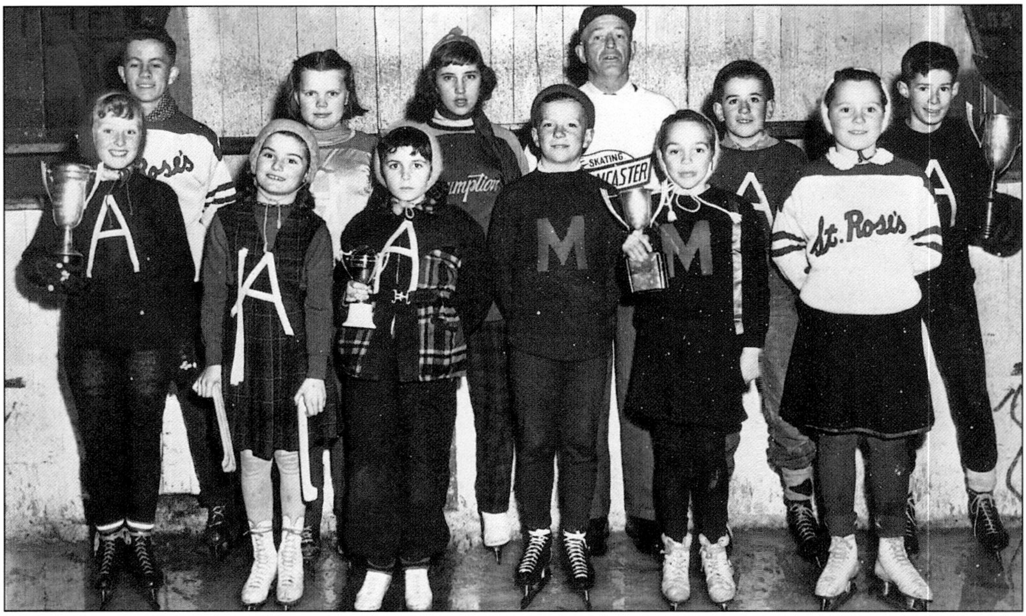

St. Rose's School Skating Club, c. 1954. Four of these skaters are holding trophies, and their sweaters identify them as being either from St. Rose's or Assumption. The only skater identified is Norm Garey (rear left). Unfortunately, many people do not record on the reverse of photos the names of those in the picture. (Garey collection, PIRP #9422.)

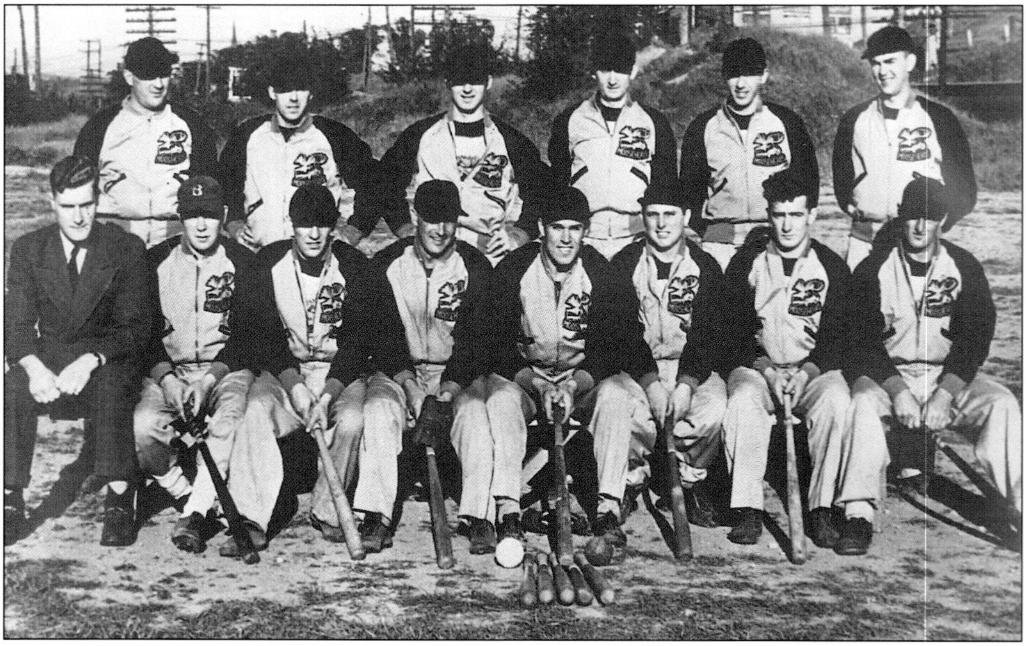

City and District Champs, c. 1950. Moosehead Breweries was, and continues to be, one of the largest sponsors of Lancaster sports from the 1940s to the present day. The Lancaster Brewers ball team was composed of, from left to right, the following members: (front row) Philip W. Oland, Moosehead, E. Rooney, G. Crilley, S. Larabie, V. Jackson, R. Crilley, G. Mason, and L. McLellan; (back row) M. McPhee, R. Reid, B. McGovern, E. Harley, R. Reid, and D. Beatty. M. McGovern is not pictured. (Buccaneers Pub collection, PIRP #9469.)

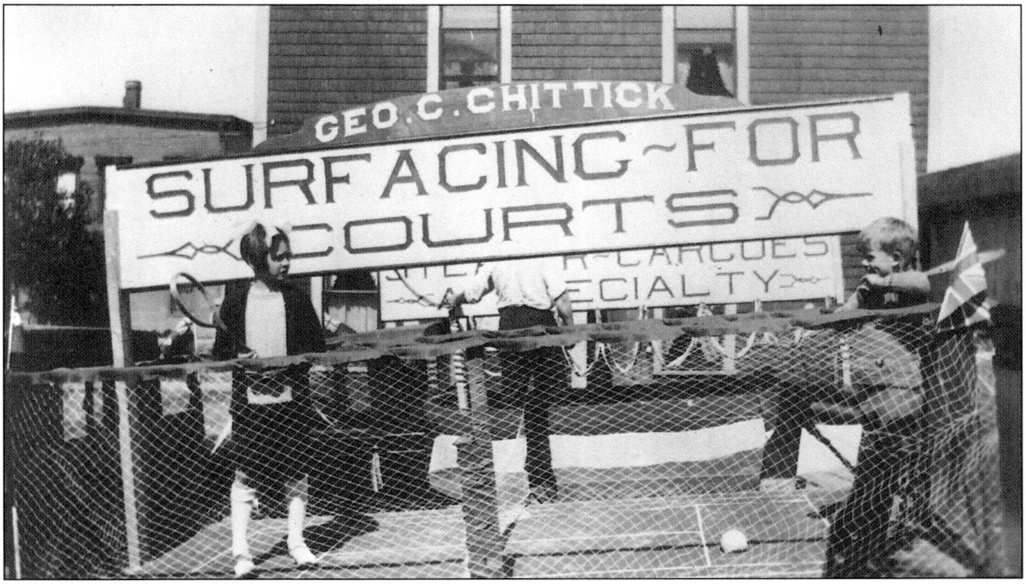

Tennis Anyone? 1935. Chittick's Transportation Day jubilee parade float, as seen earlier in the book, was this traveling tennis court. Chittick's, of course, was in the paving business . . . and thus the sign! The names of the two children are unknown. (Chittick collection, PIRP #9234.)

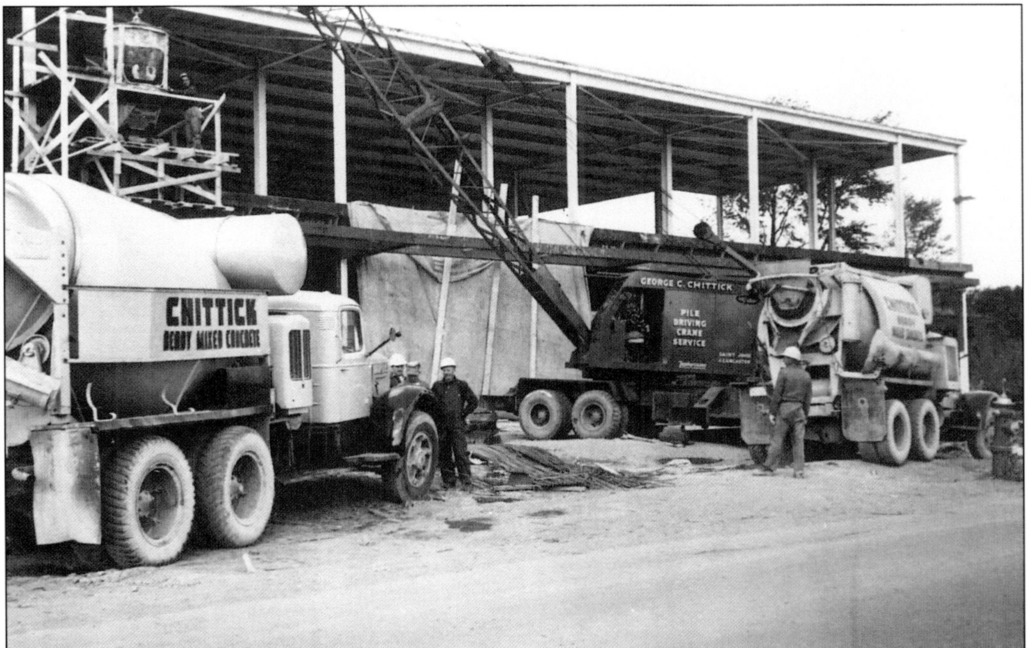

Chesley Drive Construction, c. 1965. George Chittick got the contract to erect the new Thornes building on Chesley Drive. His vehicles advertise his Ready Mix Concrete Service and his Pile Driving Crane Service. (Chittick collection, PIRP #9239.)

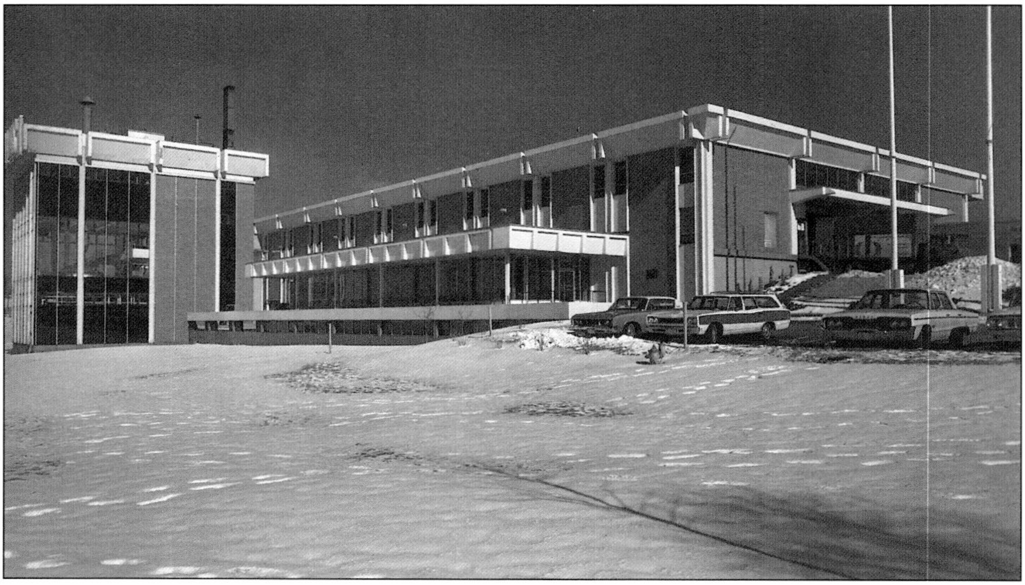

Oland's Brewery, c. 1970. Although of the same family name as the owners of Moosehead Breweries, this was competition for Moosehead in the 1970s. Oland's was bought out by Labatt's, who after several successful years of operation, closed the brewery in the early 1990s and demolished the plant. (HSJ collection, PIRP #9315.)

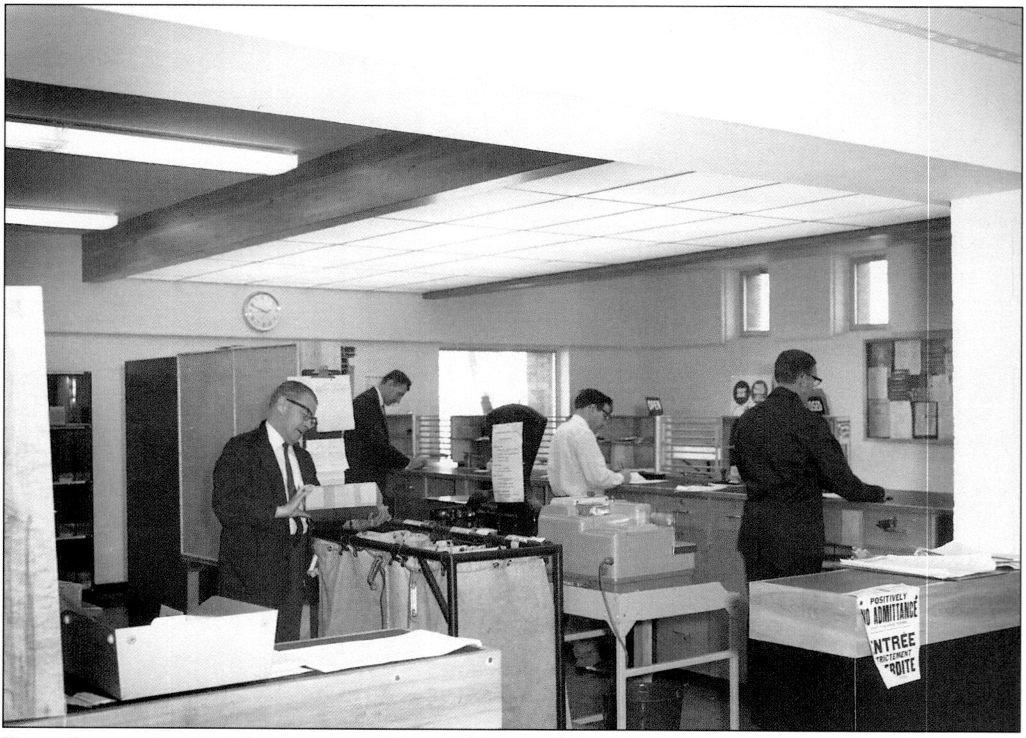

Post Office, 1972. The Lancaster Post Office on Main Street was replaced by Postal Station B on Church Avenue. The original post office is now a Deluxe French Fries Restaurant. The postal employees are actually getting ready for the Christmas rush, so this picture was probably taken in October or November. (HSJ collection, PIRP #9325.)

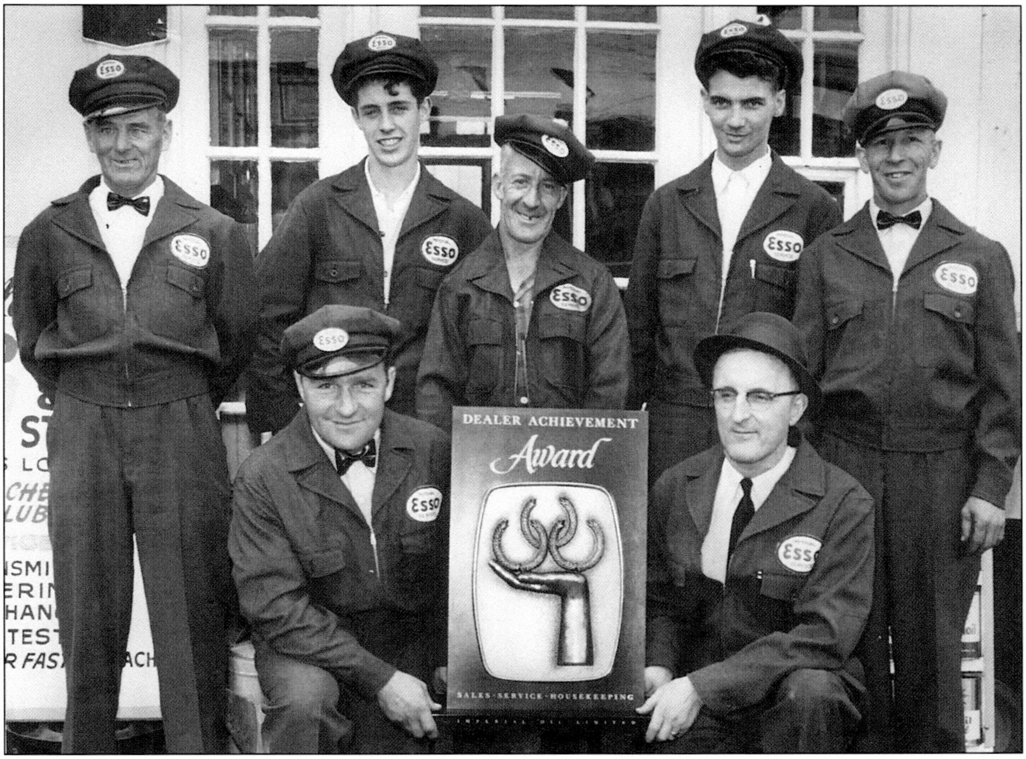

AWARD, C. 1960. Russ Webb's Esso station received the Dealer Achievement Award for sales, service, and housekeeping. Russ is easily recognized at the front right, but who are his employees? It is interesting to note that all but three of the men are wearing neck or bow ties, yet two of the three are wearing shirts appropriate for wearing a tie. Although some station attendants are back to wearing uniforms and trying to offer similar service to what we became use to receiving in the 1950s and 1960s, hats are definitely not part of the present-day uniform. (Webb collection, PIRP #9468.)

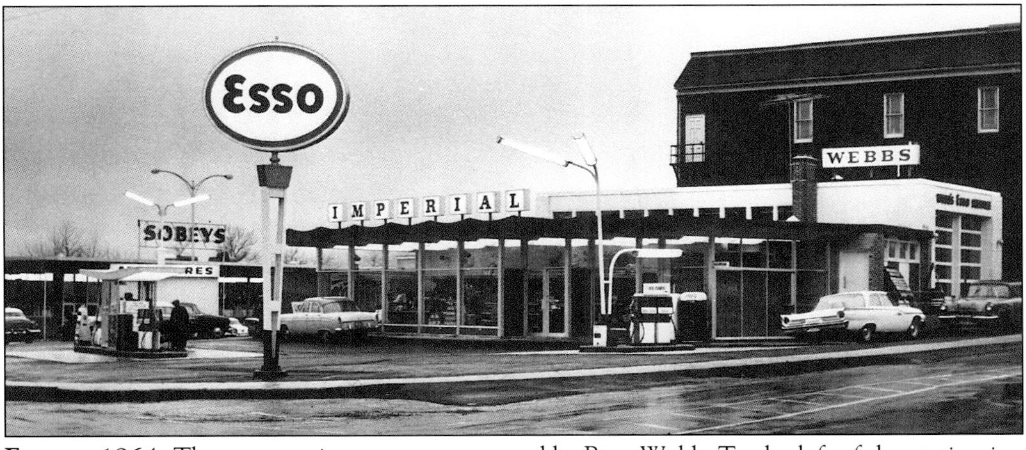

ESSO, C. 1964. The new service centre was owned by Russ Webb. To the left of the station is a c. 1954 Nash Metropolitan, today considered a rare car. At the right is a 1962–63 Ford Fairlane and a c. 1955 Pontiac. This building was recently replaced with a new service centre, complete with a Tony the Tiger and a car wash, which necessitated the demolition of the Orange Lodge Hall at the right. Note the Sobey's store in the rear. (Webb collection, PIRP #9481.)

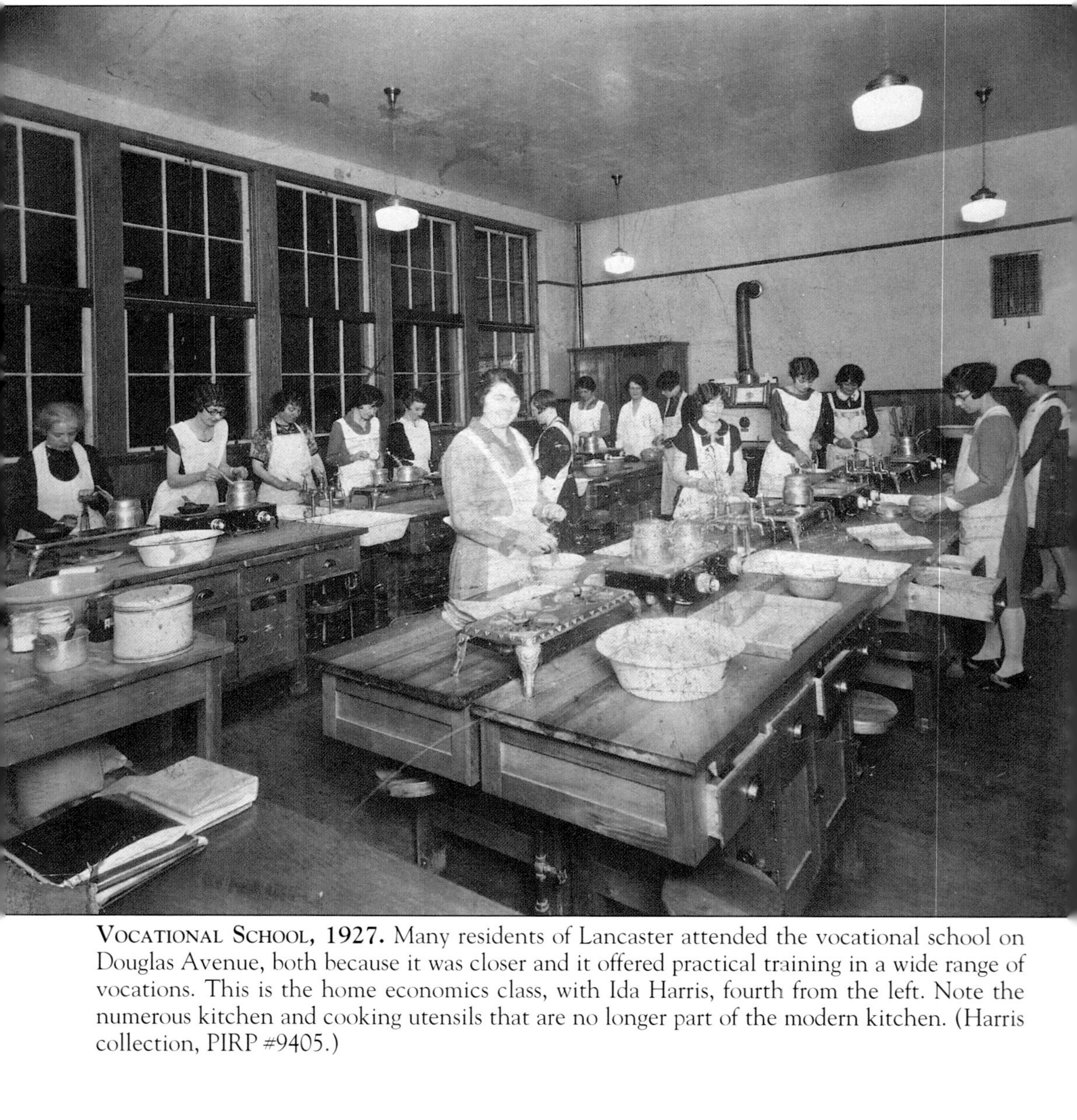

VOCATIONAL SCHOOL, 1927. Many residents of Lancaster attended the vocational school on Douglas Avenue, both because it was closer and it offered practical training in a wide range of vocations. This is the home economics class, with Ida Harris, fourth from the left. Note the numerous kitchen and cooking utensils that are no longer part of the modern kitchen. (Harris collection, PIRP #9405.)